I0147817

MY REMARKABLE LIFE

The First
Sitting Member
of Congress
to Endorse
Donald J. Trump
for President

CHRIS COLLINS

BOMBARDIER BOOKS

Published by Bombardier Books
An Imprint of Post Hill Press
ISBN: 979-8-89565-327-2
ISBN (eBook): 979-8-89565-328-9

My Remarkable Life:
The First Sitting Member of Congress to Endorse Donald J. Trump for President

Cover Design by Jim Villaflores

All people, locations, events, and situations are portrayed to the best of the author's memory. While all of the events described are true, many names and identifying details have been changed to protect the privacy of the people involved.

Post Hill Press
New York • Nashville
posthillpress.com

Published in the United States of America
1 2 3 4 5 6 7 8 9 10

To my wife, Mary Sue, who has stood by my side for over 45 years.
Through good times and bad, she is my rock and the reason
I survived the nightmare described in this book.

Table of Contents

Introduction

THE YEAR IS 2017. I'm cruising comfortably at 30,000 feet, happily ensconced on my seat aboard Air Force One. Life is good, and I can't help but marvel at the journey that brought me here. Back in early 2016, I was the first Member of Congress to endorse Donald J. Trump for president—a decision that changed the trajectory of my career. This moment in the skies, aboard the most iconic plane in the world, was one of the perks of that decision. President Trump never forgot my early endorsement, and let me tell you, it sure came in handy down the line.

My memories of Air Force One are vivid and cherished, etched in my mind like snapshots of an extraordinary time of my life. There was a sense of awe in being part of history, surrounded by the hum of the engines and the aura of power that the plane represented. I was once called to join a meeting in the plane's conference room—a room that carried the weight of monumental decisions. At another time, I found myself with Rep. Peter King, joining the president in his private office aboard the plane. Those moments were surreal, a blend of professional duty and personal honor.

Back on the ground, the privileges didn't end there. I was invited to parties at the White House—occasions that felt almost cinematic, with the grandeur of the setting and the mingling of influential figures. At speeches, President Trump would often point me out in the crowd, proclaiming, "that's my guy." The recognition was exhilarating, a momentary spotlight that made me feel special and appreciated.

Yet, as Dickens famously wrote, "It was the best of times, it was the worst of times." Beneath the veneer of success and prestige, there was a shadow—a legal predicament that would change my life. As you'll discover in these pages, I faced accusations that I believe were unfounded. In a desperate bid to protect my family, I made the painful decision to enter a guilty plea under pressure from our own Justice Department. It was a decision born of necessity, not admission, and one that left scars I carry to this day.

And then came the chapter I never imagined living—prison. The stark contrast between the heights of *Air Force One* and the confines of a prison cell is a reality I grapple with even now. In Chapter 28, you'll find the full account of that nightmare—a story of resilience, humility, and the hard truths of life.

But before diving into that, I want to share the story of my life in business and politics—the experiences that shaped me, the victories and setbacks, and the lessons I've gathered along the way. It's a journey I've been fortunate enough to live and now share, with my friends, my family, and anyone with the patience to read my story. My hope is that these pages offer insight, inspire reflection, and perhaps even spark a dialogue about the paths we take and the challenges we face.

As you read my book you will find that I have included a few political cartoons, created by Adam Zyglis, to add some levity to the trials and tribulations that I have confronted.

CHAPTER 1

The Harder You Work, the Luckier You Get

I ORIGINALLY WANTED TO CALL this chapter—and the entire book—"Serendipity," which is the occasion of achieving a happy result when you are actually looking for something different. After thinking and discussing this, it felt like I was selling myself short. It wasn't just plain "luck," but perhaps a more intentional fortune. Hence, the title of this chapter.

At some point in our lives, we all encounter moments that feel like "luck"—those happy, unexpected outcomes that seem to fall into place effortlessly. However, as I reflect on my life, I realize that these moments were anything but random. The opportunities and turning points that shaped my journey were the result of preparation, persistence, and a willingness to seize the moment.

At age eleven, a new friend in Glens Falls, NY suggested we explore Scouting. That casual suggestion set the stage for what would become an integral part of my entire life. Joining Scouting wasn't just a matter of chance, it was a commitment to a path that offered lessons, values, and relationships that I continue to cherish.

Later, adapting to high school in Hendersonville, NC, after growing up in New York, was no small feat. It took effort and resilience to navigate those changes, but a timely intervention from Coach Brown made all the difference. Noticing my struggles, he invited me to join the Key Club—a prestigious group that was highly sought after by students. Becoming a member required more than luck; it took Coach Brown's mentorship and my determination to rise to the occasion. This experience shaped my teenage years and helped me find my footing in a new and unfamiliar environment.

When I graduated from college, the choice between a design engineer position at General Electric and a sales engineer role at Westinghouse Electric wasn't merely serendipity—it was informed by my father's thoughtful counsel and my own drive to carve out a meaningful career path. Accepting the position at Westinghouse's Birmingham, AL office set me on a trajectory for growth that I could not have imagined.

My time at Westinghouse wasn't without its challenges, but each step forward was built on a foundation of preparation and readiness. For example, being promoted to an outside sales position within two months of joining the Birmingham office wasn't just a stroke of good fortune; it was the result of seizing opportunities and excelling in my work. Similarly, my decision to transfer to the Buffalo, NY facility, where I worked under Cary Mock, positioned me for rapid career advancement. His promotions created openings that I was prepared to fill, ultimately making me the youngest Division General Manager in Westinghouse history at age twenty-nine.

One of the most pivotal moments of my career came in 1982, when Westinghouse decided to shut down and sell the Gearing Division I was managing. While it may seem like luck that I was in the right place at the right time, the reality is that my relationship with Cary Mock and my readiness to embrace change turned this challenge into the opportunity of a lifetime. Purchasing the Westinghouse Gear Division, which I renamed Nuttall Gear Corporation, marked the start of my journey as a serial entrepreneur, a transformation that required vision, effort, and courage.

Looking back, I see a common thread through all these moments: the harder I worked, the more opportunities seemed to come my way. Call it preparation, persistence, or even intentional fortune—each step forward was built on the foundation of effort and a readiness to act when the time came.

Intentional Fortune and My Marriage to Mary Sue

In January 1982, a blind date that seemed destined for disaster brought me to a small restaurant and bar in downtown Buffalo where I first met my future wife, Mary Sue. I hadn't spent much time downtown, and Cole's on Elmwood Avenue wasn't a place I'd ever visited. At thirty-one, I was ten years older than Mary Sue, and our paths likely wouldn't have crossed under ordinary circumstances. But that night, what initially seemed like misfortune turned into one of the most significant moments of my life.

The blind date itself was unremarkable—I had little in common with my date and couldn't wait for the evening to end. Yet, during dinner, I noticed two women sitting at the bar who caught my attention. Gathering my courage after the meal, I struck up a conversation with Mary Sue and her best friend, Mary Mathews. It turned out Mary Sue had been hesitant about going out that evening, still navigating a difficult period in her life following the loss of her father and a faltering relationship. Our conversation that night wasn't just a product of chance; it was the result of being present, observant, and open to connection.

Mary Sue's initial reserve stemmed from past experiences, but over time, I earned her trust. We began to connect more deeply through consistent effort and persistence. Though she often seemed "busy," I remained patient, even stepping back for over ten months to let her decide when she was ready to invest in our relationship.

After not seeing Mary for almost a year, a chance encounter reignited our connection. While out with my best friend, Bill Grove, I saw Mary walking into a bar with a friend. I joked about whether she was still "busy," and this lighthearted moment opened the door for us to reconnect. From there, our relationship gained momentum, built not just on timing, but on mutual effort and willingness to engage with one another more fully.

When Mary and I decided to marry in January 1988, circumstances once again tested our resolve. With her mother's wish for a Catholic ceremony and the complexities of my prior marriage, I turned to Monsignor Robert Cunningham, Chancellor of the Catholic Diocese of Buffalo, for advice. He was a trusted confidant and good friend from our time spent together on the board of Kenmore Mercy Hospital. Father Bob, which is how I casually referred to Monsignor Cunningham, arranged for the annulment of my prior marriage, less than one week after I approached him for advice and guidance.

January 9, 1988 Wedding Photo.

On January 9, 1988, in the beautiful chapel at Saint John the Baptist Church, Mary Sue and I were married by Father Bob. Bill Grove stood by my side as best man, and Mary Mathews served as maid of honor. The day wasn't just the result of happenstance; it was the culmination of effort, determination, and the relationships we nurtured along the way.

January 9, 1988 leaving the church in my DeLorean.

Reflecting on these pivotal moments, I realize they weren't mere luck. The connection with Mary, the guidance from Father Bob, and the unwavering support of friends like Bill Grove and Mary Mathews all illustrate the importance of being proactive and prepared to embrace the opportunities life offers. Intentionality made all the difference in bringing Mary and me together—and in building the life we share to this day.

Intentional Fortune and Nuttall Gear

Throughout my ownership of Nuttall Gear Corporation, what might appear as luck was often the result of preparation and seizing opportunities. For instance, my golfing friend Jim Simpson didn't just introduce me to his professional network by chance—it was the trust and rapport we built over time that made him willing to help me secure the purchase of the Westinghouse Gear Division. Similarly, when my partners refused to sign a personal guarantee for loans, it wasn't mere fate that led to my owning 60 percent of the company—it was my readiness to take on the risk and responsibility.

Another turning point came when the manager of the Bell Aerospace facility in Niagara Falls read a *Buffalo News* story about my pending purchase. His outreach wasn't random; it was my visibility and reputation that prompted him to suggest relocating the factory to their facility—a move that turned out to be a perfect fit for Nuttall Gear.

Connections and Opportunities

In 1998, Congressman Bill Paxon's decision not to seek reelection to Congress opened a door for me to run against Congressman John LaFalce in a neighboring district. While some might call this serendipity, it was Bill's mentorship and my willingness to step into the political arena that made it possible. Even losing that race to John LaFalce proved transformative, raising my public profile and leading to new opportunities, like my eventual run for Erie County executive in 2007.

Hosting Senator Hillary Clinton at ZeptoMetrix early in 2001, after her election to the Senate in November 2000, wasn't just a lucky break—it was the culmination of years of collaboration and effort. That meeting laid the groundwork for future partnerships, including securing government funding for critical research. My investment in Virionyx, which later became Innate Immunotherapeutics, was another example of being prepared to act when the right opportunity arose.

ZeptoMetrix, Audubon Machinery, and the Pandemic

When I returned to ZeptoMetrix in 2012, after losing my reelection as Erie County executive in 2011, it wasn't chance that allowed me to uncover and address the company's challenges—it was my proactive approach and leadership. The company's eventual success, including its pivotal role during the Covid-19 pandemic, was built on years of hard work and strategic decisions. The same can be said for Audubon Machinery, whose oxygen systems became critical during the pandemic. The sale of both companies in 2020 and 2021 was the result of preparation meeting opportunity.

Business Ventures and Relationships

My investments in companies like Volland Electric, Niagara Ceramics, and Easom Automation weren't random strokes of luck. They were the result of relationships I cultivated, like my friendship with my attorney, Guy Agostinelli, and my willingness to take calculated risks. Each venture required effort, vision, and the ability to recognize potential in challenging circumstances.

Politics and Redemption

In politics, as in business, my journey has been shaped by intentional choices and resilience. Withdrawing from the New York Governor's race in 2010 wasn't just a twist of fate—it was a strategic decision that allowed me to focus on other opportunities, including my successful run for Congress in 2012, defeating now Governor Kathy Hochul. My friendship with fellow Congressman Mark Meadows, which later proved instrumental in securing a presidential pardon, was built on shared experiences and mutual trust.

Even my endorsement of Donald Trump's presidential candidacy on February 24, 2016 wasn't a matter of luck—it was a calculated decision that aligned with my values and vision. The pardon I received on December 22, 2020, which came just weeks before a Covid-19 outbreak at the prison camp, was a life-saving moment that underscored the importance of relationships and timing.

A Life of Intentional Fortune

Looking back, the events that shaped my life weren't random. They were the result of effort, adaptability, and a readiness to embrace change. While some moments may seem surreal, they are a testament to the power of preparation and the opportunities that arise when you're willing to act.

CHAPTER 2

Growing Up

MAY 20, 1950—THE DAY I was born in Schenectady, New York, the first son of Gerald Edward Collins (born January 11, 1924) and Constance Messier Collins (born April 1, 1927). My parents married on July 22, 1947. I was baptized on June 4, 1950, at the Church of Our Lady of Grace in Ballston Lake, New York. My older sister, Geraldine Edith (who changed her name to Deene as an adult), was eighteen months older than me, born on December 10, 1948.

The full weight of the Cold War descended on the American people in 1950. President Harry Truman ordered the Pentagon to begin work on a new, even more powerful nuclear weapon: the hydrogen bomb. North Korea invaded South Korea, and when the US and the UN stepped in, Mao Tse-tung hurled Chinese troops into the conflict, sending the Americans into retreat.

In 1950, America was exploring its new position as the most powerful nation in the world. Marlon Brando made his first film, *Guys and Dolls* opened on Broadway, and Coca-Cola was unleashed as a weapon mightier than any H-bomb on a world eager to embrace American tastes.

Schenectady, NY (Burnt Hills)

My dad was working in the General Electric (GE) plant in Schenectady, New York, when I was born. He was a chemical engineer, having graduated from Norwich University in 1946. Norwich is a military college located in Norwich, Vermont. My mom was a stay-at-home mom who met my dad while she attended Vermont Junior College.

Typical of many GIs following World War II, my parents had a small house situated in a suburb. Neighbors in the Burnt Hills area of Schenectady shared lawn equipment, tools, and other household items, which was typical for the times.

We didn't have a television when I was born. In 1950, only 9 percent of homes had televisions. When my family moved to Stamford, Connecticut, in 1955, they purchased their first television. By 1955, half the homes in America had televisions.

While I don't have many actual memories of my time in Burnt Hills, I've been told most of the moms gathered together every day and let all the children play together. The dads went to work in the early morning and arrived home for dinner each night. My older sister was my best friend. My sister Joyce was born on July 2, 1954. That was the beginning of the herd of children to follow: Claudia in 1956, Marilyn in 1958, Marcia in 1960, and Edward in 1962. Seven kids—five girls and two boys—born over a fifteen-year period.

We had a neighbor in Burnt Hills who had a TV. My sister and I would go to their house and watch *The Freddie Freihofer Show*. The show, produced in Schenectady, was a fifteen-minute program that ran just before *Howdy Doody*. Sponsored by the Freihofer Baking Company, it featured "Breadtime Stories" told by Uncle Jim Fisk, who wore a Freihofer deliveryman's uniform. My mom took me to the studio on my birthday, and I got to sit in the bleacher stands with about twenty-five other children who were also celebrating their birthdays.

Stamford, CT

My dad was transferred by GE to its headquarters in New York City in 1955. My parents decided to buy a house in Stamford, Connecticut, as a better place to raise kids than the city. My dad took the train each day into New York City and was home for dinner every night.

We had a television, and my favorite shows were *The Howdy Doody Show, The Lone Ranger, Leave it to Beaver,* and *I Love Lucy.*

My sister Deene and I loved to play outside. We had a very large sandbox where we would build cities, push cars on streets we constructed, and have fun pretending all sorts of scenarios.

I was in elementary school in Stamford, Connecticut—kindergarten through the middle of third grade. From what I've been told, I was always a good student.

Glens Falls, NY

In 1959, my dad was transferred by GE to Hudson Falls, New York, as the materials manager for a plant that manufactured capacitors. Tragically, this plant later polluted the Hudson River by discharging over a million pounds of PCBs (polychlorinated biphenyls) into the water over several decades. PCBs, initially used as insulation in capacitors, were later found to be extremely toxic carcinogens that persist in the environment and are linked to diseases like Parkinson's.

I finished third grade at an elementary school in Hudson Falls. We lived in a rented house as my parents built a new home in Glens Falls, New York. There were five children in the family at the time: my older sister and me, plus three younger girls aged one, three, and five. I started fourth grade at Queensbury Middle School in Glens Falls. Our new house was in a large suburban neighborhood with lots of kids our ages. I was nine years old, and my sister was eleven.

We lived close enough to the middle school to ride our bikes to school, weather permitting. The neighborhood kids all played together—dodgeball, badminton, basketball, and hopscotch. We built go-karts out of two by fours with scavenged axles and wheels. We rode our bikes a lot.

My family seemed to divide into three groups: my sister Deene and I, the next three girls (Joy, Lynn, and Claudia), and Marcia and Ted (born in 1960 and 1962). Deene and I were independent, with a four-year age gap between me and my sister Joy.

We lived a comfortable middle-class life. With seven kids and a stay-at-home mom, money was sufficient but there was nothing left for luxuries. I became active in the Boy Scouts, which was an inexpensive activity, and I had a lot of friends in my troop. I mowed lawns in the summer and shoveled driveways in the winter for spending money. I even earned money babysitting, as parents figured I could handle a couple of kids with my experience caring for five younger siblings.

Deene and I learned to snow ski and play golf. My dad joined the Glens Falls Country Club, where he and my mom learned to play golf. I occasionally got to join them, which was always fun. Deene and I participated in the junior golf program, playing nine holes before heading to the club's lake for swimming.

In June 1963, my dad took me to the US Open Golf Tournament at The Country Club in Brookline, Massachusetts. Arnold Palmer lost in a playoff to Julius Boros. Jack Nicklaus, the defending champion from 1962, didn't make the cut that year. I vividly remember the periscopes we used to watch the tournament. With seven kids, this was the only time I ever had a trip alone with my dad. It is a special memory.

In the winter, we learned to ski with two friends, Dave and Cynthia Bannon. Deene and I bought used equipment to save money, while Dave and Cynthia had the latest gear. We weren't jealous; it was simply how things were.

Every summer, we traveled from Glens Falls to South Lee, Massachusetts, where my dad was born and raised. His parents, my grandparents (Gammi and Gampa), never moved from South Lee. My dad's brother Bob, also a South Lee resident, had seven children. With fourteen grandchildren of similar ages, summers were lively.

Typical summer day at camp in Stockbridge Bowl.

My dad and Uncle Bob helped my grandfather build a cabin on Stockbridge Bowl, a small lake near Tanglewood, the summer home of the Boston Symphony Orchestra. We called our cabin "camp." There was a small five horsepower manual pull-cord motor for the rowboat, but it rarely worked well. Deene and I spent hours exploring a tiny island in the lake using the canoe. We caught frogs (which my mom cooked), fished off the dock, and swam at the beach. These summers are among my fondest memories.

My five years in Glens Falls—from January 1959 to January 1964—were some of the happiest times of my life. I often think of this period as my *Leave it to Beaver* days.

Scouting

The Boy Scouts of America (BSA) has been an integral part of my life since I was eleven years old. I joined Troop 2 in Glens Falls, NY, in the Mohican Council of Upstate New York, when I started sixth grade in 1961. I had always enjoyed playing outdoors with friends, and we collectively decided that joining the Boy Scouts for camping and hiking adventures would be fun.

Throughout my life, I've been driven by a focus on success, and Boy Scouts presented a golden opportunity to challenge myself: earning the prestigious Eagle Scout rank. The criteria for attaining Eagle Scout status were clearly defined. Scouts had to progress through the ranks—Tenderfoot, Second Class, First Class, Star, Life, and finally Eagle.

Earning the rank required completing various merit badges, as outlined in specific booklets. These included mandatory skills such as cooking, hiking, swimming, lifesaving, camping, first aid, and personal fitness. Additionally, Scouts had to choose from optional merit badges like coin collecting, skiing, astronomy, fishing, canoeing, journalism, basketry, leatherwork, woodcarving, and home repairs.

Determined to achieve my goal early, I planned to earn my Eagle Scout rank by the eighth grade—an accomplishment that was almost unheard of, as most Eagle Scouts typically achieved the rank in their junior or senior years of high school.

December 16, 1963 Eagle Scout photo.

By the end of sixth grade, I had advanced from Tenderfoot to First Class, mastering outdoor skills and participating in enjoyable activities like camping and hiking. In seventh grade, I shifted my focus to earning merit badges. By the end of that year, I had become a Star Scout and was on the verge of achieving Life Scout. During the summer of 1963, I attended summer camp, completed the mile swim, earned additional required merit badges, and advanced to Life Scout.

At the start of eighth grade, I was a Life Scout and, after earning my final required merit badge, I achieved the rank of Eagle Scout on December 16, 1963 at the age of thirteen. Alongside this achievement, I earned the Catholic Ad Altare Dei religious award as a member of Troop 2.

In January 1964, my family moved to Hendersonville, NC when my Dad was promoted by GE to be the manufacturing manager of the outdoor lighting plant. I joined Boy Scout Troop 601 in the Daniel Boone Council. I was inducted into the Tsali Lodge #134 of the Order of the Arrow, Scouting's honor society. Later that year, I attended the sixth Boy Scout National Jamboree in Valley Forge, PA, and the 1964 World's Fair in New York City as a side trip with my troop.

I remained active in Troop 601 until my junior year of high school. However, once I had a driver's license and a car, my Boy Scout career came to an end.

Camp Scouthaven with my son at summer camp.

Years later, my 1998 congressional run, though unsuccessful, brought me recognition in Western New York. In 1999, I was invited to join the Boy Scout executive board of the Greater Niagara Frontier Council (GNFC), serving as vice president for administration before being elected Erie County executive in 2007. I chaired the GNFC committee for several Boy Scout National Jamborees (2001, 2005, 2010, 2013, and 2017). My son attended the 2005 and 2010 Jamborees, following in my footsteps.

As a parent, I served as Den Leader for my son's Cub Scout Den from 2000 to 2003 and as cubmaster for Pack 568. I organized summer trips to Camp Scouthaven in western New York and later joined Boy Scout Troop 93 as an Assistant Scoutmaster. I introduced the "First Year—First Class" program, aimed at helping new Scouts achieve the First Class rank in their first year.

In 2008, I led our troop on a challenging high-adventure trip to the Philmont Scout Ranch in New Mexico, where my son and I faced demanding hikes and wilderness living. For my contributions to Scouting, I was honored with the Silver Beaver Award in 2011, along with other accolades such as the Cub Scouter, Den Leader, and Webelos Den Leader awards.

Elected to Congress in 2012, I became the chair of the Congressional Scouting Caucus, supporting both Boy Scouts and Girl Scouts. I hosted annual visits from the Boy Scouts of America chief executive and designed a unique Congressional Challenge Coin featuring the Scout Fleur-de-Lis alongside the Cub Scout and Boy Scout mottos. Additionally, I displayed the Scout flag outside my congressional office, a distinction I was proud to uphold.

In 2016, I received the National Eagle Scout Association's Outstanding Eagle Scout Award, a rare and prestigious honor. My son, inspired by his own Scouting journey, became the youngest Eagle Scout in New York at age twelve in seventh grade. He ultimately earned sixty-seven merit badges and nine Eagle Palms—an extraordinary achievement.

Scouting profoundly shaped my life over the past sixty-five years, starting with my time in Troop 2 in 1961. The memories, lessons, and values gained through Scouting remain a cornerstone of my life, and the time spent with my son during his decade in Scouting remains one of my greatest joys.

Hendersonville, NC

When my dad came home one day in 1963 and announced we were moving to Hendersonville, North Carolina, I was very upset. I was in the middle of eighth grade, but my sister, Deene, in the middle of her sophomore year in high school, was even more distraught. Moving during middle school is hard, but moving during high school felt catastrophic to her. My five younger siblings, ranging in age from one to nine, adapted more easily.

We moved to Hendersonville in January 1964. Deene and I attended Hendersonville High School, which at the time was segregated, while my younger siblings went to a private Catholic school. My initial impression of Hendersonville High was bleak. The building was old and run-down, a stark contrast to the modern Queensbury Middle School I had attended. The sight of men shoveling coal into the school's basement on a snowy day only added to the dreariness.

I was assigned to Mr. Swofford's algebra class. He was, quite frankly, in my opinion an awful human being. The moment I walked into the classroom, he asked, "Who are you?" I introduced myself and explained that the principal, Mr. Lockaby, had assigned me to his algebra class. Without missing a beat, he interrogated me about my background and questioned why anyone would think I was qualified to be there.

I told him I had moved to Hendersonville from Glens Falls, NY. With a smirk, he turned to the class and announced, "We've got a Yankee in our midst." He then asked about my previous math class. I replied that I had been in "modern math."

He sneered, snorted, and chuckled simultaneously. "Let's see how good this Yankee is with algebra," he said. "Modern math sounds like a bad joke to me."

He called me to the blackboard, directing me to solve equations in front of the class. I solved them all, one after another. The class sat in silence, staring at me. This routine continued for five days straight. Isolated and without friends, I didn't tell my parents about the ordeal.

On the fifth day, he finally stumped me with a complex problem well beyond standard algebra. Turning to the class, he proclaimed, "I know Mr. Collins doesn't belong in this class, but we'll have to put up with him as he catches up to all of you." He then told me to sit down. My classmates looked at me like I was from another planet.

When I started my junior year of high school, I was sixteen, had a driver's license, and owned a car. I worked at Holly-Swofford Shoe Store to pay for the car, gas, and insurance. Earning straight commission at 10 percent motivated me to become an excellent shoe salesman. I worked five days a week after school and all day on Saturdays.

In a letter of recommendation dated May 31, 1968, Mr. John Holly wrote:

> "Chris Collins is punctual, loyal, and has developed into the best part-time salesman we have ever had. He handles men, women, and children professionally and seldom needs help with fittings. His quickness, intelligence, and patience usually make him the top person on the floor. Chris is a high-type young man, consistently on the honor rolls during his high school years, and one who will be sorely missed by our organization. We recommend him highly."

During high school, I played on the golf team, joined several clubs, was inducted into the National Honor Society, and served on the Student Council for three years. Despite being a Yankee, I had many good Rebel friends.

In January 1968, my dad was promoted to General Manager of GE's Somersworth, NH facility. At age forty-four, he relocated the family to Durham, NH. My sister, Deene, was a freshman at the University of North Carolina at Chapel Hill (UNC), and I was in my senior year at Hendersonville High School. I refused to move mid-year, and surprisingly, my parents didn't insist. They found me an apartment, helped furnish it, and moved to New Hampshire with my five younger siblings.

Living alone to finish high school was almost unheard of. The administration didn't know how to handle me. When I skipped school (occasionally), I wrote my own notes: *"Please excuse Chris Collins' absence from school. Signed, Chris Collins."*

My apartment became a social hub. Parents warned their daughters against going there, but teenage girls are the same in every generation—they followed their instincts, not parental warnings.

One wall of my apartment was stacked with empty beer cans, floor to ceiling. In 1968, the legal drinking age was eighteen, so getting beer at sixteen or seventeen wasn't difficult. It's safe to say my senior year of high school was memorable—for me and many others.

I graduated near the top of my class of 135 students. After graduation, I drove to Durham, NH, where I got a job selling shoes. Not knowing anyone, I spent most of the summer working. It was a lonely, uneventful time.

NC State University (Raleigh, NC)

In the fall of 1968, I began engineering school at N.C. State University in Raleigh, NC. Freshmen weren't allowed to have cars, so I flew from New Hampshire and shipped my belongings in a trunk. I lived in a dormitory my first year, in the Sigma Pi fraternity house my second year, and in an off-campus apartment for the remaining two years.

The year 1968 was tumultuous. The Vietnam War escalated, marked by the Tet Offensive. Martin Luther King Jr. and Robert Kennedy were assassinated. Richard Nixon was elected president, and on Christmas Eve, Apollo 8 became the first manned spacecraft to orbit the moon.

As a Mechanical Engineering major, my coursework was rigorous, encompassing math, engineering, and science. Classes included Analytical Geometry Calculus, Applied Differential Equations, Thermodynamics, Fluid Mechanics, and Heat and Mass Transfer. To meet humanities requirements, I also took courses in Accounting, Economics, Corporate Finance, Business Law, Religion, and Science and Civilization.

I made the Dean's List every semester except for two—those coincided with the year I pledged Sigma Pi. Fraternity life proved to be a distraction, albeit a memorable one.

On December 1, 1969, the Selective Service held its first Vietnam draft lottery. My fraternity brothers and I gathered to watch as 366 numbers, one for each day of the year, were drawn. We each contributed five dollars to a pot, which went to the person with the first number drawn—or, as we jokingly put it, "the loser." The first number, assigned to September 14, became lottery number one. My birthday, May 20, was drawn as number 183.

Draft boards called the first 195 numbers in 1970. Fortunately, my college draft deferment protected me. After I graduated in 1972, the war was winding down, and my draft number was never reached.

After my freshman year, my parents moved from Durham, NH to Rochester, NY, when my dad left General Electric and became president of General Railway Signal Company. That summer, I moved to Rochester and worked two jobs: designing filters as a draftsman by day and selling shoes in the evenings and on Saturdays. When Neil Armstrong walked on the moon on July 20, 1969, I was driving from Rochester, NY back to Raleigh, NC for the fall semester in college.

I stayed in Raleigh the following summers, avoiding the isolation of Rochester. I sold shoes and spent time with college friends who also stayed in Raleigh.

On May 29, 1972, tragedy struck at the North Hills Shopping Mall where I worked. A sniper killed three people and injured eight before taking his own life. Among the victims was my fraternity brother, Mel Harrison, who was picking up his wife, Brenda, from work. Mel was shot as he drove toward the shopping center. It was a heartbreaking loss.

College during the Vietnam War was fraught with protests and demonstrations. At N.C. State, we looked to the more liberal University of North Carolina at Chapel Hill for cues on activism. My junior year, a campus-wide protest led to the cancellation of final exams.

When I graduated in 1972, calculators were a new innovation, and personal computers were still years away. Engineering students relied on slide rules for calculations. I like to say we sent a man to the moon using slide rules.

Our graduating class was the last at N.C. State not required to take a computer science course. On May 13, 1972, I received my Bachelor of Science in Mechanical Engineering. In 2015, I was honored to be inducted into the N.C. State Mechanical and Aerospace Engineering Hall of Fame.

The recession in 1972 made engineering jobs scarce, but I was fortunate to receive six job offers through on-campus interviews. After careful consideration, I chose to start my career at Westinghouse Electric.

CHAPTER 3

Westinghouse Career

WHEN I BEGAN WORKING FOR Westinghouse Electric in 1972, I envisioned a lifelong career, with the ultimate goal of becoming the president and CEO of the company. Starting an entrepreneurial career was far from my imagination.

My father had a successful career with General Electric, rising through the ranks in manufacturing. Every four or five years, he would receive a promotion, which often meant relocating the family to begin a new role. A chemical engineer by training, he started his GE career as a purchasing agent in Schenectady, NY, where I was born. Later, he was transferred to GE headquarters in New York City, prompting the family to move to Stamford, CT, where he commuted daily by train. In 1959, when I was nine, he was transferred to Hudson Falls, NY, as the manufacturing materials manager. By 1964, he was promoted to manufacturing manager for the outdoor lighting factory in Hendersonville, NC. His final role at GE came in 1968, as the General Manager of the Outdoor Metering and Instrument Transformer Division in Somersworth, NH. At just forty-four years old, he left GE to become president of General Railway Signal Corporation in Rochester, NY.

As my graduation from NC State approached, I sought my father's advice regarding my career. The job market in 1972 was tough, but I was fortunate to have received five or six solid offers. My top two choices were General Electric and Westinghouse Electric. GE offered a role as a mechanical engineer, while Westinghouse proposed a sales engineer position. I turned to my father for guidance.

He advised me to accept the position at Westinghouse. He explained that while GE was a better-managed company, a successful engineering career there would be highly competitive and challenging. He shared that, during his time at GE, he had often struggled to demonstrate his ability to handle customer-facing responsibilities. By contrast, a sales engineering role at Westinghouse would allow me to establish that skill set early in my career. Moreover, Westinghouse, unlike GE, didn't have a reputation for top-tier management, giving me an opportunity to differentiate myself and advance more quickly.

Following my father's advice, I accepted the sales engineer role at Westinghouse—a decision that ultimately altered the course of my life.

Sales Engineer

As a new hire, the sales engineer career path at Westinghouse involved short, month-long assignments at various sales offices. Most new employees found a permanent position after completing four to five assignments. I began in the Greensboro, NC, office, followed by stints in Charlotte, NC, and Tampa, FL, before securing a permanent role in Birmingham, AL.

My career took an unexpected turn early on. After only two months as an assistant sales engineer in Birmingham, I was offered the opportunity to step into the outside sales engineer role—a position usually attained after two years of training. This rapid advancement came when the sales manager fired two outside sales engineers and offered me the chance to fill one of their roles. This unexpected promotion accelerated my career trajectory by at least two years, presenting both a significant opportunity and a challenge; I was in the spotlight and had to either succeed or fail spectacularly.

While performing my duties as an outside sales engineer, I simultaneously attended training programs designed to prepare inside sales engineers for this position. My assignment involved selling the full range of Westinghouse Electric products to user accounts—companies that purchased equipment for their own manufacturing operations. Other sales engineers specialized in selling to distributors, consulting engineers, or original equipment manufacturers (OEMs).

Alabama, with its robust base of heavy industrial manufacturers, provided a rich territory. My region spanned roughly half the state, covering Montgomery in the south to the Tennessee border in the north, and from the Georgia border in the east to the Mississippi border in the west. Key clients included Gulf States Paper, Kimberly-Clark, US Steel, Republic Steel, Reynolds Metals, Union Camp Paper, and many others.

To excel in my role, I needed comprehensive knowledge of a wide range of products, including AC and DC electric motors, industrial gears, switchgear, transformers, relays, capacitors, circuit breakers, controls, and more. Sales ranged from $300 for a 5-HP motor to $1 million for an electrical substation for a major plant expansion. I joined professional organizations like the Association of Iron and Steel Engineers (AISE) and the Institute of Electrical and Electronics Engineers (IEEE) to network with engineers and enhance my professional development.

From 1973 to 1976, life as a sales engineer had its challenges. Without modern tools like cell phones, personal computers, or word processing software, much of my work involved driving several hours to meet clients, listening to AM radio during the drive, and taking clients to lunch. These trips, while sometimes monotonous, laid the groundwork for my future success.

Always forward-thinking, I sought opportunities to enhance my qualifications and position myself for advancement. In November 1973, I applied to the MBA program at the University of Alabama at Birmingham (UAB). Scoring in the top 3 percent on the Admission Test for Graduate Study in Business (ATGSB), I was accepted into the program in Spring 1974. With a flexible schedule, I was able to attend afternoon classes while working full-time. I focused my MBA studies on finance and accounting and completed the program in two years, earning my degree in June 1976.

By this time, I had over three years of experience as an outside sales engineer and consistently exceeded my sales quotas, often doubling my targets. With my MBA in hand, I requested a transfer to one of Westinghouse's factories and was offered a position as a market research analyst in the Buffalo, NY, Medium Motor & Gearing Division.

Market Research Analyst

I arrived in Buffalo in August 1976, just five months before the infamous Blizzard of 1977—a frosty welcome to the city. My supervisor, Cary Mock, became a mentor to me. He was a brilliant strategist and manager, and I worked closely with him for eighteen months on various projects aimed at driving growth for the Medium Motor & Gearing Division.

The energy crisis of the 1970s created a demand for energy-efficient solutions, and Cary and I identified electric motor efficiency as a key marketing opportunity. While electric motors were generally efficient, there was room for improvement, especially in industrial applications where motors often ran twenty-four/seven. I led the development of the MAC-II line of high-efficiency motors, which ranged from five to 250 horsepower. These motors provided significant energy savings for heavy-duty users in industries like paper and steel manufacturing.

By 1977, we launched the MAC-II motors, which quickly became the industry standard for high-efficiency motors. To promote the product line, I traveled extensively, presenting at industrial conventions and writing technical papers that explained the improvements we made and their cost-saving benefits. The MAC-II line was a resounding success, and in December 1977, the US Department of Energy recognized Westinghouse with an Energy Excellence Award for the development of these motors.

This achievement brought me recognition from Westinghouse's upper management and reinforced my reputation as a key contributor to the company's success.

Cary and I also worked on a strategic plan to elevate the Gearing Product Line, which had long been an afterthought compared to the company's primary focus on motors. Gears and gearboxes, which were essential to transmitting power from motors to machinery, received little marketing or sales support. We proposed spinning off the Gearing Product Line into a standalone profit-and-loss (P&L) division. The plan was approved, and on January 5, 1978, Cary Mock was appointed General Manager of the newly formed Gearing Product Line Division.

Strategic Planning Manager

Typical Westinghouse management meeting.

With Cary's promotion, I was appointed Strategic Planning Manager for the Medium Motor & Gearing Division at just twenty-seven years old—a corporate-level management position that placed me in a pivotal role. Over the next two years, I supported Cary's efforts to reposition the Gearing Division, creating new marketing materials, introducing innovative products, and refining cost analysis tools to focus on more profitable sales.

One of my key responsibilities was managing the division's centralized computer systems, which housed production, sales, and cost data. In the late 1970s, personal computers and tools like Excel didn't exist, so I taught myself to write computer programs that provided actionable insights for the sales and marketing teams. These efforts helped the division identify sales trends, improve profitability, and streamline operations.

Cary's exceptional leadership earned him a promotion to Westinghouse's Mergers, Acquisitions, and Divestitures department at corporate headquarters in Pittsburgh in December 1979. At just thirty-six years old, he left behind a well-positioned Gearing Division. Once again, I was in the right place at the right time, stepping into the role of General Manager of the Gearing Product Line Division. At twenty-nine years old, I became the youngest manager in Westinghouse history to hold a P&L corporate position.

General Manager: Gearing Division

Under my leadership, the Gearing Division experienced significant growth:

Year	Sales	Profit
1978 (Mock)	$6,255,000	$0
1979 (Mock)	$7,734,000	$0
1980 (Collins)	$14,107,000	$2,000,000
1981 (Collins)	$23,254,000	$3,500,000
1982 (Collins)	$15,973,000	$1,000,000

The growth in 1980 and 1981 was driven by increased demand for gearmotors used in offshore oil rigs during the oil crisis, and the development of rapid rail transit systems in major cities, including New York, Washington, and San Francisco.

In mid-1982, Westinghouse formed a joint venture with Francorail, a French company, to manufacture railcars for New York City's R68 subway project. Francorail built the cars in France, and Westinghouse supplied the propulsion systems, including DC traction motors and gearboxes. I was offered the position of president of Westinghouse-Francorail—a role that came with apartments in Paris and New York City. At just thirty-two years old, I had the opportunity to oversee a high-profile project that aligned perfectly with my goal of becoming president and CEO of Westinghouse.

I accepted the position and began working with the Westinghouse Transit Division to prepare for my new role. Since the official start of my presidency was set for 1983, I continued to manage the Gearing Division in Buffalo in the interim.

After a decade at Westinghouse, I had firmly established myself as a fast-track leader within the company, consistently achieving results and surpassing expectations. My unconventional career path and relentless focus on advancement had positioned me to realize my ultimate ambition.

CHAPTER 4

Purchase of Westinghouse Gear Division

ON SEPTEMBER 13, 1982, I received an unexpected call from Cary Mock. He informed me that Westinghouse planned to phase out operations at the Buffalo plant, beginning with the closure of the Gearing Product Line Division. He asked me to keep this information confidential.

Cary suggested that I consider purchasing the division and offered his assistance if I was interested. His proposal left me speechless—stunned, confused, and unsure how to respond.

Sensing my hesitation, Cary elaborated, promising that Westinghouse would be fair and reasonable in supporting a Leveraged Buyout (LBO). He reminded me of the job offer to serve as president of Westinghouse-Francorail, assuring me that the position would remain available if the LBO didn't materialize.

I told Cary I needed time to consider my options and promised to call him back the next day. The idea of owning a company had never crossed my mind, and the prospect both intrigued and overwhelmed me. Successfully executing an LBO seemed daunting, yet the potential rewards were compelling.

After weighing the challenges against the potential financial upside—and buoyed by Westinghouse's offer to hold the joint venture opportunity open—I decided to proceed. The next day, I called Cary and confirmed my interest. He expressed confidence in my ability to succeed and encouraged me to move forward.

I began researching LBOs and discreetly consulted four trusted colleagues at Westinghouse, whom I also considered potential partners:

- Carl Becker, sales manager of the Gearing Product Line Division;
- Dave Ashman, manufacturing manager of the Gearing Product Line Division;

- Lou Masciantonio, manager of Repair Parts for the Gearing Product Line;
- Chuck Kolkebeck, field sales manager in Birmingham, AL.

They were as shocked as I was by the news of the division's closure, but expressed interest in exploring roles in the potential new company.

Negotiating Terms and Building the Plan

I met with Cary Mock to discuss the logistics of relocating the operation from the existing factory. Several key issues needed addressing:

- Union negotiations with the International Union of Electrical Workers (IUE),
- Timing for vacating the factory,
- Coordination of manufacturing operations to fulfill existing orders,
- Sales force restructuring since Westinghouse sales representatives were dispersed across the US,
- Partnerships with Westinghouse Electric Supply Company and Industrial Services for distribution and repairs, and
- Payment terms and purchase price.

Cary estimated the purchase price at $5–6 million and promised to draft a preliminary letter of intent.

To navigate these complexities, I reached out to Al Hill, a corporate attorney at Moot & Sprague. We discussed financing options, including Industrial Revenue Bonds, bank loans, and SBA guarantees. Al emphasized the need to secure 20 percent of the purchase price from private investors, equating to roughly $1 million—a daunting figure for me and my prospective partners, none of whom had substantial funds.

On October 19, I met with the Erie County Industrial Development Agency (ECIDA) to explore financing options, including bonds and Regional Development Corporation loans. An appraisal of the machinery was required as collateral.

Meanwhile, Cary presented a concise four-page letter of intent. The terms included a purchase price of $3.1 million for assets and $1 million for inventory, with Westinghouse covering rigging costs for relocating machinery. These terms exceeded my expectations, and I agreed without negotiation.

Incorporating the Company

As I delved into the division's history, I learned that Westinghouse had acquired the R.D. Nuttall Company in 1928. A respected name in the gearing industry, Nuttall pioneered the involute gear tooth and in 1916 founded the American Gear Manufacturers Association. Inspired, I decided to revive the Nuttall name, incorporating Nuttall Gear Corporation on November 4, 1982, as a Subchapter S Corporation in Delaware.

Dave Ashman, Carl Becker, and Chuck Kolkebeck joined as founding shareholders. We set a fundraising target of $1 million for 20 percent equity, valuing the company at $5 million.

Securing Financing and Facilities

Over the next two months, I held numerous meetings with banks, the local Industrial Development Agency (IDA), the SBA, and potential investors. Despite challenges, progress was steady. I also began searching for industrial real estate and discovered the vacant Bell Aerospace plant in Wheatfield, NY. The facility, with its high ceilings and ample space, was ideal for our needs.

Textron, the plant's owner, offered favorable lease terms:

- Two dollars per square foot for ten years, with a ten-year renewal at $2.50 per square foot.
- Free heating and access to surplus office equipment at no charge.
- Dedicated parking for 125 employees.

The deal was extraordinary, reducing our costs significantly.

Finalizing the Deal

By year's end, Westinghouse pressed to finalize the Letter of Intent. However, fundraising remained a hurdle. Marine Midland Bank required

$1 million in equity for a $3.5 million demand loan and a $1.5 million line of credit.

After negotiations, Marine Midland agreed to reduce the equity requirement to $300,000, alleviating some pressure. We raised $100,000 from outside investors with a private placement stock offering. I provided $100,000 and my three partners provided the remaining $100,000.

We finalized the allotment of founder's stock as follows:

1.	Chris Collins	50.70%
2.	Dave Ashman	14.15%
3.	Chuck Kolkebeck	14.15%
4.	Carl Becker	11.50%
5.	Outside Investors	9.50%

On December 28, 1982, I signed the letter of intent.

Westinghouse, as a public company, issued a press release to announce the letter of intent agreement to sell the assets of the Westinghouse Gearing Products Division to Nuttall Gear Corporation. *The Wall Street Journal* published a short article titled "Westinghouse to Sell Its Gear-Making Assets."

On January 7, 1983 *The Buffalo News* published a more in-depth story titled "Westinghouse will lose another division, but the Buffalo area will gain an independent manufacturer."

The following months were a whirlwind of legal agreements, financing approvals, and operational planning. My team worked tirelessly to ensure a seamless transition.

Closing the Deal

The final agreement was signed on April 4, 1983, marking the official launch of Nuttall Gear Corporation.

That evening, we celebrated at my home, coinciding with the NCAA basketball championship—a serendipitous victory for my alma mater, NC State, who defeated Houston 54–52. The ending of the game is one of the most famous in college basketball history, with a buzzer-beating dunk by Lorenzo Charles off a desperation shot from thirty feet out by Derek

Whittenburg. The NC State victory has often been considered one of the greatest upsets in college basketball history.

It was an unforgettable day, symbolizing both professional and personal triumphs.

At thirty-two years old, I was a self-made millionaire on paper. Though challenges lay ahead, I felt confident in the future of Nuttall Gear and the journey we were about to embark on.

CHAPTER 5

Nuttall Gear Corporation

Start-up and Transition to Bell Aerospace

Prior to the closing on April 4, 1983, we spent considerable time at Bell Aerospace reviewing surplus office equipment offered to us at no charge. Most of the furniture was from the WWII era, consisting of gray and green metal desks, filing cabinets, and simple, utilitarian tables and chairs. We also utilized an older phone system, which sufficed during our start-up phase.

Nuttall Gear Corporation company brochure.

Our rented office space was a standalone 7,000-square-foot building on Niagara Falls Boulevard with a convenient adjacent parking lot. With the help of Bell Aerospace personnel, we moved the furniture we selected into our rented office. The main office housed me, Chuck Kolkebeck, and Carl Becker. There was ample space for design engineers, purchasing, sales and marketing, and accounting. Additional office space in a mezzanine area of the factory was designated for salaried production personnel, including quality assurance, production planning, manufacturing engineering, and Dave Ashman's office. Surplus furniture from Bell Aerospace furnished all these offices.

Our purchase from Westinghouse included drafting tables, blueprint machines, and filing cabinets filled with engineering drawings. I made an investment in three new IBM personal computer XT computers, which had been released just one month prior, on March 8, 1983. Each computer, featuring floppy disk drives and 128 KB of memory, cost $7,545—a significant expenditure at the time. These were assigned to Carl Becker, Chuck Kolkebeck, and me. Reflecting back, it's amusing to think how revolutionary those computers seemed then.

The Lotus 1-2-3 spreadsheet program, introduced on January 26, 1983, was a game-changer. Recognizing its potential, I ensured Nuttall Gear became one of the first companies in the USA to utilize IBM XT computers running Lotus 1-2-3 for daily tasks in sales, marketing, and accounting.

We persuaded retired Westinghouse manufacturing executive Bill Meier to join Nuttall for one year to oversee the relocation of the Westinghouse machinery. This was no small feat—350 pieces of machinery, some so large they had to be disassembled, transported, and then reassembled at the Bell Aerospace plant. The largest, an Ingersoll planer mill, weighed one hundred tons. Several gear-cutting machines required pits beneath them for collecting metal filings, necessitating foundation excavations about six feet deep.

Bill Meier's experience proved invaluable. Having supervised the relocation of gear machinery from Pittsburgh to Buffalo in 1960, when Westinghouse moved the industrial gear product line, he was familiar with many of the same machines we moved in 1983.

To ensure a smooth transition and maintain production continuity, we manufactured additional inventory at the Westinghouse facility to fill the gap during the machinery move. Dave Ashman and his production planning team did an excellent job coordinating production to meet customer shipping dates despite the upheaval.

Within days of our April 4 closing, we had salaried personnel operating from the Bell Aerospace facility. We convinced four Westinghouse gear engineers to join Nuttall Gear, as they recognized their careers at Westinghouse were effectively over. Additionally, several Westinghouse sales support personnel transitioned to Nuttall. Hiring machinists for our new facility was straightforward, as many experienced workers from the Gearing Division, and even some from the Motor Division, were available due to prior layoffs at Westinghouse.

Cash flow, however, was a major concern. Following the closing, we had approximately $300,000 cash on hand. Legal and financing costs exceeded expectations, including fees for the Niagara County Industrial Development Bond, the N.F.C. Development loan, the SBA-guaranteed Marine Midland Term Note, and the Marine Midland Accounts Receivable Line of Credit.

Additionally, while Westinghouse covered rigging expenses for removing machinery, we were responsible for transportation and installation costs at Bell Aerospace. We had to pay the rigger $250,000 as a 50 percent down payment on the total $500,000 contract to move all the machinery from the Westinghouse facility to our new location at the Bell Aerospace facility.

After paying the rigger, Nuttall was left with only $50,000 in our bank account on April 5.

The cost to maintain production at Westinghouse was $75,000 per week, payable weekly. With the Marine Midland Line of Credit accessible only after invoicing customers, our cash flow remained precarious. It felt as though Nuttall Gear was bankrupt on the day of the LBO closing.

Fortunately, Westinghouse was slow in invoicing us for weekly production, which allowed us to limp along. By shipping and invoicing approximately $500,000 worth of products in April, we were able to borrow $400,000 against our $1.5 million line of credit. Although cash flow remained tight over the next five months, we managed to stay current with vendor payments and employee payroll. We worked tirelessly to vacate the Westinghouse facility by August 31, 1983.

Nuttall Gear—Independent of Westinghouse: The Journey Begins

By August 31, 1983, Nuttall Gear had completely vacated the Westinghouse facility. All machinery was installed and operational in the Bell Aerospace plant. Our focus shifted to securing orders from existing and new customers, establishing ourselves as a reliable supplier of industrial gearing products. With one hundred years of history as a major gear supplier, and permission to use the Westinghouse name for one year, we referred to Nuttall Gear as the "successor to the Westinghouse Gearing Product Line" during this transition period.

Nuttall Gear had the capacity to produce gears ranging from four to 105 inches in diameter, serving industries such as: steel, aluminum, paper, chemical processing, bulk material handling, water and sewage treatment, mass transit, offshore oil, textiles, coal crushing, cranes and hoists, wood debarking, food machinery, wind turbines, hydro turbines, and nuclear reactor plants.

Continuing to utilize the Westinghouse national sales force was crucial for maintaining customer loyalty. Many customers visited our new Niagara Falls facility and were impressed with its organization and cleanliness. Every machine moved from Westinghouse was cleaned and repainted. Early on, I implemented visual management practices, including signage identifying machines and their capabilities, painted floor lines, and branded work shirts for employees, complete with our logo and their names.

This foundation set the stage for Nuttall Gear's journey as an independent company, ensuring a seamless transition while preserving customer trust and operational excellence.

I considered $9–10 million in sales to be our baseline objective for the standard product line sold to existing customers. We had a small backlog of transit drives for the Buffalo NFTA mass transit system and one offshore oil rig project as we embarked on our new future. Additional sales volume was essential for achieving solid profitability.

Having been offered the position of president at Westinghouse-Francorail, I was well acquainted with the R68 New York City transit project, which required 219 new rail cars with 876 gear drives. In June 1983, I traveled to Pittsburgh to initiate negotiations for Nuttall Gear to secure the contract for the 876 WNT-44 gearboxes. The discussions progressed smoothly, and on October 18, 1983, Westinghouse awarded Nuttall Gear the contract.

Wind turbines were emerging as a significant market for power generation, each requiring a gearbox to drive the turbine. In November 1983, Nuttall Gear secured a $1 million contract from Dynergy for gear drives for 200 wind turbines, supplementing our baseline sales.

International Paper (IP) had long been Westinghouse's primary customer for traditional gear drives, with every IP paper machine relying on them. Known for their reliability, these gear drives operated continuously year-round. We secured a new two-year contract to supply all of International Paper's gear drives for 1984 and 1985, providing much-needed assurance that our new venture was on the right path.

Westinghouse Electric, the world's largest supplier of nuclear reactors, utilized gear drives produced in Buffalo, including critical speed increasers for reactor cooling pumps. In March 1984, Nuttall Gear was certified as an approved manufacturer of nuclear 1-E equipment. This certification enabled us to continue manufacturing safety-related components for nuclear power plants.

By May 1984, Nuttall Gear had partnered with thirteen independent sales representative organizations, increasing to twenty by October 1984. With most of the country covered, we were prepared for the end of our relationship with the Westinghouse Industrial Sales Organization on December 31, 1984.

In October 1984, Nuttall invested in a Prime Computer 2250-012 system and Manage-2000 software from ROI Systems in Minneapolis. This technology supported material requirements planning (MRP), order entry, purchasing, invoicing, and accounting. The new system ensured a seamless transition from Westinghouse's computer systems by the end of 1984.

Our involvement in the wind turbine market expanded in 1984, including a subsequent Dynergy order for 160 additional gearboxes, totaling 480 units since 1983. We also received a $1 million contract from Fayette Manufacturing for speed increasers for their wind farm in Altamont Pass in Northern California.

In July 1985, I was elected to the American Gear Manufacturer's Association (AGMA) board of directors for a four-year term. The twelve-member board oversaw an organization representing 300 companies with over 32,000 employees and annual sales exceeding $2 billion.

On September 30, 1985, we completed our second profitable year of operations independent of Westinghouse, entering fiscal year 1986 with growing sales and a healthy backlog.

Starting October 1, 1985, we decided to allocate 80 percent of profits to the four founders, 20 percent split equally as compensation for managing the company, and 60 percent based on ownership. Though this caused some tension due to my substantial ownership, the decision was implemented without significant disputes.

International Paper extended its contract for another year, including a project to provide gear drives for a $200 million expansion in Pine Bluff, Arkansas. With 168 Nuttall/Westinghouse gear reducers already installed there, our reliability record helped secure the extension. Additionally, E.I. DuPont approved Nuttall Gear as a supplier, awarding a $200,000 contract for synthetic fiber production lines in October 1985.

The offshore oil business saw a significant downturn with plummeting oil prices. In March 1986, we secured one order for a jack-up rig with Petrobras, Brazil's national oil company. However, the offshore oil market never regained its former momentum.

During 1984–1985, Nuttall successfully fulfilled the 876 WNT-44 gear drive contract for Westinghouse-Francorail, boosting our base load. Despite steady industrial business, competition intensified as foreign manufacturers entered the US market. In November 1986, we secured a new transit contract with General Electric for 432 WNT-44 gear drives for a New York City subway car overhaul project. This contract, influenced by New York State's financial incentives, provided a thirteen-month sales boost from May 1987 to June 1988.

In October 1986, AGMA honored Nuttall Gear with a Founders Award for seventy years of commitment to the association, tracing back to the R.D. Nuttall Company, which helped establish AGMA in 1916. This recognition surprised competitors, as Nuttall Gear had been in existence for just three years.

After Dave Ashman's passing from lung cancer in 1986, we fairly negotiated with his estate to purchase his shares.

Sales grew consistently from fiscal years 1988 to 1991. We focused on niche markets underserved by traditional gear manufacturers, specializing in custom-engineered products often produced in small quantities. We invested in computer-aided design (CAD) software to modernize our engineering department, transitioning from traditional drafting methods to advanced computer technology.

On April 15, 1990, Nuttall Gear paid off the $3.5 million Industrial Revenue Bond used to finance the 1983 leveraged buyout of the Westinghouse Gearing Division. This milestone marked a significant rite of passage for the company.

The three remaining founders enjoyed competitive salaries and profit-sharing distributions. With the bond repaid, the company generated positive cash flow, providing financial flexibility for future growth.

Employee Stock Ownership Plan (ESOP)

I explored options to enable the three founders to leverage the seven-year success of Nuttall Gear into a cash distribution for ourselves. The ultimate win-win I identified was an Employee Stock Ownership Plan (ESOP), benefiting not only the three founders of Nuttall Gear but also all the employees.

In 1974, Congress recognized ESOPs as qualified employee benefit plans and granted them tax advantages.

Marine Midland Bank agreed to fund our ESOP, fully understanding the benefits it brought to both the founders and the employees. Prior to this, Nuttall Gear had negotiated with several minority owners to buy back their stock. When we closed the ESOP transaction on January 1, 1991, the ownership of the company was structured as follows:

ESOP	38.0%
Chris Collins	37.0%
Chuck Kolkebeck	10.0%
Carl Becker	8.5%
All Others	6.5%

An independent appraisal valued Nuttall Gear's equity at $8 million. We financed the ESOP's 38 percent ownership stake with a $3.0 million seven-year term loan from Marine Midland.

The $3.0 million loan was distributed among the original founders and minority shareholders as follows:

Chris Collins	$1,800,000
Chuck Kolkebeck	500,000
Carl Becker	400,000
All Others	300,000
	$3,000,000

Nuttall Gear regularly shared quarterly sales and profit information with employees, ensuring no surprises during the annual ESOP valuation. Employees understood that the value of their ESOP holdings was directly tied to the company's profitability, fostering a culture of motivation and productivity. This alignment also removed concerns about employees voting to organize a union.

Seven Years of Success Leading to the Sale

The ESOP became effective on January 1, 1991, marking nearly eight years of Nuttall Gear's existence. With solid profitability and growth potential, the ESOP aligned management and employees towards a shared goal of increasing profitability and company value.

Between 1991 and 1997, Nuttall Gear maintained steady and consistent sales and profit growth. The company earned numerous accolades, including:

- Business First "Top 100" list of private companies (1987–1994)
- "Future 50" company award in 1995
- Western Region Small Business Showcase Award for Manufacturing in 1996, presented by Empire State Development.

Nuttall Gear continued to thrive by focusing on custom-engineered gear drives, a niche with limited competition and robust profit margins. Our emphasis on customer service and quality set us apart from competitors.

Acquisition by Constellation Capital Partners

On February 19, 1997, I received a call from Philip Knisely, CEO of Constellation Capital Partners LLC, a private equity firm based in Richmond, VA. The firm, founded in 1995 by Philip Knisely, Mitchell Rales, and Steven Rales, sought to develop world-class industrial manufacturing platforms. Their initial focus was on power transmission through Ameridrives International.

Nuttall Gear, a well-known custom manufacturing company in the power transmission industry, was identified as an ideal acquisition candidate. This call came at an opportune time as Chuck, Carl, and I had just decided it was time to sell Nuttall Gear.

During the conversation, I expressed interest and sent preliminary information, including all thirty-three *News From Nuttall* newsletters, product literature, and financial details. On March 19, 1997, we hosted Knisely and Executive VP John Young at our Niagara Falls plant. The meeting was productive, with Knisely expressing strong interest and requesting additional financial information.

After further discussions and document exchanges, we reached a tentative agreement on April 11, 1997, less than two months after the initial call from Phil Knisely. The deal's complexity stemmed from the ESOP, which required dissolution before the sale. Constellation Capital led the drafting of the necessary documents, and the closing date was set for July 1, 1997.

Closing and Aftermath

The ESOP was terminated, and employees received $3,292,695 for their stock. All employees were immediately 100 percent vested, with some receiving life-changing amounts exceeding $100,000. Many expressed gratitude for this windfall.

For my part, I received $3,406,335 for my ownership stake, plus $1,080,000 for my shareholder loan, representing undistributed profits. Including the cash that I received when the ESOP was established, I felt well-compensated for my efforts and contributions to Nuttall Gear.

By the time of the sale, Constellation Capital had already acquired four other manufacturing companies. Subsequently, Constellation Capital rebranded as Colfax Corporation, establishing two platforms: Power Transmission and IMO Pump. In 2004, Colfax's Power Transmission Group merged into Altra Industrial Motion Inc.

Today, Nuttall Gear remains operational in its original Bell Aerospace facility as part of Altra Industrial Motion Inc. As the co-founder of Nuttall Gear, it is gratifying to see the company continue to provide good-paying jobs in Western New York.

CHAPTER 6

Transition to Politics

President Nuttall Gear LLC

After closing the sale of Nuttall Gear Corporation to Constellation Capital, I began a new career as the president of Nuttall Gear LLC, a wholly owned subsidiary of Constellation Capital. Chuck Kolkebeck and Carl Becker joined me in their new roles as employees of Nuttall Gear LLC.

I felt a little strange as I pulled into my parking space on July 2, 1997. I was no longer the majority owner of Nuttall Gear Corporation. I was back to being a corporate employee, with a boss. The difference now was that I had a substantial net worth and a lot of cash in the bank.

The entire company had shared in the success of Nuttall Gear, so the mood in the shop was very positive. Several employees admitted to me that they never fully understood the ESOP and never thought they would see anything substantial from it. One employee shook my hand and "apologized" for saying anything negative about me. That was pretty funny.

Nuttall Gear was considered a first cousin to Danaher Corporation. Mitch and Steve Rales, co-founders of Danaher, were also co-founders of Constellation Capital. Two weeks after our sale, I was sent to a Danaher facility to be trained in the Danaher Business Systems (DBS) that Danaher used to manage and operate their various divisions. Total Quality Management (TQM) which I utilized at Nuttall Gear, was completely compatible with and complementary to DBS. When I attended the training at Danaher, it was an extension of the TQM training I had already experienced.

Just one month after Constellation Capital purchased Nuttall Gear, they acquired Boston Gear, headquartered in Quincy, MA. Boston Gear was a large manufacturer of small, standardized gear drives. Delroyd Worm Gear, owned by Boston Gear, operated in a facility in Trenton, NJ. Following the acquisition, Constellation Capital changed its name to

Colfax Corporation. Boston Gear operated as a division of Colfax, while Ameridrives, including Nuttall Gear, operated as a separate division.

Phil Knisely asked me to oversee the relocation of all Delroyd Worm Gear machinery from Trenton, NJ, to the Nuttall Gear factory. He wanted Delroyd to operate as a division of Nuttall Gear. Boston Gear focused on standardized gear drives, whereas Delroyd Worm Gear specialized in custom gear drives. Moving Delroyd to Nuttall made a lot of sense, as the synergy was obvious. The overhead expenses of Delroyd would be reduced by 75 percent after the move.

I secured additional space in the Bell Aerospace facility and, on an expedited basis, had all the machinery moved to Niagara Falls by Thanksgiving.

In January of 1998, Phil Knisely called and asked me to take the position of president of Boston Gear and relocate to Quincy, MA. Boston Gear had sales exceeding $100 million annually and was much larger than Nuttall Gear. They had factories in Quincy, MA, Charlotte, NC, and Raleigh, NC.

From Phil's perspective, this was a substantial promotion for me and confirmed my role as a key employee in the Colfax operation.

I respectfully turned down the offer and told Phil I wanted to remain president of Nuttall Gear LLC. Phil was dumbfounded that I would decline such an opportunity. His offer, and my refusal, marked a turning point for me.

I came home after my conversation with Phil and told my wife that my time with Colfax was limited. I didn't fit the mold of an aggressive, career-driven executive at Colfax. It was time for me to consider other options. Money was not an issue after selling Nuttall Gear. I could pursue any number of opportunities without time constraints.

I had signed a three-year employment contract, but there were no "golden handcuffs" incentivizing me to stay with Colfax.

Congressman Bill Paxon

I was acquainted with Bill Paxon, a congressman from Western New York who lived in my town, Clarence, NY. Bill Paxon was the chairman of the National Republican Congressional Committee (NRCC) and one of the top four leaders in the House of Representatives. Newt Gingrich was Speaker, Dick Armey was Majority Leader, and Tom DeLay was Majority Whip.

In the summer of 1997, several House Republicans saw Newt Gingrich's public image as a liability. There was an attempt to force Gingrich to resign as Speaker, with Bill Paxon proposed as his replacement. Dick Armey balked at the proposal to make Bill Paxon the new Speaker and warned Gingrich of the coup.

Gingrich retaliated against Bill Paxon and forced him to resign as chairman of the NRCC. Gingrich had appointed Bill to the position, so he had the authority to remove him.

On February 28, 1998, Bill Paxon announced he would not seek reelection to Congress. This was big news in Western New York, and I heard the announcement on the radio. Although I had never considered running for Congress or any public office, Bill Paxon's decision not to run for reelection presented an opening for me to pursue a complete career change—moving from the private sector to the public sector as a Member of Congress.

The NY-27 congressional seat held by Bill Paxon was a solidly Republican seat, previously held by Jack Kemp. Any Republican running for that seat was almost guaranteed to win. This was an opportunity for me to resign as president of Nuttall Gear LLC and run for Congress.

The day after Bill's announcement, I called him to express my desire to replace him in Congress. His response was disappointing. He told me that Tom Reynolds, a fellow Republican, had already been chosen by the Republican county chairs as the 1998 candidate for Congress in NY-27. Tom was the Minority Leader in the NY State Assembly and a longtime politician.

Bill was intrigued by my offer and suggested I run for Congress in NY-29 against incumbent Democrat Congressman John LaFalce. John LaFalce had been elected to Congress in 1974 and served for twenty-four years without a significant challenge. He was a pompous individual, not well-liked in his district, but so well-entrenched that no Democrat would challenge him. Republicans who ran against him were always underfunded and unable to wage a credible campaign. Although I didn't live in NY-29, Nuttall Gear was located there, giving me a credible reason to run. There is no requirement that a congressional candidate live in the district they're running in.

Bill expected Republicans to gain forty seats in the House of Representatives in the 1998 mid-term election. Bill Clinton's scandal involving Monica Lewinsky was tabloid fodder in January 1998. As the former head of the NRCC, Bill believed the scandal would hurt Democrats much like the Richard Nixon scandal hurt Republicans in 1974, costing them forty-eight seats in the mid-term election.

Bill was confident I could defeat John LaFalce with a properly funded campaign. I told Bill I was willing to provide a substantial initial loan to my campaign. Bill assured me that as long as Republicans won at least ten seats, I would be a new Member of Congress by January 2, 1999.

Bill offered to help me assemble a campaign staff with personnel loyal to him, who were seeking opportunities because he wasn't running for reelection.

I accepted Bill Paxon's help and decided to run for Congress in NY-29 in the 1998 mid-term election. This was a bold, unexpected, and life-changing move.

CHAPTER 7

1998 Congressional Election

Campaign Team

To get my campaign started, Bill Paxon recommended that I hire Michael Hook, co-founder of the political consulting firm Greener and Hook. Michael Hook had served as Paxon's chief of staff from 1993 to 1995 and was most recently chief of staff at the Republican National Committee (RNC).

Trusting Paxon's recommendation, I hired Michael Hook as my campaign consultant to develop a strategy to defeat Rep. John LaFalce in the 1998 midterm election. Michael had strong connections with GOP county chairs in Western New York, and a deep understanding of the demographics and politics of NY-29.

I assured Michael that my campaign would be well-funded, even if it required my own financial support. A candidate can loan money to their campaign and later repay it if the campaign generates enough cash.

Collins For Congress

Campaign Button for 1998 Congressional campaign in NY-29.

With Michael's assistance, I completed the necessary paperwork to run for Congress. I registered "Collins for Congress" as my campaign committee, opened a bank account, and arranged for office space at Bell Aerospace, where Nuttall Gear was located.

Michael accompanied me to meet the four GOP county chairmen of NY-29, representing Niagara, Erie, Monroe, and Orleans counties. As a political novice, I relied on Michael's established credibility from his time as Paxon's chief of staff. This connection gave me instant credibility with the county chairmen.

Yard sign promoting my campaign.

Although I wasn't ready to announce my candidacy publicly, word leaked that I was meeting with GOP committees across NY-29. On March 29, 1998, *The Buffalo News* published a top-of-the-fold lead article titled, "LaFalce could face tough GOP challenge." The sub-title read, "Ex-Paxon aide signs on with campaign."

Bob McCarthy, the lead political reporter for *The Buffalo News*, reported that I had secured support from leaders of all four GOP county organizations in NY-29 and committed to raising $1 million for the campaign. Erie County Republican Chairman Robert Davis was quoted saying, "This is without question the most serious challenge John LaFalce has ever had. This is for real."

Palm Card for 1998 congressional campaign.

The article also highlighted that I had been in Washington the prior week meeting with party and congressional leaders, and attending candidate sessions sponsored by the NRCC. It noted Michael Hook's involvement as a key figure in my campaign.

Over the next five weeks, I prepared campaign materials, including palm cards, bumper stickers, and campaign finance literature. To jumpstart fundraising, I loaned my campaign $150,000, signaling to potential donors my commitment to funding the campaign adequately.

I formally announced my candidacy on May 6, 1998, at a press conference with my family standing in front of Nuttall Gear. I emphasized my background as the founder, president, CEO, and chairman of Nuttall Gear. Holding a large sign that read, "Chris Collins for Congress," I articulated my vision:

"My vision of Western New York in the 21st century is a region that is dynamic, vibrant, and full of energy—a family community that is the envy of the entire country. I will devote all my energy to making that vision a reality."

Two headlines in local newspapers helped define my candidacy:

- "Collins opens bid against LaFalce with big cash supply"
- "Businessman announces candidacy"

These articles highlighted my business background, contrasting it with John LaFalce's long political career. One article noted that I was launching my campaign with over $250,000 already in the account.

Campaign

From May through August, I focused on fundraising and grassroots campaigning. I traveled extensively across NY-29, participating in parades, visiting county fairs, touring small businesses, and meeting as many voters as possible.

A friend who owned a car dealership helped locate a 1974 Chevrolet Impala for use in parades. The car symbolized how long Rep. John LaFalce had been in Congress. On one side, it read, "74—The year John LaFalce went to Congress." On the other, "Retire this car—Retire John LaFalce."

The car's symbolism resonated with people and helped reinforce my campaign's message that it was time to retire LaFalce. I was told the car's presence unsettled him, which I took as a good sign.

Campaign literature for 1998 congressional campaign.

Our campaign literature struck a balance between introducing me positively to voters (30 percent) and criticizing John LaFalce's record (70 percent). Negative mailers focused on his voting record and support for liberal, tax-and-spend policies.

One standout piece of literature was a four-page positive mailer, designed to look like a *Time* Magazine cover, highlighting my business achievements and vision. Additionally, we produced 5.5" x 10" mailers with bold titles that caught voters' attention in their mailboxes. Each negative mailer carried the title "The John LaFalce Report," followed by pointed critiques of his record:

1. **"Votes five times against the Balanced Budget Amendment."** "John LaFalce says Congress shouldn't have to live within its means like every American family."
2. **"Says no to reforming welfare and no to welfare recipients working for their check.**" "John LaFalce voted no when Bill Clinton and Congress changed 'welfare as we know it.'"
3. **"Votes yes to the largest tax increase in U.S. history."** "… one of the best votes I've cast in my entire 20 years in Congress."
4. **"Why is this man smiling?"** "If your pay increased from $44,600 to $136,672 per year, you'd be smiling too."

These materials effectively framed the choice for voters, drawing a stark contrast between my vision for the future and LaFalce's lengthy political career and voting record.

We mailed a 5.5" x 10" comparison mailer that compared my stance on issues to John LaFalce's. On the front of the mailer, there was a title in large, bold font. Inside were four issues:

LaFalce vs. Collins
Who best represents you?

Chris Collins	**John LaFalce**
- Supports a balanced budget amendment	- Voted against the Balanced Budget Amendment
- Will support tax cuts	- Voted for the largest tax increase in US. history
- Welfare recipients should work for a check	- Voted against the welfare reform law that passed
- Will never vote for a pay raise	- Voted yes to raise his pay six times

We started spending money in September on TV ads and mailers. *The Buffalo News* reported on our first ad with the headline:

"Collins challenges LaFalce with personally financed TV ads"

Bob McCarthy reported, "Republican congressional candidate Christopher Collins transforms a low-key campaign into a high-energy effort today with the debut of television commercials financed by almost a half a million dollars of his personal funds. The thirty-second spots will air during newscasts every day between now and Election Day. Collins' first buy cost six figures."

McCarthy continued the article, quoting me as saying, "In Washington, they don't ask where the money came from, or care that it came from my personal checking account. This is my way of sending a message to Washington and the local community that I've done my part."

We ran TV commercials non-stop from September 1, 1998, through Election Day, November 3, 1998. The TV ads were hard-hitting negative commercials attacking John LaFalce. We had fun detailing his many trips to Europe at taxpayer expense, misrepresenting the trips as official government business. We noted that most of these trips occurred during the Christmas season. At one point, John LaFalce had been quoted as saying his wife liked to go to Europe around Christmas each year.

The TV commercials showed John LaFalce flying a biplane with a red scarf trailing behind him in the wind, as though he was Snoopy impersonating the Red Baron from WWI. People really enjoyed those commercials. We made our point with a very funny portrayal of John LaFalce. However, we heard that John LaFalce and his wife did not find the commercials amusing at all.

John LaFalce refused all my demands for a public debate. I finally corralled him at an event on October 24, 1998, sponsored by the Niagara Business Alliance in Tonawanda, NY. They tricked John into attending and ambushed him with two podiums set up for a debate. The press was in attendance, having been tipped off that Collins and LaFalce were going to debate. John LaFalce couldn't duck out the back door and was finally compelled to face me in a debate.

We went at each other, back and forth. At one point, John tried to take credit for my success with Nuttall Gear. He actually said, "Chris did a great job creating jobs with Nuttall Gear, but what he doesn't tell you is that he did it with a Small Business Administration loan I authorized the legislation for."

The newspaper story covering the debate noted that LaFalce's assertion angered me, and I replied, "I can't let John LaFalce take credit for the success of my business. My business was a success in spite of John LaFalce and the other liberals in Washington."

The newspaper coverage of the surprise debate largely favored me. They reported that on the subject of raising the minimum wage, LaFalce was pro, and I was con. One reporter said she was surprised I did as well as I did in a debate against a veteran politician like John LaFalce. She wrote that I had a very direct and solid presentation, and that both of us exhibited good knowledge and touched briefly on each other's records, with neither backing down from the other.

Headlines reported:

- "LaFalce, Collins face off on issues"
- "LaFalce, Collins square off"
- "LaFalce, Collins differ sharply at forum over ways to improve the local economy"

Other than the one debate late in the campaign, we battled each other with press releases and press conferences that were always covered. Our race had tightened, and the public was interested in all the details surrounding my campaign to unseat a twenty-four-year incumbent who had never faced a serious challenger.

Some of the newspaper headlines tell the story of our race coming down to the wire:

- "A novice is giving LaFalce a tough fight"
- "Candidate says he has right stuff to beat 'ultraliberal' LaFalce in the 29th District"
- "LaFalce fights battle of career versus Collins"
- "LaFalce duels with Collins over trips"

On September 18, 1998, I became the first congressional candidate to call for President Clinton's resignation in the wake of the Monica Lewinsky scandal. The newspaper headlines were clear:

- "LaFalce challenger first to call for president's resignation"
- "Congressional candidate blasts president's conduct"

Polling conducted early in October indicated that I had closed the gap with Rep. John LaFalce and even held a slight lead. My campaign was hitting on all cylinders. We had succeeded in our strategy to portray Rep. John LaFalce as an arrogant, anti-job, anti-business, tax-and-spend liberal who represented the failed policies of the past.

The Clinton Impeachment Inquiry

I was blindsided on October 8, 1998, when Speaker Newt Gingrich launched a formal impeachment inquiry into President Bill Clinton, stemming from his denial that he had engaged in a sexual relationship with White House intern Monica Lewinsky. The inquiry focused on potential perjury and obstruction of justice during Bill Clinton's testimony in a sexual harassment lawsuit filed by Paula Jones.

With less than four weeks to go before the November 3, 1998, election, this "October Surprise" turned into a nightmare for Republicans. Clinton's nationally televised speech from January 26, 1998, where he famously stated, "I did not have sexual relations with that woman, Miss Lewinsky," was still fresh in voters' minds.

The decision of Speaker Gingrich to launch the inquiry united Democrats and many Independents to show their disapproval by turning out in the mid-term elections. Over sixty years, between 1938 and 1998, the president's party had lost seats in every Congress during mid-term election cycles. However, this backlash resulted in Republicans losing five seats in the 1998 mid-term election—a stark contrast to their anticipated gains.

I lost the election to incumbent Rep. John LaFalce on November 3, 1998. I remain convinced that I would have defeated him had Speaker Gingrich waited until after the election to launch the impeachment inquiry. Life is full of surprises, and this one backfired on me and many other Republicans in 1998.

Campaign Finances

Raising money as an unknown challenger taking on a twenty-four-year incumbent is very difficult. People don't want to contribute to a candidate they think has no chance of winning. Additionally, many people hesitate to upset a sitting Member of Congress by contributing to their opponent.

I primarily self-financed my campaign with loans. Later in the campaign, as my race tightened, I raised what you might call defensive money. While people don't want to contribute to a losing campaign, they also don't want to be left out of a winning one. I raised over $150,000 in the last couple of weeks of my campaign.

I spent $937,900 on my 1998 campaign. I had committed to spending $1 million and came very close to hitting that target. I would have actually spent more than $1 million, but as the election approached, all available advertising spots were already taken by other candidates running for statewide offices.

I raised a total of $398,112, with $299,436 contributed by individuals and $98,676 contributed by the NRCC. I loaned my campaign $539,821.

John LaFalce spent $1,026,000 on his campaign. He raised $739,399, with $298,302 coming from individuals and $441,097 from PACs. Even though he only raised $739,399 in 1998, he ended his campaign with a significant cash-on-hand balance.

John LaFalce never faced another serious challenger. While I lost, I'm proud of running a first-rate campaign that nearly succeeded against a twenty-four-year incumbent.

CHAPTER 8

Cobblestone Enterprises LLC

AFTER LOSING THE ELECTION FOR Congress on November 3, 1998, I was uncertain about where my future would take me. I had been confident I would win the election and was unprepared for the loss. Having spent fourteen years as the president and CEO of Nuttall Gear Corporation, I didn't feel inclined to pursue another opportunity as a full-time president and CEO of a company.

However, I was confident I could bring value to small companies that might be struggling for various reasons. I had financial resources at my disposal, and through raising money via private placement to finance the purchase of Nuttall Gear from Westinghouse Electric, I had gained experience interacting with individuals seeking investment opportunities in small businesses.

I was friends with Geoff Rosenberger, co-founder of Clover Capital Management in Rochester, NY, a highly successful investment firm. Geoff had invested the proceeds from our 1991 ESOP at Nuttall Gear and, like me, had also run for Congress and lost. We shared similar experiences and perspectives.

I reached out to Geoff and arranged a lunch meeting to discuss my options. I valued his opinion and wanted his insights. During our conversation, Geoff shared his experiences investing in small businesses and mentioned friends who collaborated as a group to invest in companies seeking outside funding. He highlighted how many small businesses were undercapitalized and struggled to grow due to a lack of resources for marketing, inventory, computer systems, or quality employees.

Geoff was familiar with my efforts in Total Quality Management (TQM) at Nuttall Gear and highlighted my experience to illustrate how I could help small businesses become more efficient. Our discussion left me feeling energized and focused. I envisioned a future where I could act as an advisor and investor in multiple small businesses. Inspired by this, I decided to form an investment company. Since I lived on Cobblestone Drive, I named it Cobblestone Enterprises LLC and structured it as a single-member LLC.

Business Plan

I developed a business plan with clear objectives and a strategic focus. I outlined the profile of potential target companies:

- Undercapitalized small companies serving a sustainable market niche
- Strong management
- Collateral available to secure loans
- Good variable margins on incremental growth
- Potential for strategic add-on acquisitions or roll-ups

I also established guidelines for strategic loans I would offer:

- Interest rate of Prime +2 percent, with a floor of 8–9 percent, paid monthly on a secured loan
- Five to ten year amortization of principal, with interest-only payments in the first year if needed
- Collateral to secure the loan, with a subordinated position to the company's bank or principal lender
- Personal guarantees from the owners, if appropriate but not critical
- Equity stake of 20–49 percent at no cost as an incentive for providing a secured loan

To protect my investments as a minority investor, I would implement the following measures:

- Appointment to the board of directors
- Shareholder agreements specifying covenants and management compensation and benefits

- Board resolutions requiring unanimous approval for major decisions, such as real estate purchases or asset disposals
- Agreements ensuring minority shares are sold under the same terms as majority shares in case of a sale
- Yearly stock valuation agreed upon by shareholders

Incentives for management:

- A bonus of 20 percent of operating profits, coupled with a living salary
- Stock incentives tied to achieving specific objectives, such as aggressive growth targets in the first or second year after the investment

Key considerations for all investments included:

- The investment must be a win-win for all parties involved
- Partners must be honest, hardworking, and motivated to succeed
- Partners must have a significant personal stake in the company's success

In cases involving real estate, I explored setting up a separate holding company to own the real estate, with the business paying rent equal to the mortgage payment. This arrangement also ensured that the company would handle maintenance, repairs, taxes, and utilities. After the mortgage period, typically fifteen years, the real estate would be owned outright, providing a substantial return at no cost. Depending on the situation, real estate investments might not be shared with partners. I also considered personally financing real estate or equipment at slightly above-market rates.

Financing

- As a subordinated lender, collateral was available if banks lent at 75 percent of receivables or 50 percent of inventory
- Secondary mortgages on real estate often provided solid collateral

- Machinery and equipment owned outright by the company could serve as valuable collateral
- Properly structured loans with collateral ensured precedence over unsecured creditors in bankruptcy scenarios

While I was uncertain about finding investment opportunities, I saw potential in engaging with the Center for Entrepreneurial Leadership (CEL) at the State University of New York at Buffalo (UAB). The CEL program allowed small business owners to pay a tuition fee for a year-long program that included studying business principles and crafting strategic plans with input from advisors and peers. I anticipated enjoying the interactions with other small business owners and knew my positive reputation as an entrepreneur would benefit me.

My investment in Nuttall Gear had garnered publicity, including recognition as a top one hundred business in Western New York, various manufacturing awards, and four years of service on the Small Business Advisory Council to the Federal Reserve Bank of New York.

Summary and Profile of Cobblestone Enterprises LLC Investments

Over time, my investments spanned various industries and followed a consistent logic. Each investment involved a collateralized loan subordinated to the primary lender, an equity stake at no cost, and an operating agreement that provided robust protection for my loan and minority ownership.

Categories of Investments

My nineteen investments fell into seven categories:

1. **Management Buyout:**
    - Nuttall Gear
    - ZeptoMetrix (Cellular Products)
    - Easom Automation Systems
    - Niagara Ceramics

2. **Strategic Rollup:**
    - Mead Supply
    - Lang & Washburn Electric
    - Electric Motor Supply
    - Chautauqua Millwork
    - By Design
    - Buffalo Casual Furniture
    - X-Bats
3. **Recapitalization:**
    - Oakwood Woodworks
    - Volland Electric
4. **Bankrupt Company Asset Sale:**
    - Bloch Industries
5. **Secured Lender UCC Article 9 Asset Sales:**
    - Frontier Supply
    - BioClinical Partners (BCP)
6. **Shareholder-Approved Bulk Sale of Assets:**
    - Schlyer Machinery
    - OGSI
7. **Strategic Investor:**

Virionyx, Ltd / Innate Immunotherapeutics

Platform Companies

1. **Nuttall Gear Corporation**—Sold to Constellation Capital
2. **ZeptoMetrix Corporation**—Sold to Private Equity Group
    - Cellular Products
    - BioClinical Partners (BCP)

3. **Bloch Industries LLC**—Shut Down and Liquidated
    - Oakwood Woodworks
    - Chautauqua Millwork
    - By Design
    - Buffalo Casual Furniture
    - X-Bats
4. **Volland Electric Equipment Corporation**—Still Operating Profitably
    - Mead Supply
    - Frontier Supply
    - Lang & Washburn Electric
    - Electric Motor Supply
5. **Easom Automation Systems**—Sold to Lincoln Electric
6. **Audubon Machinery Corporation**—Sold to NOVAIR
    - OGSI
    - Schlyer Machine
7. **Niagara Ceramics Corporation**—Shut Down and Liquidated
8. **Virionyx, Ltd / Innate Immunotherapeutics**—Now Amplia Therapeutics Ltd

Chapter 9 - Chapter 16 cover my entrepreneurial career, purchasing a number of companies starting in 1999.

CHAPTER 9

Bloch Industries LLC

SHORTLY AFTER LOSING THE ELECTION for Congress in NY-29 to Representative John LaFalce on November 3, 1998, I received a call from my brother-in-law, Brian Geary. Brian informed me that Bloch Industries in Rochester was being auctioned off by a bankruptcy trustee overseeing the company's bankruptcy proceeding since August 1998.

Bloch Industries was a well-known custom kitchen cabinet company that had been in business since 1956. Lee Bloch originally founded the company in 1952 as a shower-door firm. In 1956, the company transitioned into custom cabinetry after moving into a facility with leftover cabinet-making machinery. By the time Lee Bloch sold the company in 1986, custom cabinets had virtually eclipsed the shower-door business.

The company's most recent owner, Samuel Yacono, tragically committed suicide shortly after the SEC began investigating Bloch Industries in August 1998. The investigation centered on allegations of $780,000 in employee retirement funds being diverted. Following the death of Yacono, Bloch Industries shut down and entered bankruptcy, with Douglas Lustig appointed as the bankruptcy trustee. At the time of its closure, the company employed eighty-five people.

Under the guidance of the bankruptcy judge, Lustig reopened Bloch Industries in October 1998 with a smaller staff of thirty employees. The company's products, sold under the Quaker Maid brand, were highly regarded within the kitchen cabinet industry.

After touring the facility with Brian Geary, I saw the potential in the business and agreed to help finance its purchase from the bankruptcy court.

Purchase of Bloch Industries

Bloch Industries operated out of two adjoining buildings with a combined total of 53,000 square feet. The buildings were connected by a walkway.

The first building, 140 Commerce Drive, was relatively new and modern, housing the showroom and offices. The second building, 130 Commerce Drive, was much older and contained most of the woodworking machinery.

In a bankruptcy auction conducted by Lustig, we successfully acquired all of Bloch Industries' assets for $1.8 million. Brian and I only had to put up $400,000 in cash to close the deal. M&T Bank provided $1.1 million as a first mortgage on the two buildings, and the bankruptcy trustee agreed to a payment schedule for $300,000 spread over three years.

We finalized the purchase on February 11, 1999. At that point, Brian and I officially owned a custom cabinet company, and the journey to bring Bloch Industries back from bankruptcy began.

Business Operations

To assist Brian, I commuted to Rochester four days a week to address the various challenges of stabilizing our new company. Drawing on my background in Lean Six Sigma, I implemented strategies to enhance efficiency. A critical component of Lean Six Sigma is the 5S methodology, which promotes organizing, cleaning, developing, and sustaining a productive work environment. The 5S pillars are:

- **Sort:** Remove unnecessary items from each area.
- **Set in Order:** Organize and identify storage for efficient use.
- **Shine:** Clean and inspect each area regularly.
- **Standardize:** Incorporate 5S into standard operating procedures.
- **Sustain:** Maintain and improve upon established practices.

I found myself deeply involved in manual labor, working on ladders, moving ductwork for the dust collection system, running conduit and wiring for machines, and installing compressed air piping for air tools. I enjoyed the hands-on work and believed it sent a strong message to employees: if I could get my hands dirty doing these tasks, I was committed to the company's success.

Bloch Industries shop photo.

Our hard work began to pay off. Home builders placed initial orders, and after receiving high-quality products delivered on time, they returned with more orders. However, we faced significant challenges, including a sluggish market and intense competition from low-cost cabinets manufactured in China. Retail giants like Lowe's and Home Depot offered standard cabinets at prices far below those of our custom products. Bloch's niche became higher-priced custom homes, as lower-priced homes and apartments typically utilized the cheaper options from big-box retailers.

In 1999, Bloch Industries achieved sales of approximately $3 million in custom cabinetry, generating a nominal profit. To expand our business and diversify our product offerings, we acquired several other companies that were struggling financially, including Chautauqua Millwork, Buffalo Casual Furniture, By Design, and X-Bats.

Oakwood Woodworks

In May 2000, Brian Geary met with John Yetter at John's millwork and door company in East Rochester, NY. During the meeting, John expressed his desire to move into a larger facility but mentioned that Oakwood Woodworks lacked the financial resources needed for expansion. After discussions, Brian and I agreed to assist Oakwood in expanding its operations in exchange for an ownership stake in the company.

A 27,000-square-foot building adjacent to Bloch was for sale and seemed like the perfect facility for Oakwood Woodworks. On June 1, 2000, Brian and I purchased the property at 160 Commerce Drive for $1 million. John moved Oakwood Woodworks into the new facility over three weeks. In return, Brian and I acquired a 50 percent equity stake in Oakwood by providing the necessary space and financing for the company's growth.

We also supported John in designing the layout for new machinery and helped implement Lean Six Sigma and 5S methodologies into Oakwood's operations.

Over the next four years, Oakwood's sales grew from $1.8 million in 2000 to $3.5 million in 2003. However, the high costs of goods sold led to slim profit margins, and the company remained unprofitable. Oakwood failed to pay interest on my loans, which were in default. Consequently, I called in the loans, merging Oakwood Woodworks into Bloch Industries on January 27, 2005.

Bloch and Oakwood

Following the merger, Bloch and Oakwood operated as a single entity. Bloch retained its cabinetry division, while Oakwood continued its millwork and door division. The combined operation became a fully integrated wood manufacturing company with modern facilities and skilled craftsmen. Bloch earned certification from the Architectural Woodwork Institute (AWI) as a premium-grade manufacturer, producing high-end woodwork for residential and commercial clients across the US. Its product line included kitchen cabinets, vanities, entertainment units, commercial casework, architectural millwork, stile and rail doors, and home bars.

Challenges and Closure

The 2008 financial crisis severely impacted Bloch Industries. New home construction in upstate New York virtually ceased, remodeling projects dwindled, and commercial work slowed significantly. Competition intensified as struggling companies began bidding on jobs at cost just to stay afloat, eroding profit margins. Sales dropped from $5 million in 2009 to $3.5 million in 2011.

Front door manufactured by Oakwood Woodworks.

Competition from China added further challenges, as Chinese products were priced at least 30 percent lower than comparable US-made goods.

As sales continued to decline, Bloch faced mounting financial difficulties. To keep the business afloat, I provided additional loans to cover cash flow shortages and payroll. Despite Brian Geary's efforts to find a buyer, no success was achieved.

By spring 2016, it became clear that Bloch Industries could not continue. The company owed me approximately $2 million and was unable to pay even the interest on its loans. Bloch Industries ceased operations on June 30, 2016. The equipment and machinery were auctioned on July 20, 2016.

Bloch Industries was my first entrepreneurial venture following my election loss to Congressman John LaFalce on November 3, 1998. The company operated for over seventeen years, from February 11, 1999, until its closure in 2016, providing well-paid jobs to its employees during that time. Brian Geary did his best as president of Bloch Industries, but external factors proved insurmountable. Unfair competition from China, the financial crisis of 2008–2011, and the economic decline of upstate New York collectively led to the company's demise.

CHAPTER 10

ZeptoMetrix Corporation

I RECEIVED A CALL FROM Sandra O'Loughlin on May 20, 1999—my birthday. Looking back, it was one of the most impactful days of my life, which is saying a lot.

Sandy, a partner at Hiscock & Barclay, had previously assisted me during the sale of Nuttall Gear Corporation to Constellation Capital in July 1997. After leaving Constellation Capital in April 1998 to run for Congress against incumbent Congressman John LaFalce in NY-29, I named Sandy as Treasurer for my campaign.

On this occasion, Sandy was calling because she'd been hired by James Hengst and Michael Durski to help them secure a private placement to purchase an infectious disease biotechnology company in downtown Buffalo. Cellular Products Inc., the company in question, was owned by Hemagen Diagnostics Inc., a small publicly traded biotechnology company in Waltham, MA. Hemagen had purchased Cellular Products for $600,000 on November 1, 1996, during a bankruptcy proceeding. Hemagen—a manufacturer of medical diagnostic kits—found itself in financial trouble and was now seeking to sell Cellular Products for $800,000 to raise cash and fend off a hostile takeover.

Jim Hengst and Mike Durski, who had been running Cellular Products under Hemagen, saw an opportunity. Jim, the Chief Scientist and COO since 1993, and Mike, the CEO and CFO since 1995, needed outside investors to raise the $800,000. They hired Sandy to facilitate the transaction, and on May 18, 1999, signed a letter of intent with Hemagen to purchase Cellular Products, agreeing to close the deal by July 23, 1999—just sixty days away.

When Sandy called me on May 20, she described a unique opportunity and invited me to meet her at Cellular Products. I knew little about biotechnology, infectious diseases, or virology, but I agreed to meet.

Cellular Products

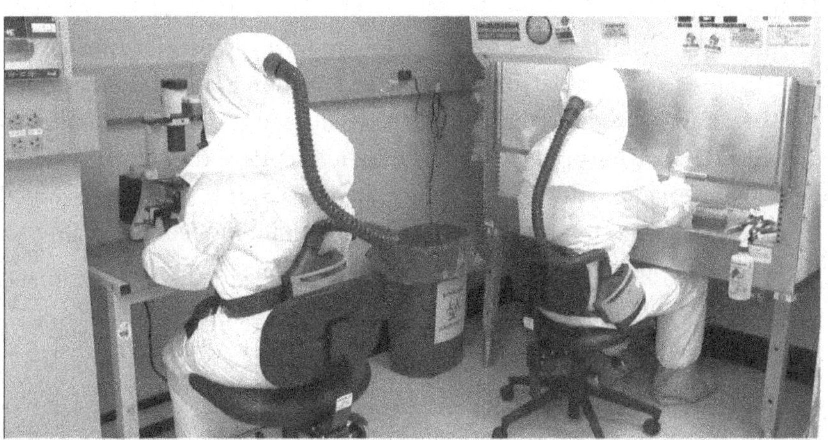

Workers in BSL-4 lab working with HIV virus.

Upon arriving, I was stunned by what I saw. On the second floor of a nondescript cinderblock building were two large biocontainment labs. Workers clad in spacesuits worked in what resembled scenes from the movie *Outbreak*, where such labs were designated Biosafety Level 3 (BSL-3) and Biosafety Level 4 (BSL-4). At Cellular Products, one lab was BSL-3, and the other was BSL-4—the highest safety level. I couldn't help but think, *Holy shit.*

In the conference room, I sat with Sandy, Jim, and Mike to discuss the opportunity. Cellular Products had been founded in 1982 to develop tests for HTLV (linked to leukemia) and HIV/AIDS. At the time, there was no test for HIV and no treatment for AIDS. Initially, it was unclear whether HIV was airborne or bloodborne, so the company built a BSL-4 lab for maximum containment. Later, when it was confirmed that HIV was bloodborne, they constructed a BSL-3 lab. Over $10 million had been invested in these labs to develop diagnostic test kits.

Despite these efforts, Cellular Products was not the first to market. Abbott Labs and Ortho Pharmaceutical received FDA approval for HIV tests in March 1985, leaving Cellular Products far behind when their test was finally approved in January 1986. Struggling financially, the company declared bankruptcy in 1994 and was ultimately purchased by Hemagen in 1996.

By 1999, Cellular Products focused on producing viruses for research use only (RUO), a less regulated market. This transition reduced overhead but left the company with minimal sales. To avoid associations with cell phones and past negative press, Jim and Mike sought to rename the company. They envisioned a name reflecting the holy grail of diagnostics: the detection of antibodies at the zeptogram level (0.000000000000000000001) grams, so they chose ZeptoMetrix as the new name for Cellular Products.

ZeptoMetrix Corporation

ZeptoMetrix intrigued me. The variable profit margin for virus production was an impressive 85 percent. The cost of building and maintaining BSL-3 labs created high barriers to entry for competitors, and the RUO virus market was too small to attract large biotech companies. Additionally, the company required minimal new capital investment. However, sales were low, and the aggressive timeline to close the purchase added risk.

After listening to their pitch, I made a decisive offer: I would provide the entire $800,000 in exchange for one-third of the company. My investment would be structured as a loan from Cobblestone Enterprises, collateralized by all company assets, plus personal guarantees from Jim and Mike. They quickly accepted. Sandy expressed interest in a 1.5 percent stake, which we agreed to, leaving 98.5 percent of the equity split equally among the three of us. We also agreed on roles: I would be chairman and CEO, Jim would be president, Mike would be CFO, and Sandy would serve as secretary.

On June 15, 1999, ZeptoMetrix signed a stock purchase agreement with Hemagen, with the closing scheduled for July 23, 1999. I financed the deal through a five-year, $800,000 loan at Prime +2 percent interest, plus a $200,000 line of credit for working capital. We closed on time, and the purchase received positive press coverage.

With my limited biotechnology experience, I initially considered my involvement with ZeptoMetrix a passive investment. However, by early

2001, sales remained stagnant at around $1 million annually, and I had to reassess my role. Jim and Mike had projected growth that had not materialized, prompting a difficult but necessary "come-to-Jesus" meeting to address the company's challenges.

Restructure Ownership

I informed Jim and Mike that I was reducing their salaries by one-third to alleviate the company's financial strain. Their reaction was, to put it mildly, explosive. As chairman and CEO, I had the authority to implement this change. Furthermore, despite having provided additional funding to sustain the company, I was not receiving any interest or principal payments on my Cobblestone loans.

In the following week, I had several conversations with both Jim and Mike. Each blamed the other for the company's poor performance, creating intolerable tension within the organization. I realized I had to make a difficult decision to ensure the company's survival.

I decided to terminate Mike Durski. As the CFO, Mike's role was replaceable, whereas Jim, the chief scientist, was irreplaceable. I knew I could reduce my time in Rochester with Bloch Industries and spend a few days a week at ZeptoMetrix, managing the company's finances and accounting.

Mike was understandably upset, though his anger seemed more directed at Jim Hengst than at me. He blamed Jim for failing to develop new products to boost sales. Two days after his termination, Mike returned to the company accompanied by an attorney.

In a meeting with Mike and his attorney, Mike expressed his desire for the company to buy his one-third ownership stake in ZeptoMetrix. I explained that the company lacked the resources to buy him out, suggesting instead that he could retain his stake and treat it as an investment, similar to owning stock in Ford or GM.

Mike, however, was adamant. Mike set his price at $2 million—a ludicrous figure for a company struggling financially. I countered with an offer of $100,000, which Mike initially dismissed. However, after a brief discussion in the hallway with his attorney, they returned and agreed to my offer, provided I also paid for two weeks of unused vacation and covered his health insurance for three months.

Flabbergasted but relieved, I agreed. I informed Jim of the deal, suggesting that we each contribute $50,000 to buy out Mike, making us equal fifty/fifty owners while Sandy O'Loughlin retained a minor 1.5 percent stake. However, Jim said he couldn't come up with $50,000. Despite my suggestions to explore options like a second mortgage or borrowing from his IRA, Jim declined. Consequently, I decided to buy Mike out myself, giving me two-thirds ownership of ZeptoMetrix.

That night, I had an idea. Instead of me buying out Mike, I would have my two children, (ten-year-old daughter and eight-year-old son), purchase his shares. Both had over $50,000 in their accounts from annual gifts under the Uniform Gifts to Minors Act. Using these funds, my kids each acquired a 16 percent stake in ZeptoMetrix in 2001. This investment, which seemed modest at the time, eventually yielded a multi-generational payday when the company was sold on December 31, 2020. Thanks, Dad!

Sales Growth

In the years that followed, Jim gradually increased company sales, producing new viruses like simian immunodeficiency virus (SIV), used in primate research for understanding HIV and AIDS. Although demand for SIV was limited, ZeptoMetrix's exclusivity in growing SIV made the sales vital to our bottom line.

Jim also developed a confirmatory test for HIV and SIV which was used by blood testing labs to test for these diseases. These assays, being highly sensitive, did occasionally produce false positives. Despite this, they were crucial in ensuring no false negatives, which would be far more detrimental. By 2002, we reached a breakeven point on cash flow, a significant milestone.

BioClinical Partners (BCP): Impath

Jim's collaboration with Greg Chiklis, a fellow PhD in chemistry, began in the late 1990s. Greg worked in Franklin, MA for BioClinical Partners (BCP), which was owned by Impath, Inc. Together, they explored ways to render viruses inactive while preserving their molecular genetic structure. This innovation led to the creation of NATrol, patented in 2001. The product, safe for researchers, retained the RNA and DNA of the pathogens intact, making it invaluable for molecular diagnostics.

Initially, we partnered with Impath, Inc. to sell NATrol while ZeptoMetrix focused on manufacturing. However, Impath sales efforts were disappointing. Eventually, we took over sales and marketing ourselves, recognizing NATrol potential as our flagship product.

The main Impath business was providing cancer treatment recommendations, which was unrelated to NATrol. The company's fraudulent financial practices ultimately led to a Chapter 11 bankruptcy in 2003. Following this, we hired Greg Chiklis as our VP of research & development under a ten-year contract that incentivized him to drive growth and innovation at ZeptoMetrix.

Purchase of BCP

In 2004, a significant opportunity arose. The Impath bankruptcy trustee informed us that the BCP division, housing valuable assets like Sub-Zero freezers and bottling equipment, was up for sale. Acquiring BCP would also resolve legal disputes over the NATrol patent. After a thorough evaluation, we concluded that purchasing BCP was a transformative opportunity for ZeptoMetrix, solidifying our position in the molecular diagnostics market.

I called the bankruptcy trustee and informed her that ZeptoMetrix would purchase the BCP division if Impath agreed to pay ZeptoMetrix \$500,000. There was a brief silence on the line before the trustee asked why she should consider paying ZeptoMetrix to take the division. I explained that disposing of 5,000 liters of infected plasma would cost Impath \$1 million. By paying ZeptoMetrix \$500,000, Impath would actually save \$500,000—a win-win proposition.

The trustee responded that my offer was insulting and unacceptable. She added that the asset sale included \$1 million in accounts receivable, which made my proposal nonsensical. Realizing the accounts receivable might indeed be part of the deal, I pivoted. I told her that ZeptoMetrix would pay \$500,000 if the assets included all equipment, inventory, and accounts receivable. I specified that the offer would be adjusted at closing based on the most recent aging of the accounts receivable, with reductions for any accounts aged over sixty days.

To my surprise, the trustee agreed and promised to have a contract delivered by Monday, March 8. Greg and Jim were stunned that I had negotiated a deal where Impath effectively paid ZeptoMetrix $500,000 after factoring in the accounts receivable included in the assets.

The price we paid was later reduced by $120,000 when the trustee informed me that they planned to retrieve ten negative-eighty degree freezers used to store the Impath cancer samples. I pointed out that the freezers belonged to ZeptoMetrix. While they could remove the cancer samples, the freezers were off-limits unless they were willing to purchase them. I offered to sell the freezers for $12,000 each, a non-negotiable price. Though initially unhappy, the trustee had no choice but to agree, resulting in a $120,000 reduction in our purchase price. We finalized the sale in early April 2004.

Proficiency Panels: Infected Plasma

With the purchase, ZeptoMetrix acquired the world's largest repository of infected plasma. In the 1980s, during the height of the AIDS epidemic, BCP had established a unique blood draw operation, compensating gay men for weekly blood donations. The assumption was that some donors would later contract HIV, providing a sequential progression of blood samples—a priceless resource for research.

ZeptoMetrix now owned this inventory of HIV-infected plasma. As researchers and pharmaceutical companies sought to develop HIV tests, the ability to detect the virus earlier than competitors became a critical advantage. ZeptoMetrix created "panels" of plasma showing the progression from HIV-negative to highly infected. These panels sold for $1,000 each, cost ZeptoMetrix nothing, and became highly sought after by researchers and pharmaceutical companies. An inventory from a single donor could yield over 500 panels.

With the advent of antiretrovirals in the early 1990s, HIV-infected individuals began treatment immediately upon diagnosis, making the collection of such sequential plasma samples impossible. The seroconversion panels from BCP's inventory became irreplaceable and remain available today, alongside similar panels for HBV and HCV.

Under Greg Chiklis' guidance, ZeptoMetrix expanded into creating proficiency panels for labs testing for various diseases. As PCR molecular diagnostics gained traction, labs such as Quest and LabCorp, as well as hospital labs, needed to demonstrate testing proficiency. ZeptoMetrix developed NATrol panels—inactive, safe samples yielding accurate results when tested correctly—and became the leading supplier for proficiency testing organizations worldwide, including:

- College of American Pathologists (CAP)
- American Proficiency Institute (API)
- LabQuality (Finland)
- BioNuclear (Puerto Rico)
- QCMD (partnered with Qnostics)

ZeptoMetrix provided influenza panels to labs three times a year, shipping over 1,000 panels per cycle and becoming one of New England's largest FedEx customers. To maintain integrity, ZeptoMetrix prepared five different panels (A, B, C, D, E) with varying virus concentrations, ensuring labs couldn't compare results among themselves. CAP graded the labs based on the actual concentrations.

ZeptoMetrix customers included prominent diagnostic companies such as Cepheid, BioFire, Luminex, Abbott Molecular, Ortho, Roche, Siemens, and others. The company developed NATrol controls for over fifty viruses, including Influenza A, HIV-1, Zika, SARS, and over 100 bacteria, fungi, and parasites.

Rapid Sales Growth

Between 2003 and 2012, ZeptoMetrix sales grew from $3 million to $10 million, and profits increased from zero to $1.5 million. Greg's contributions were recognized with a $200,000 bonus in 2012, in addition to his $130,000 salary.

In November 2007, I was elected Erie County executive, assuming office in January 2008. I will discuss this and my other campaigns for public office in later chapters. Overseeing a bankrupt county with 6,000 employees and a $1.5 billion budget kept me occupied until my unexpected reelection loss in November 2011. Shortly afterward, tragedy struck when Karen Hengst passed away in January 2012 from an aggressive flu bug. Days later, Jim Hengst became critically ill with the same flu. Greg Chiklis flew to Buffalo, took Jim to the hospital, and likely saved his life.

Following my election loss in 2011, I returned to ZeptoMetrix as chairman and CEO to oversee its operations while Jim was hospitalized.

Jim Hengst—President of ZeptoMetrix Retires

After I returned to ZeptoMetrix, employees approached me to express their concerns about Jim Hengst as president of ZeptoMetrix. The primary issues were his tendency to procrastinate on decisions, micromanage departments, and isolate the Franklin operation. I shared their frustration, as I had been disappointed with the company's slow growth over the previous two years.

In search of clarity, I consulted Greg Chiklis, who admitted to a strained relationship with Jim. Although they were peers, Greg technically reported to Jim. When I asked Greg how he would manage the company differently if he were president, he provided insights that made a lot of sense.

When Jim returned to work, I summoned him to my office to discuss the future of ZeptoMetrix. We ultimately agreed that Jim would retire with Greg taking over as President of ZeptoMetrix.

Greg Chiklis, President (2012–2017)

Greg quickly took charge and, at the end of 2012, we agreed to a five-year contract extension. He became president and COO, while I remained chairman and CEO. I increased his salary to $250,000, and adjusted his bonus structure to 10 percent of pre-tax profits up to $1 million and 15 percent above that threshold. In 2012, with profits at $1.5 million, this formula felt fair and motivating. Additionally, we agreed to a clause awarding Greg 10 percent of any sale of the company above $5 million.

In November 2012, I was elected to Congress, limiting my direct involvement with ZeptoMetrix. From 2013 to 2017, Greg excelled in growing the company. Sales surged from $9.6 million in 2012 to $23 million in 2017, while profits climbed from $1.5 million to $6.1 million. Greg's compensation reflected his success with his total earnings over $1 million in 2017.

Greg's contract was set to expire on December 31, 2017. As we entered October, Greg and I began negotiations for a new contract. We struggled to agree on a mutually acceptable formula with a base salary and bonus structure.

Greg grew impatient. When he demanded a 15 percent equity stake in ZeptoMetrix as part of a new contract, I firmly refused. Equity is a cornerstone for entrepreneurs, and gifting 15 percent ownership—valued at $15 million—was out of the question. I pointed out the tax implications of such an arrangement, but negotiations stalled.

Greg Chiklis Resigns

On October 26, 2017, Greg submitted his resignation, effective December 26, 2017. Anticipating a dispute, I initiated binding arbitration on December 18, 2017, per his employment contract. In response, Greg filed a lawsuit against ZeptoMetrix on January 16, 2018. With my reelection campaign underway, I did not what to deal with an extended lawsuit. I proposed a settlement to Greg, that if he agreed to withdraw the lawsuit he filed, I would pay him $100,000 for the bonus he forfeited by resigned prior to year-end. Greg accepted, ending the ordeal.

Shawn Smith, President (2018–2020)

Jim and I brainstormed options to replace Greg. We found an excellent candidate in Shawn Smith, who started on January 1, 2018. His contract mirrored the terms I had offered Greg, emphasizing profit growth without a sales clause tied to the sale of the company. Shawn proved to be exactly what ZeptoMetrix needed.

Under Shawn's leadership, sales rose from $23 million in 2017 to $27 million in 2019, and profits grew from $6.1 million to $9.8 million. As 2020 began, ZeptoMetrix was thriving, valued between $100 million and $150 million based on our 2019 profits.

My legal nightmare had resulted in me pleading guilty to two felonies on October 1, 2019, and resigning from Congress. More on that whole ordeal later.

I moved to Marco Island, Florida, focused entirely on my legal issues. Shawn Smith continued to run ZeptoMetrix with very little involvement on my part.

Covid-19

On March 11, 2020, the World Health Organization declared Covid-19 a global health emergency. The world was in turmoil, and no one could foresee the profound impact COVID-19 would have on our lives.

At ZeptoMetrix, our lab was frantically working to grow, purify, and inactivate the COVID-19 virus that would be used by blood testing labs. We received the virus cells on March 16, 2020, and immediately began production. The demand was unprecedented. Typically, we would grow a virus for six to eight weeks, stockpile enough inventory to last three years, then sterilize the line and switch to another virus. In contrast, our COVID production line ran twenty-four/seven and was never shut down. We shipped the virus worldwide, with exponential sales growth and profit margins nearing 85 percent, yielding profits that bordered on obscene.

Negotiation to sell ZeptoMetrix

On June 22, 2020, Shawn Smith received an unsolicited inquiry from a private equity firm, expressing an interest in acquiring ZeptoMetrix, likely intrigued by our booming COVID-19 virus production.

Shawn sent them documents, including financial statements. Negotiations began, and on October 5, 2020, the private equity firm sent a non-binding letter of interest to acquire ZeptoMetrix. This offer was based on sales data through August. COVID sales had surged from April to August, and we projected continued growth.

As negotiations continued, I was languishing in Marco Island, waiting for a firm date to report to prison. I reported to the federal prison camp in Pensacola, FL on October 13, 2020. My daughter, who is an attorney, was the point person as negotiations continued with me in prison.

While incarcerated at Pensacola Prison Camp, she handled the negotiations with the private equity firm without any involvement of my wife or son.

A deal was reached with the private equity firm, with a closing date set for December 31, 2020.

Closing on the Sale

On December 22, 2020, President Trump issued me a full, unconditional pardon, ending my incarceration after just ten weeks. Merry Christmas indeed. The pardon likely saved my life, as a COVID outbreak at the Pensacola Camp infected 100 percent of inmates in January 2021. Given my health conditions, I can't imagine how severe my symptoms might have been. The prosecutor and judge's willingness to risk my life for a prison sentence was shameful.

I was released from prison at 7:00 PM on December 22 and stayed overnight at a hotel in Pensacola. On December 23, I drove home to help finalize the ZeptoMetrix sale.

We had to register a new company name, as the seller. We opened a new bank account in Marco Island, and on December 31, 2020, the cash from our sale was wired into our account.

My twenty-one-year journey with ZeptoMetrix had concluded. From a shaky startup company with $800,000 in loans, I had built a company that sold for a multi-generational payday. Few, if any, companies with 125 employees have achieved such a monumental sale.

CHAPTER 11

Volland Electric Equipment Corporation

VOLLAND ELECTRIC WAS FOUNDED BY Alexander Volland in 1943 as an electric motor and transformer repair shop in downtown Buffalo, NY, on Ellicott Street. The company quickly expanded and relocated to a new facility at 1511 Niagara Street in 1946, which remains operational as an auxiliary site. In 1991, a new state-of-the-art plant was built at 75 Innsbruck Drive. Mr. Volland served as president of the company for thirty-two years until his untimely death in 1975 at age fifty-five.

Upon his death, the company's management transitioned to Dick Wagner and Ron Graham. Dick Wagner was married to Norma Volland, and Ron Graham to Ann Volland, who were the two daughters of Alexander Volland. Dick Wagner led the company as president until his retirement in 1985, at which point Ron Graham assumed the role of president and CEO. Ron retired in 2020, and his son Chris Graham now serves as president, with his other son, Kirk Graham, as vice president of operations.

Western New York has undergone significant changes over the past eighty years since Volland Electric's founding. In 1950, Buffalo was the fifteenth largest city in the United States; today, it is the third poorest. During the 1950s through the 1970s, Buffalo and Western New York were hubs for heavy industries, including steel, automotive, aerospace, and electric motor manufacturing. Companies such as Bethlehem Steel, Buffalo Forge, Westinghouse Electric, Bell Aerospace, Ford, and General Motors collectively employed over 100,000 factory workers. Bethlehem Steel alone had 22,000 workers before closing in 1983, and Westinghouse Electric employed over 6,000 workers before shutting down in 1986. Manufacturing jobs in Western New York have declined by over 70 percent since 1950.

Despite these challenges, Volland Electric remains a success story, reinventing itself as traditional heavy industry customers shuttered. As the saying goes, "If you are the last restaurant in town, you will be busy on

Saturday night." This sentiment aptly describes Volland Electric in 2025. While the company thrives today, many competitors have either been acquired by Volland or gone out of business.

My Involvement with Volland Electric

My association with Volland Electric began in the summer of 2001. I was playing golf one Saturday with Guy Agostinelli, a local attorney and good friend, who mentioned that one of his clients, Volland Electric, was experiencing financial difficulties and required a cash infusion to navigate a rough patch with their bank. Guy knew of my investments in Nuttall Gear, Bloch Industries, Oakwood Woodworks, and ZeptoMetrix, and wondered if I would be interested in meeting with Ron Graham to learn more about the business.

I've always been drawn to investment opportunities, particularly turnarounds. Although risky, turnarounds offer potentially lucrative financial returns if structured correctly. My business model through Cobblestone Enterprises involved structuring loans with strong collateral and security, while acquiring significant equity stakes at minimal or no cost. This approach provided a fair interest rate on loans and the potential for substantial equity returns.

After researching Volland Electric, I discovered it had an excellent reputation as a premier electric motor repair shop and distributor of electrical products. I decided to meet Ron at the company's Cheektowaga, NY facility. The plant, built in 1991, was impressive, and although Ron described dire financial conditions—maxed-out loans with HSBC Bank, overdue vendor payments, and difficulties securing new material—the shop's appearance didn't reflect this reality.

Ron's honesty and the strong reputation of Volland convinced me the company aligned with my investment criteria, provided the terms were favorable. I acted quickly, as I'm thorough in my due diligence but don't procrastinate. Ron not only wanted my financial investment, but also sought my advice to help return Volland to profitability. My prior success with Nuttall Gear and increased public profile after running for Congress in 1998 made me a compelling partner.

Volland Electric shop photo.

Ron and I reached a mutually beneficial agreement: I would provide a loan of $450,000 to address the immediate financial crisis in exchange for a 22.5 percent ownership stake. The deal closed on August 10, 2001. I committed two days a week to Volland Electric, balancing this with time spent in Rochester assisting my brother-in-law with Bloch Industries and Oakwood Woodworks.

Addressing Financial Challenges

Ron provided me with an office next to Chris Graham, then vice president of sales. Ann Graham worked as the receptionist, while Kirk Graham managed the shop. My primary focus was on the company's financial issues, but I was also available for broader advisory roles.

Volland Electric's financials were in disarray. My approach to understanding a company's financial health begins with the balance sheet. If it is accurate and reconciles, the profit and loss (P&L) statement will also be correct. Although my background is in mechanical engineering, I've developed exceptional accounting expertise. Unlike CPAs who adhere strictly to Generally Accepted Accounting Principles (GAAP), I employ pragmatic, out-of-the-box thinking to ensure practical financial management.

For example, certain expenses are classified as operating costs in the P&L, including salaries for shop personnel, manufacturing engineers, purchasing staff, and property-related expenses like electricity, rent, and taxes. Meanwhile, commissioned salespeople's salaries are categorized under sales, general, and administrative (SG&A) expenses, reflecting overhead. This nuanced understanding of financial reporting is vital for strategic decision-making and effective business management.

I reconfigure the P&L for all my companies to focus on "variable margin." This concept is often foreign to college-educated accountants and CPAs. Once I explain it to other small business owners, they often react as though I've unveiled a genius strategy for managing their businesses more effectively.

Knowing the profit margin on every new order is essential. It allows me to determine when to walk away from a bid to avoid losses—a fundamental aspect of business management. Making smart decisions, however, requires understanding variable margins. Without this knowledge, poor decisions are inevitable.

To calculate variable margin, I exclude substantially fixed expenses from operating cost calculations, unlike traditional accounting practices that include them in the cost of goods sold (COGS). For example, if you receive an additional order, does it change your rent, property taxes, electricity usage, or the number of foremen and manufacturing engineers needed? Of course not. These are fixed expenses. In my COGS calculation, I include only the costs of raw materials, direct labor, and expendable tooling—the true variable costs associated with any new order.

But what about sales commissions? Accountants typically categorize these under SG&A, excluding them from margin calculations. However, sales commissions are direct expenses related to new orders and must be included in the COGS calculation to determine the real variable margin.

Volland Electric shop photo of large motor repair.

This principle became especially relevant when I joined Volland Electric in 2001. Volland had no clear understanding of the variable margins on new orders. As a result, they sometimes rejected orders deemed unprofitable based on traditional accounting, even though these orders were actually highly profitable when evaluated using variable margins. Conversely, they sometimes accepted orders with margins that were deceptively low when commissions were factored in.

Volland Electric operated two main businesses: repairing electric motors, and selling new electric motors and controls. Their services spanned AC and DC motors, ranging from fractional HP to 10,000 HP, and included twenty-four-hour emergency field service. Despite their reputation for quality and customer service, they occasionally lost orders due to price sensitivity. Customers sometimes offered them the chance to match a competitor's lower price, but Ron Graham, the owner, often declined.

Using my variable margin approach, I found that many rejected orders had acceptable margins and would have been profitable. On the distribution side, traditional accounting showed a typical margin of 20 percent on new orders, which seemed reasonable. However, factoring in an 8 percent sales commission reduced the actual margin to only 12 percent.

Chris Graham shared that his father, Ron, disliked losing orders. Salespeople often persuaded him to lower prices to secure business, which sometimes resulted in unprofitable deals. Emergency repairs were also priced using standard cost estimates, leaving substantial money on the table. For emergency jobs, where downtime was the customer's primary concern, I suggested significantly increasing prices.

Additionally, I highlighted that the standard margin for industrial distributors was in the low thirties, far higher than current Volland margin. Underpricing undermined profitability, and I emphasized the importance of training customers to value quality and service over price alone. Losing an order to a lower-quality competitor could teach customers the value of paying a premium for better service.

The market for motor repair in Western New York was declining as large customers shut down. Volland needed to diversify beyond motor repair and electric product distribution. The company already offered a comprehensive range of electrical products, including motors, transformers, controls, switches, conduit, and enclosures. They also had a crane and hoist department that serviced overhead cranes, often during holiday shutdowns. Their market extended within a four-hour radius of Buffalo, covering Albany, Pittsburgh, and Cleveland.

Recognizing the need for growth, I knew Volland had to expand its services. An opportunity to do so presented itself just three months after I invested in the company.

Frontier Industrial Supply

A local industrial distributor, Frontier Industrial Supply, faced financial difficulties, leading M&T Bank to declare the company in default on its credit facilities. The bank was prepared to seize the company and sell it at auction.

I toured Frontier Industrial Supply with Ron and Chris Graham, who were familiar with the company. They remarked that Frontier was founded by a friend of Alexander Volland in 1943, the same year Alexander established Volland Electric. It truly is a small world.

The shop was well-organized, with supplies neatly arranged on the shelves. We negotiated with M&T Bank and purchased Frontier's assets through a secured party private sale under New York's Uniform Commercial Code (UCC). I provided the necessary cash to finalize the transaction.

At the time, I owned 22.5 percent of Volland Electric, which entitled me to 22.5 percent of the company's profits. I provided a loan of $300,000 to help purchase Frontier Supply. Ron Graham agreed to a side agreement granting me 35.5 percent of the profits from Frontier Industrial Supply. To measure Frontier's profitability, we kept its financial results separate from Volland financials.

With my cash infusion into Volland in August 2001 and the acquisition of Frontier in December 2001, Volland Electric was breaking even as we entered 2002.

Mead Supply

In March 2002, I received a call from Clint "Chip" Ivins III, the owner of Mead Supply, Inc., another industrial distributor. Unlike Frontier, which focused on road contractors, Mead targeted industrial contractors and also rented scaffolding and other equipment. Chip had read about Volland purchasing Frontier and expressed interest in selling Mead Supply to Volland.

Although Chip's call was unexpected, we recognized the growth potential of combining Mead Supply with Frontier under the Volland umbrella. We finalized a deal with Chip and closed the purchase on April 8, 2002, less than four months after acquiring Frontier.

Lang & Washburn Electric

Two years later, in 2004, another opportunity arose: the chance to acquire Lang & Washburn Electric, located in Amherst, NY. Lang & Washburn distributed electrical components and operated a panel shop that built custom OEM electric panels for machinery manufacturers.

Lang & Washburn competed indirectly with Volland Electric, primarily serving OEMs. Volland, Frontier, and Mead sold similar electrical products but primarily to contractors. While Lang & Washburn was breaking even, it wasn't profitable.

Ron Graham, Chris Graham, and I toured the Lang & Washburn facility. The premises were tidy and well-maintained, and the electric panels being assembled were of exceptional quality.

We negotiated a purchase price of $1.1 million, which included all assets, inventory, and accounts receivable. After agreeing to the terms, we closed the acquisition on April 2, 2004. I provided a loan of $400,000 to help finance this purchase.

Twenty Years of Profitable Growth

Following the Lang & Washburn acquisition, I met with Ron Graham to renegotiate my various agreements regarding Volland, Frontier, Mead, and Lang & Washburn. We agreed to increase my ownership stake in Volland to 49.25 percent.

The Lang & Washburn panel shop became the fastest growing and most profitable segment of Volland Electric. On July 23, 2015, we purchased a new building on Nagle Drive in Cheektowaga, near our main facility, to house the panel shop. The property is owned jointly by me and the Graham family, with each holding a 50 percent stake.

Over my twenty-four years with Volland Electric, the company has grown substantially and remains highly profitable. I continue to look forward to receiving profit distributions every quarter. The traditional motor repair and electric motor distribution business is steady and predictable and the industrial supplies segment—comprising Frontier, Mead, and Lang—is equally stable. The Western New York market is stagnant, making significant growth unlikely, but on the upside, we don't anticipate any new competitors entering the market.

Of all the more than twenty companies I've invested in over the past twenty-five years, Volland Electric is the only one I'm still involved with. I envision my grandchildren and Ron Graham's grandchildren continuing as partners in Volland for the next fifty years.

CHAPTER 12

Easom Automation Systems

CHUCK KOLKEBECK, MY FORMER BUSINESS partner at Nuttall Gear Corporation, called me on January 3, 2003, to discuss a potential business opportunity. Chuck had received a call from Reg Kelley, who wanted to know if he was interested in investing in a management buyout of Easom Automation Systems in Detroit, MI. Reg and Chuck had served together on the Power Transmission Representatives Association (PTRA) board of directors when Chuck was the VP of marketing for Nuttall Gear.

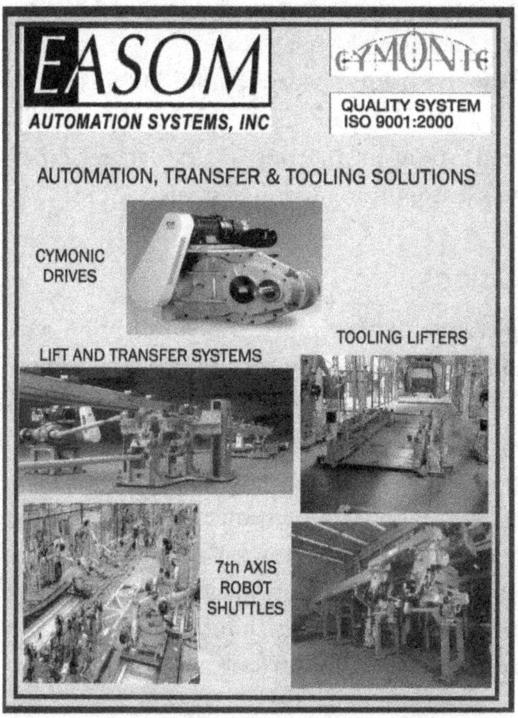

Easom Automation Company Brochure.

The Besl family, owners of Easom Automation Systems, offered Reg and his management team the opportunity to purchase the company through a management buyout. The patriarch of the Besl family had passed away, and the family was not interested in continuing ownership of Easom.

Easom was a combination of two businesses, both established in 1945. George Easom started Easom Engineering Co., providing engineering design and detailing services to tool builders in the greater Detroit area. Around the same time, the Jack Haines Company began operations in a garage shop, offering detail-machining services to machine tool builders. Both startups served the large and small tool builders in Detroit's machine automation market. Easom focused on engineering services, while Jack Haines Company specialized in machining small parts.

The two companies operated independently until 1983, when Easom Engineering contracted Jack Haines Company to manufacture their patented Cymonic Drive, a specialized indexing device. Jack Haines Company had developed a unique planetary transmission used by automobile manufacturers in their final assembly plants.

The companies remained separate until 2000, when the Besl family acquired Jack Haines Company from ERG Industries. The Besl family, having purchased Easom Engineering in 1996, merged the two companies in 2001, forming Easom Automation Systems.

Easom Operations

Easom is a full-service turnkey provider of automation systems. The company designs and builds handling systems for large components used in vehicular and aerospace assembly plants. Their offerings include multizone weld systems and cells, robotic transfer units, conveyors, drives, and positioning systems. Easom operates three plants in Michigan, including an engineering, sales, and technical center in Madison Heights, MI.

The Easom product line features: Cymonic Drives, Digi-Dog programmable limit switches, transfer systems, tool shuttles, conveyors, lifters, robot slides, indexing devices, programmable turntables, weld positioners, precision fixtures, weld cells, and special equipment.

Their systems automate welding, machining, drilling, and assembly of heavy, complex components where precision and speed are critical. The company is recognized as a leader in custom, precision-designed laser welding cells and other large-component applications. Easom serves heavy fabrication, aerospace, automotive OEMs, and suppliers as both an integrator and manufacturer of automation and positioning solutions.

Easom Purchase

Reg Kelley and his team raised most of the funds needed for the buyout but were still short $750,000. Reg's team offered 10 percent of the company in exchange for a $750,000 loan, paying 8 percent interest. Chuck Kolkebeck wanted to know if I was interested in joining the investment opportunity. He believed Reg was an exceptional manager and that Easom was a well-run, highly respected company in the power transmission field.

I expressed interest and asked Chuck how much he planned to invest. He said he was committing $225,000 for a 3 percent stake and hoped I would invest $525,000 for a 7 percent stake. I was a bit surprised that Chuck only wanted to invest $225,000 but agreed to the allocation, provided I could review the financials that justified the $7.5 million pre-money valuation.

The management team at Easom consisted of:

Reg Kelley	President
Brian Mabee	VP of Engineering
Gary Stade	VP of Manufacturing

Chuck and I flew to Detroit to visit the factory and meet with Reg, Brian, and Gary. I was extremely impressed by the factory and equipment, the office and computer-aided design capabilities, and the personnel.

We finalized the management buyout on January 31, 2003. Chuck and I were appointed to the board of directors and each elected as vice president of Easom Automation Systems, Inc.

Profitable Growth and Sale to Lincoln Electric

Over the next eleven years, I traveled to Detroit four times a year for board meetings. Reg and his team consistently pursued complex systems orders from the big three automobile companies (GM, Ford, and Chrysler) and their tier-one suppliers. The lift and transfer systems provided by Easom would pick up a car on the assembly line and transfer it to the next station. Computer chips on the cars communicated with the Easom system, ensuring the tools aligned precisely with the car at each assembly station.

Robots performed all the welding on the assembly lines, and Easom provided the robots as part of their systems. Lincoln Electric supplied most of the welding equipment used in EASOM systems.

By 2013, EASOM's sales reached approximately $30 million. That year, Lincoln Electric approached Reg about purchasing the company. An agreement was reached, and the sale to Lincoln Electric for $25 million closed on October 6, 2014.

I thoroughly enjoyed the eleven years I spent working with Reg, Brian, and Gary on Easom's profitable growth. Chuck Kolkebeck and I contributed valuable input as Easom expanded. Our shared background in managing technical, engineering-intensive businesses proved beneficial.

While my investment in Easom provided a substantial financial return, the experience was even more rewarding for the opportunity to reconnect with Chuck and build strong friendships with Reg Kelley, Brian Mabee, and Gary Stade.

CHAPTER 13

Schlyer Machine

I RECEIVED A CALL FROM Dale Schlyer on June 30, 2003. I didn't know who he was until he explained the reason for his call. He knew of me through various newspaper articles and was familiar with my background as the founder, president, and CEO of Nuttall Gear Corporation.

He told me that his company, Schlyer Machine Corporation (SMC), was in a precarious financial position, and he hoped that I would consider making an investment in his company. His company manufactured vivarium washing and sterilization equipment for animal research facilities. He started SMC in 1981 and was well known in the vivarium cage and rack washing market.

I had no idea what he was referring to; the word "vivarium" was not part of my vocabulary. I looked it up and saw that it referred to "an enclosure for keeping or raising and observing animals, especially for laboratory research."

Dale explained that most medical universities have animal research facilities affiliated with their programs. He told me that approximately 100 million mice and rats are used in biomedical research each year. Like humans, mice are mammals, and their bodies undergo many similar processes, such as aging, and have similar immune responses to infection and disease.

He explained that the cages housing the mice and rats need to be kept very clean, with fresh bedding and a water bottle in each cage. The cages must be sterilized during cleaning before new bedding is placed inside them. The racks also have to be sterilized before clean cages are stacked on them.

Schlyer Machine served this niche market, predominantly making washing equipment for research facilities conducting animal testing in laboratory environments. This equipment was designed for washing and sterilizing animal cages, and any additional parts and components involved.

Schlyer Machine cage and rack washer.

The list of products manufactured and sold by SMC was extensive. These included:

- cage and rack washers
- cage and bottle washers
- bottle washers
- bottle fillers
- tunnel washers
- bedding dump stations
- bedding dispensing systems
- glassware washers

Schlyer Machine Financial Difficulties

I agreed to meet Dale Schlyer at his shop in Wilson, NY, on July 2, 2003. The shop, a WWII-era Quonset Hut measuring approximately twenty by forty-eight feet (960 square feet), was made of corrugated steel.

I had to admit, I'd never seen a factory inside a Quonset Hut—or even a Quonset Hut at all. The shop was all but empty. There were shelves with pipe fittings, various pieces of angle iron, nuts and bolts, electric wire and switches, and conduit. The manufacturing equipment consisted of steel cutting saws, iron workers, and welders.

Dale showed me an extensive and impressive binder with photos of equipment he had manufactured over the past twenty-plus years. Everything was stainless steel and looked like it belonged in a sterile laboratory.

Dale got straight to the point and admitted that he was effectively out of business. He had struggled for years, often using down payments on new orders to purchase the material needed to complete orders already in production. His current predicament was that he had a substantial $200,000 order from Duke University with a 50 percent down payment, but he had used their down payment to complete another order. He didn't have any money to purchase the raw materials needed to build the equipment for Duke.

Dale's predicament was not uncommon among small businesses that "steal from Peter to pay Paul." However, his problem was that he didn't have a new order with a down payment that would allow him to complete the Duke order.

I told Dale I was somewhat interested but needed to think more about his business before making any decisions.

Purchase of Schlyer Machine

After my meeting with Dale, I called my former partner and VP of engineering at Nuttall Gear Corporation, Carl Becker. Carl had decided not to continue working for Constellation Capital after we sold the company in 1997. He worked for them for a couple of years and then quit.

I didn't have the time to commit to a turnaround of Schlyer Machine, but I thought Carl might be interested. SMC had an impressive history.

They served a sustainable niche market with limited competition, and the products they manufactured had good margins.

Carl agreed to meet me back at SMC a week later. He saw the opportunity and the risk. Dale wanted and needed a job. He knew his company was basically worthless. It didn't take long for us to work out a mutually acceptable deal.

Carl and I decided to provide the capital to complete the Duke University unit. We also hired Dale Schlyer as an engineer and salesman for our new company. Dale accepted a "bulk sale of assets" agreement covering all Schlyer Machine's assets for a nominal $10,000.

We shook hands. No "real" money was changing hands, so we agreed to close on the transaction on August 6, 2003.

Carl Becker, President

Carl was happy to be involved in another venture with me. There was definite upside and very little downside. Carl had an hour's drive from his home in Amherst, NY, to the SMC factory on the shore of Lake Ontario in Niagara County.

Carl and I decided to try and get some money from Duke University, in addition to the 50 percent they still owed on the machine ordered from SMC, payable when the cage and rack washer was completed.

Carl set up a meeting with the purchasing agent at Duke. The meeting was tense. Carl explained that he had just purchased the assets of SMC, and that Dale Schlyer had been hired as an employee and no longer had any ownership interest in the company.

He clarified that Dale had not purchased any raw materials with the $100,000 down payment. He explained that our new company had no obligation to complete the cage and rack washer that Duke had ordered.

Carl told the purchasing agent that we would complete the order for an additional $50,000 on top of the $100,000 balance due upon completion. That would make the total $250,000 for Duke University—$50,000 more than the original order. Carl assured him that no additional funds needed to be advanced, and the entire $150,000 would be due upon completion of the order.

This was a win/win of sorts for Duke and SMC. If Duke didn't accept our offer and ordered the unit they needed from a competitor, it would cost them $200,000 on top of the $100,000 they had already paid Dale as a down payment. Duke would be out-of-pocket $300,000.

If Duke agreed to our offer, they would be out-of-pocket $250,000. We were saving them $50,000.

The purchasing agent at Duke was between the proverbial "rock and a hard place." He reluctantly agreed to our offer.

With that negotiation completed, the new SMC was off and running. Carl and I advanced the cash needed to order the parts for the Duke machine. Dale Schlyer was relieved to have a job and focused solely on getting new orders, free from the burden and stress of running the shop.

Dale succeeded in bringing in a number of new orders. We didn't make any money on the Duke order, but we didn't lose any money either. The $150,000 we collected from Duke when the machine was completed covered the total cost of production. The $50,000 reduction we offered Duke was essentially the profit margin on the machine.

Carl Becker managed SMC for about eighteen months. The company was marginally profitable. However, the limited space in the Quonset Hut was a definite constraint. Carl's health declined as his diabetes worsened.

In early 2004, I partnered with Joe McMahon and Bob Schlehr to form a new company named Audubon Machinery. Audubon absorbed a company they owned, Oxygen Generating Systems International (OGSI). The assets of OGSI were acquired by Audubon in a bulk sale of assets transaction similar to the one Carl and I used to acquire the assets of SMC.

On December 17, 2004, Carl and I transferred the assets of SMC to Audubon Machinery Corporation. Audubon assumed all the obligations of SMC without any additional payment for its limited assets.

Carl Becker retired to focus on his health issues. Dale Schlyer went to work for Audubon Machinery.

Audubon Machinery then had two divisions: OGSI and SMC.

CHAPTER 14

Audubon Machinery Corporation

OGSI oxygen generator.

DURING MY TIME AS PRESIDENT and CEO of Nuttall Gear Corporation, I became friends with the owners of another business located in the Bell Aerospace facility in Niagara Falls, NY. Joe McMahon and Bob Schlehr owned Oxygen Generating Systems International (OGSI). They formed OGSI in 1995 and began operations as a tenant in the Bell plant.

OGSI manufactured large oxygen-generating machines for hospitals, fish farms, water and sewage treatment plants, and companies needing to burn toxic chemicals in a smokestack before emitting the gas into the atmosphere.

The technology behind oxygen-generating machines is called Pressure Swing Adsorption (PSA), which produces medical-grade oxygen at 90–93 percent purity. A molecular sieve material acts as an adsorbent to remove nitrogen from the air. PSA systems have two tanks filled with sieve material. Compressed air is forced into one tank, and as the air passes through, the sieve absorbs nitrogen, discharging 93 percent pure medical-grade oxygen. The remaining 7 percent is argon, an inert gas. The system is designed to alternate between tanks continuously, ensuring a steady output of medical-grade oxygen.

Hospitals in the United States and Europe primarily use liquid oxygen, produced by temperature separation of air. Companies such as Praxair or Linde utilize this process to produce 99 percent pure oxygen, nitrogen, argon, and other gases. However, hospitals in third world countries, lacking infrastructure for liquid gas transport, rely on PSA technology. Regions like Africa, China, the Middle East, Indonesia, parts of South America, as well as remote areas in Alaska and Canada, utilize PSA oxygen systems.

Mentor to Joe McMahon

After losing my 1998 congressional election and returning to the private sector, I received a call from Joe McMahon in 1999. He asked me to mentor him in an entrepreneurial program offered by the State University of New York at Buffalo (UB) Center for Entrepreneurial Leadership (CEL).

The CEL program was a twelve-month initiative where around twenty business owners met weekly to brainstorm how to improve their companies. Each participant was assigned a mentor to assist in crafting a strategic plan addressing strengths, weaknesses, and growth opportunities.

I agreed to mentor Joe, marking my introduction to CEL. Over the next twelve years, I mentored a different business owner annually.

During my mentorship with Joe, I gained insight into OGSI and its global potential. Around 90 percent of OGSI's business was in Africa and China, with limited competition and good margins. However, the company faced significant financial challenges. Joe and Bob had raised funds from various unsophisticated private investors, leading to a convoluted ownership structure. It was unclear who were investors, who were lenders, and their respective roles within the company.

At the end 2000, I wished Joe well but expressed skepticism about OGSI's long-term viability without resolving its financial issues.

Purchase of OGSI

In early 2004, Joe called again, acknowledging my earlier concerns. OGSI was struggling under financial strain and needed help. He gave me free rein to salvage the company. By this time, OGSI had moved to a larger facility in the Audubon Industrial Park, located in Amherst, NY.

Upon reviewing their finances, I realized that a complete financial reset was necessary. OGSI was burdened with debt, unable to pay bills or loans, and struggling to acquire raw materials. Despite these challenges, I saw potential and decided to proceed, safeguarding my investment where possible. Joe and Bob accepted my asset purchase proposal, and we finalized the transaction on February 6, 2004. I loaned the company $175,000 to repay HSBC Bank, which was the only secured creditor.

When the deal closed, I became OGSI's largest creditor. I purchased a $400,000 note from one of the OGSI investors for $50,000. With the purchase of the note, I became a secured creditor. This secured creditor status placed me ahead of unsecured creditors, which included all the vendors who would not be paid on their outstanding balances.

With my investment, OGSI emerged from its crushing debt load, owing money only to me. We agreed on a three-way split of the company's equity, with Joe, Bob, and I as equal partners.

Audubon Machinery

I established Audubon Machinery Corporation to acquire OGSI's assets. Retaining the OGSI name was essential for brand recognition, as it was globally known for manufacturing oxygen-generating systems for third world hospitals. I registered OGSI as a trademark of Audubon Machinery, the name based on its location in the Audubon Industrial Park.

Joe McMahon traveled extensively, booking orders and engaging with customers and sales representatives worldwide. He visited China and Africa at least six times a year. As the president of Audubon, Joe was the face of the company. Bob Schlehr, the VP of sales and marketing, traveled less than Joe. Bob focused on preparing proposals and supervising the inside sales team.

Massive medical equipment trade shows were held annually in Dubai and Dusseldorf, Germany. MEDICA, held in Dusseldorf, was the largest trade show, featuring several thousand exhibitors from more than fifty countries. The Arab Health Exhibition in Dubai catered specifically to the Middle East.

Before joining Audubon, I had not traveled internationally with Westinghouse or Nuttall Gear. The other companies I was involved with did not conduct international business. My involvement with Audubon Machinery/OGSI gave me the opportunity to travel to China, Dubai, and Dusseldorf. I became well-versed enough in PSA technology to man our trade booth at these international medical equipment trade shows.

China Trip

My trip to China with Joe McMahon in May 2004 was eye-opening. We traveled to Guangzhou to meet our primary Chinese sales representative, blending business with pleasure. We visited several Chinese hospitals that used OGSI oxygen generators, giving me the opportunity to see our systems in operation. I was pleasantly surprised to find that most of the hospitals were modern and well-equipped.

During the trip, we explored the Great Wall, walking a significant portion of it. Joe McMahon, who is over six feet tall and on the heavier side, often became an attraction for young Chinese boys who wanted their picture taken with him. Joe was a tourist attraction himself.

Traveling on Chinese roads was an unforgettable experience. Many of the expressways were newly built, with cars speeding alongside animal-drawn carts and three-wheeled vehicles in the same lanes. Drivers constantly honked their horns in a chaotic free-for-all. On local roads without stoplights, intersections became a test of nerves, with every driver for themselves.

My week in China was a wonderful experience. Traveling with Joe and spending time with our sales representative gave me a unique perspective on the country, very different from that of a typical tourist. I interacted with Chinese businessmen and locals, which enriched my understanding of the culture.

Dusseldorf Trip

In November 2004, I traveled with Joe and Bob Schlehr to Dusseldorf, Germany, for the MEDICA trade show. Having attended numerous trade shows with Westinghouse and Nuttall Gear, I found nothing comparable in size to MEDICA. Even the Offshore Oil Technology Conference (OTC) in Houston, TX, paled in comparison.

Dubai Trip

In January 2005, I joined Joe and Bob on a trip to Dubai for the Arab Health Exhibition. This experience was mind-blowing. The Middle Eastern men wore traditional Thobes—white, ankle-length robes with long sleeves—and either white or red-checkered Ghutras on their heads. Women wore Abayas, black loose-fitting robes covering their entire bodies except for the head, feet, and hands. Some women also wore Burkas to cover their faces. Dubai is often referred to as the Middle East's playground, with less stringent rules than countries like Saudi Arabia, Iran, or Iraq. Traffic in Dubai was notoriously congested, with Maserati, Ferraris, Bentleys, and other exotic cars creeping along at twenty MPH on the highways. Bumper-to-bumper traffic was a constant, twenty-four hours a day.

The Burj Al Arab is the most iconic hotel in Dubai, symbolizing wealth in the UAE. During our visit, we explored the Burj and even went snow skiing at a large indoor ski resort located within the Mall of the Emirates.

I traveled with Joe and Bob to Dusseldorf and Dubai annually from 2004 to 2007, until I was elected Erie County executive. While I retained ownership interests in all my companies during my term as County executive, I avoided attending trade shows to prevent potential media scrutiny.

Schlyer Machine

Carl Becker's health issues caused challenges at Schlyer Machine. I proposed to Joe and Bob the idea of merging Schlyer Machine into Audubon Machinery. Despite having no product or industry overlap, the skills required for manufacturing Schlyer cage and rack washers aligned closely with those needed to build oxygen generators.

Both Schlyer and OGSI purchased most of the components for their products and relied on skilled employees to assemble the finished machines. For Schlyer, external suppliers provided stainless steel enclosures, washing mechanisms, and electronic controls for cage and rack washers. Similarly, OGSI sourced air compressors, oxygen compressors, cast-iron molecular sieve tanks, and electronic controls for oxygen generators.

Merging Schlyer into Audubon Machinery spread overhead expenses across both companies, improving profit margins for Schlyer and OGSI products. Joe and Bob agreed, and on December 17, 2004, Audubon Machinery purchased the assets of Schlyer Machine. Dale Schlyer joined Audubon, focusing on sales.

We quickly relocated the Schlyer machinery and equipment from its Quonset Hut factory in Wilson, NY, to the Audubon factory in Amherst, NY. The transition went smoothly, and the Audubon factory workers swiftly adapted to assembling cage and rack washers.

LEED Certified New Factory

In early 2005, we embarked on the ambitious project of building a new 40,000-square-foot factory for Audubon in North Tonawanda, NY. The chosen site was a remediated brownfield, previously known as the

Wurlitzer Hazardous Waste Dump Site. The New York State Department of Environmental Conservation had removed 16,000 tons of contaminated soil from the four-acre Wurlitzer Drive location.

To finance the new building, we formed a real estate holding company named Wurlitzer Capital Group, inspired by the factory's address at 814 Wurlitzer Drive. We committed to constructing an energy-efficient factory, thoroughly researching available incentives. LEED (Leadership in Energy and Environmental Design) certification, governed by the US Green Building Council, became our goal.

Achieving LEED certification for our factory was particularly challenging due to the large open spaces in the factory that limited opportunities for energy efficiency. We focused on innovative features to earn the credits for certification.

We used one hundred tons of recycled steel, wood, and paper during construction. Locally produced materials reduced transportation emissions, and we installed recycled drywall, steel, and carpeting. Energy-efficient lighting illuminated the shop floor. We installed an electric vehicle charging station powered by solar panels and a wind turbine, bike racks to encourage cycling to work, and showers for employees. Additionally, we lobbied the county to extend a bus line past our new factory to promote public transportation. Low-maintenance shrubs minimized water usage, and an energy-efficient variable-speed compressor powered air tools in the factory.

Innovative features earned us the maximum LEED credits for innovation. After a year of construction, our factory became the first LEED-certified green factory in New York State, meeting the required points for certification by a narrow margin.

On May 7, 2007, we received recognition and an award from the US Environmental Protection Agency (EPA) for building New York's first LEED-certified green factory. I traveled to Newark, NJ, to receive the award from then-Mayor Cory Booker, now a US Senator. It's a small world—he served in Washington, DC, as a Democratic Senator during my tenure as a Republican congressman.

Operating In Our New Factory

OGSI proudly displayed flags in our factory representing the more than 110 countries where our oxygen generators were installed. China and Africa were our two largest markets, though we also reached many isolated and far-flung places worldwide.

Joe McMahon engineered a compact oxygen generator for fire companies to fill EMT oxygen bottles. This was a significant cost savings for fire companies, which previously relied on vendors to supply full liquid oxygen tanks and remove the empty ones. He also developed small oxygen generators for veterinary clinics and nursing homes, and designed a novel package that could be airlifted to disaster zones following earthquakes and hurricanes. These innovations allowed us to reduce our dependence on overseas sales from 90 percent to 60 percent, which helped mitigate challenges like currency fluctuations and exchange rates.

Our largest single customer was Intel, which designated us as their oxygen supplier for all new plants under construction worldwide.

In 2012, we had an opportunity to acquire Roe Biomedical, a company with complementary products to Schlyer Machine. Roe manufactured equipment and systems to remove and replace bedding in mice and rat cages. Following this acquisition, we renamed the Schlyer division of Audubon as SMC-Roe.

Despite our efforts, Audubon Machinery struggled to achieve consistent profitability. Periodically, I extended loans to cover cash flow shortfalls, believing the company would eventually break free from its financial challenges and become profitable like ZeptoMetrix, Volland Electric, and Easom Automation. Unfortunately, that vision never materialized.

After my election as Erie County executive in 2007, and subsequently to Congress in 2012, I had little time to devote to my private business investments. I relied heavily on my business partners' management skills and entrepreneurial talents, though I was always available for advice when needed.

COVID-19

The COVID-19 pandemic hit on March 11, 2020, when the WHO declared it a worldwide crisis. The pandemic had unexpected positive impacts on my businesses.

ZeptoMetrix saw a surge in demand, as it was instrumental in growing and purifying the COVID-19 virus for companies developing diagnostic tests. Similarly, OGSI faced unprecedented demand as countries worldwide clamored for oxygen generators to combat respiratory issues caused by COVID-19. Production ramped up dramatically during 2020 and 2021 to meet this surge.

Sale of Audubon to NOVAIR

Over fifteen years from 2004–2019, Audubon Machinery muddled along. We had profitable years and unprofitable years. When we lost money, I was able to use the loss to offset income from ZeptoMetrix, Volland Electric, and Easom Automation. I always considered the federal government my silent partner. Being in a 40 percent tax bracket, any loss from Audubon reduced my taxable income, with the Federal Government offsetting 40 percent of my loss.

With the surge in demand resulting from COVID-19, Audubon became marginally profitable in 2020. Profitability increased in 2021 as sales grew substantially with worldwide demand for our oxygen generators.

In August 2021, we received a call from NOVAIR SAS, a French competitor, expressing interest in purchasing Audubon Machinery Corporation. NOVAIR's market focus differed slightly from ours, as they provided complete oxygen systems to hospitals, including the necessary piping to deliver oxygen to hospital rooms. In contrast, OGSI only sold the generators, leaving hospitals to manage their own piping systems.

I was elated by NOVAIR's interest. Audubon hadn't paid me interest on my loans for over four years. While I hadn't loaned additional funds since 2015, the outstanding loans had been accruing interest at 8.5 percent compounded annually. Before COVID-19, I would have accepted a 50 percent repayment of the loan principal and forfeited all accrued interest to resolve the financial deadlock.

We reached an agreement with NOVAIR and signed an asset purchase agreement on December 9, 2021. The sale included Audubon Machinery and Wurlitzer Capital Group. By then, the mortgage on our factory in North Tonawanda was nearly paid off, providing substantial equity. Joe and Bob had agreed in writing that proceeds from a factory sale would first be used to pay off my outstanding loans before any owner distributions.

The deal with Novair closed on December 31, 2021. All my loans, including four years of compounded interest, were paid in full. NOVAIR also paid cash for our building. We agreed to a two-year earnout based on audited profits from 2021 and specific sales targets for 2022. For me, any earnout payments were just "frosting on the cake." I was relieved and grateful to recover my loans, accrued interest, and a share of the building's equity.

I had long worried that my investment in Audubon Machinery might end poorly. While I wasn't overly concerned about losses, I feared any financial return would be negligible.

Timing is everything in life. COVID-19 profoundly impacted both ZeptoMetrix and Audubon Machinery, positioning them perfectly to address the pandemic's challenges. I take pride in the fact that the companies I was involved with played an essential role in saving lives during 2020 and 2021.

CHAPTER 15
Niagara Ceramics Corporation

Buffalo Pottery

The story of Niagara Ceramics Corporation is the story of Buffalo Pottery, founded in 1901 in Buffalo, NY, and the story of John Larkin, Elbert Hubbard, and Darwin Martin. John Larkin was the founder of Larkin Soap Company in 1875, manufacturing Sweet Home Soap in his Buffalo factory. Larkin's brother-in-law, Elbert Hubbard, worked in the company since its founding, handling marketing and merchandising. Darwin Martin joined the Larkin Company in 1878.

Historic Deldare Ware manufactured in 1909.

Elbert Hubbard conceived the idea of including a "premium" in each box of soap, such as a lady's handkerchief. He packaged one hundred cakes of Sweet Home Soap in a box with perfume and cold cream, selling the "combination box" for ten dollars. The premium was either a Chautauqua desk or lamp, both valued at ten dollars. The Larkin Company grew rapidly, becoming the world's largest manufacturer of soaps.

As the company expanded, Larkin produced a catalog of premium items that women could order with their combination box purchase. Included were dishes and other ceramic items. To meet the demand for ceramics, John Larkin founded Buffalo Pottery in 1901.

The eight original buildings on Hayes Place formed the largest pottery in the world at the time, spanning 80,000 square feet with over 400 windows and skylights for natural light and ventilation. With the advent of electricity in Buffalo, provided by Nikola Tesla and George Westinghouse, Buffalo Pottery became the world's only pottery entirely operated by electricity.

Elbert Hubbard and his wife tragically died when the Lusitania was torpedoed by a German submarine in 1915.

The largest and most critical equipment at Buffalo Pottery was the kiln, used to "fire" pottery during the production of dinnerware, mugs, bowls, and pitchers. The two main kilns, each half the length of a football field, were heated with natural gas. Lined with firebricks, these kilns ran continuously. Shutting one down required a gradual reduction of heat over several days to prevent damage.

Buffalo China

In 1956, Buffalo Pottery changed its name to Buffalo China. The company grew further, becoming a dominant supplier of dinnerware to restaurant chains, hotels, country clubs, cruise lines, and airlines. In 1983, Buffalo China was acquired by Oneida, Ltd., which specialized in dinnerware, flatware, and glassware.

Oneida faced serious financial difficulties in 2003, missing interest and principal payments to noteholders and requiring waivers from lenders. On October 31, 2003, Oneida announced the closure of the Buffalo China plant and four other facilities.

Purchase of Buffalo China

Bob Lupica, Oneida's Senior VP and GM of the Buffalo China plant, was approached in November 2003 to gauge his interest in a management buy-out of the operation. Alongside his management team, Bob negotiated the purchase and raised capital for the new company.

Niagara Ceramics shop photo.

Bob Lupica's friend, Guy Agostinelli, a legal expert, became involved in the buyout process. Guy also reached out to potential investors, including me, to support the effort.

At the time, I was deeply involved in other ventures, including Bloch Industries, Oakwood Woodworks, ZeptoMetrix, Easom Automation, and Schlyer Machine. Despite my busy schedule as a serial entrepreneur, I agreed to meet with Bob and his team to explore the opportunity.

The Buffalo China management team included Tom Ziolkowski (Plant Manager), Karl Franz (Manufacturing Engineering Manager), Joe Bronco (Manager of Decorating Services), and Richard Reichard (Finance Manager). They presented me with the terms of the asset agreement with Oneida.

Niagara Ceramics Corporation (NCC) was formed to acquire the assets—machinery, inventory, accounts receivable, and real estate—for \$5.5 million. I provided the necessary cash as a loan to supplement a bank loan for the purchase.

Niagara Ceramics Corporation finalized the purchase on March 12, 2004. I received a 24.75 percent equity stake.

I was a passive investor in Niagara Ceramics. The management team, experienced from their years running Buffalo China for Oneida, handled operations. Sales during the first four years averaged \$20 million annually, with modest profits. This success relied on a five-year supply agreement with Oneida, which was part of the purchase agreement.

Unfortunately, after the agreement expired, sales declined significantly. From 2008 to 2012, Niagara Ceramics operated at a loss. Natural gas prices soared from \$5.00 per million Btu in 2004 to over \$13.00 per million Btu in 2008, exacerbating the challenges. The factory, designed for large production runs for chain restaurants, struggled with smaller-volume orders.

I supported the company as much as possible, loaning an additional \$1 million during its cash-strapped years. Despite these efforts, it became clear that Niagara Ceramics could not survive. I arranged to surrender my stock back to the company, at no cost, effective December 3, 2012.

At the time, I was running a competitive congressional race in NY-27 against incumbent Democrat Kathy Hochul (now New York Governor Hochul). Avoiding the negative press of a potential closure was crucial. By the time Niagara Ceramics officially shut down on September 9, 2013, I was a sitting Member of Congress, having won the 2012 election.

When it was announced that Niagara Ceramics was shutting down, my official statement read: "I am sorry to hear of the closure of Niagara Ceramics, something I learned about today for the first time from the media. I transferred my ownership interest in Niagara Ceramics in 2012, at no cost, to the management team in an effort to give them the best chance possible at future success. I have had no involvement in the company since that point. Prior to 2012, I had not been involved in the day-to-day management of the company since 2007 when I was elected Erie County Executive."

I wrote off my unpaid loans upon transferring ownership. Considering the initial profits, tax benefits from losses over seven years, and new hire tax credits received when we first acquired Buffalo China, my overall investment broke even. Today, I cherish the historic Buffalo Pottery collection that decorates my home, along with three exquisite sets of Frances Palmer dinnerware manufactured by Niagara Ceramics.

CHAPTER 16

Innate Immunotherapeutics Ltd.

TO UNDERSTAND THE VALUE PROPOSITION that existed when I invested in Virionyx in 2005, it's important to detail the progress that had already been achieved by Virionyx before I became an investor. Virionyx was located in Auckland, New Zealand, and was a non-public, closely held company.

Approximately 1,500 investors were shareholders in Virionyx. The structure of Virionyx was unique to New Zealand and could not exist in the United States. In the US, investors must be "sophisticated" and meet certain net worth and income criteria. That wasn't a requirement in New Zealand, and Virionyx had raised a significant amount of money from unsophisticated investors.

HIV-AIDS

Virionyx was formed to develop and bring to market a drug to treat HIV. The drug they developed was referred to as HRG215. HRG215 consisted of goat-produced polyclonal antibodies that the human immune system would recognize to kill HIV infected cells. HIV is masked in the human immune system, so humans don't create antibodies to fight the virus.

When HIV was first detected in the early 1980s, it was primarily affecting marginalized communities—men who have sex with men, people who inject drugs, and people who exchange sex for money. The public and policymakers were slow to respond to this new health threat. There were no tests for HIV, and by the time patients presented with symptoms, they often had only months to live.

In 1982, the CDC labeled the condition that caused death in this newly identified disease as "acquired immunodeficiency syndrome" (AIDS).

In 1984, researchers identified the cause of AIDS as a virus they named "human immunodeficiency virus" (HIV).

By 1985, there was a test for HIV that could identify those who had the virus before they developed symptoms. Treatments for HIV did not exist initially, and when treatments were developed, HIV's rapid mutation rendered them ineffective over time. The first effective treatment for AIDS was "highly active antiretroviral therapy" (HAART), introduced in 1996. Even this therapy had limited long-term efficacy due to the virus's mutation rate.

Dr. Frank Gelder, the founder of Virionyx, started the company in 1994, prior to the introduction of HAART. Dr. Gelder's impressive resume included:

- 1975: PhD in Biology from Ohio State University
- 1978–1997: Director of Transplantation Immunology, Department of Pathology, Louisiana State University

Dr. Gelder was well aware that HIV caused AIDS. Infected individuals experienced destruction of their immune systems, ultimately dying from infections a healthy immune system would eliminate. Dr. Gelder determined that the only way to treat AIDS was to introduce antibodies capable of fighting the HIV virus that was destroying the immune system.

MDP/DNA-Microparticle Adjuvant (MIS416)

Dr. Gelder recognized that treating poisonous snakebites involved using antibodies produced in animals. Small doses of venom were injected into an animal to stimulate antibody production. These antibodies were then purified for use in humans. Drawing from this knowledge, Dr. Gelder developed a treatment to activate the innate immune system in humans, referring to his discovery as an MDP/DNA-microparticle adjuvant. This microparticle could activate the innate immune response, releasing at least one immune or pro-inflammatory cytokine.

Although Dr. Gelder developed his MDP/DNA-microparticle in the mid-1990s, he didn't file for a patent until April 1, 2009. The patent (number 20110033494) was issued on February 10, 2011. Today, this microparticle is known as MIS416. MIS stands for Microparticle Immunostimulant, and the name reflects its discovery date: April 16 (416).

HRG214

Dr. Gelder realized that producing polyclonal antibodies for AIDS patients required using animals in a disease-free environment. New Zealand, recognized by the World Organization for Animal Health (WOAH) as being animal disease-free, was an ideal location.

Male goats, which are relatively inexpensive and abundant in New Zealand, were chosen for antibody production. Dr. Gelder contracted Cellular Products (now ZeptoMetrix Corporation) to provide HIV that was produced in bio-containment labs in Buffalo, NY. By injecting goats with his MIS416 microparticle to stimulate their innate immune systems, followed by a small dose of HIV, the goats' hyper-stimulated immune systems produced HIV antibodies. The HIV virus was not masked in goats as it was in humans. These polyclonal antibodies were trademarked as HRG214.

Goats were processed twice weekly through plasmapheresis to extract antibodies from their blood. This process was efficient and humane, with goats showing no adverse reactions to the injections. A small herd could produce large amounts of HIV antibodies.

Compassionate Usage

At the time, conventional wisdom suggested that continuous antibody treatment would cause patients to develop anaphylactic shock due to their immune system's reaction to foreign bodies. However, Dr. Gelder's understanding of HIV's destruction of the immune system led him to believe otherwise. In individuals with CD4 cell counts below 200, anaphylaxis was not a concern as their immune systems were too compromised to trigger such a reaction.

Dr. Gelder treated seventy-seven late-stage AIDS patients with HRG214 under compassionate use protocols during the 1990s. The results were remarkable; some patients who had been given only months to live recovered to the point of leading active lives, including one patient who successfully ran a marathon.

HRG214 FDA Approved Trials

Dr. Gelder incorporated Virionyx Corporation on May 31, 2000, and began operations in August. After further development of HRG214, he initiated an FDA-approved Phase 1 safety trial in 2001 at Beth Israel Deaconess Medical Center in Boston. The results confirmed HRG214's safety.

In 2004, the FDA approved a Phase 2 efficacy trial for HRG214, which began in June 2007, with fifty patients across seven testing sites. The trial cost was estimated at $2 million, requiring Virionyx to secure additional funding.

At the time, nineteen anti-HIV drugs were approved for use in the US, but HIV's resistance to existing treatments created an ongoing need for new therapies. HRG214's unique mechanism of action as a polyclonal antibody treatment made it a promising candidate for salvage therapy and potentially a first-choice therapy. Unlike traditional antiretroviral drugs, HRG214 targeted multiple HIV epitopes simultaneously, enhancing its effectiveness and reducing the likelihood of resistance.

Simon Wilkinson served as CEO of Virionyx during this critical period, and I knew Simon from the collaboration between Virionyx and ZeptoMetrix.

Virionyx Investment

Simon Wilkinson was planning a trip to New York City to meet with a potential investor group to raise the funds needed for the HRG214 Phase 2 trial, and to sustain the company for at least fifteen months. He had prepared a Private Placement set of documents detailing the $5 million fundraising effort.

Virionyx was positioning HRG214 initially to treat salvage therapy patients, but it also anticipated significant use in the failing therapy patient population. By 2008, Virionyx projected the salvage and failing therapy patient markets in North America to be 52,500 and 472,500 patients, respectively, with similar numbers expected in Western Europe. HRG214 was to be priced at $10,000 per patient compared to $20,000 per patient for existing HIV cocktails of antiretroviral drugs. The potential for Virionyx and HRG214 was immense.

The prospectus Simon prepared detailed the HRG214 human trials conducted so far. It highlighted collaborations with the Hauptman-Woodward Medical Research Institute (HWI) in Buffalo, the Wadsworth New York State Biodefense Lab in Albany, and ZeptoMetrix to develop emergency passive immunotherapies for SARS, West Nile, and Anthrax. Pharmaceutical-grade antibody preparations were shipped to and tested by ZeptoMetrix and the Wadsworth Biodefense laboratory, where they demonstrated the ability to neutralize SARS, West Nile, and Anthrax toxins at concentrations achievable in humans.

The offering was limited to individuals defined as "accredited investors" under SEC Regulation D requirements, ensuring that only sophisticated investors participated.

I persuaded Simon to delay his New York trip and instead come to Buffalo to present to my friends, many of whom were qualified accredited investors. I organized a meeting at Brookfield Country Club, where Simon presented the Virionyx opportunity to thirty of my friends.

Simon explained the rationale behind a pre-money valuation of $35 million, projecting a valuation of $150–$300 million after a successful Phase 2 trial. He estimated the valuation could reach $1–$2 billion following a fast-tracked FDA Phase 3 trial. Merck and Pfizer had already expressed interest in investing after the Phase 2 trial, should additional funds be required for the Phase 3 trial.

My investor group posed many questions, all of which Simon answered effectively. We successfully closed the Private Placement on December 31, 2005, raising $6 million—$1 million more than the target—from twenty-five of my friends and their families. My family's investment was $1 million, including contributions from my daughter and son.

The Phase 2 FDA drug trial was approved and scheduled to begin in June 2007. However, delays—common with FDA trials—pushed back the start date. Issues arose with contract negotiations at potential trial sites, as they required organizational approval to conduct an HIV trial.

I agreed to provide loans to Virionyx to keep the company operational as the delays consumed cash at an alarming rate.

Timing is everything, and for Virionyx, delays proved catastrophic. In early 2008, two new antiretroviral drugs received accelerated FDA approval.

It is unethical for a doctor to enroll a patient in a drug trial if FDA-approved treatments are available. Because HIV rapidly mutates, our potential trial patients were in the "failing therapy" category, where existing cocktails had failed. The new drugs offered an alternative, rendering our trial patients ineligible. Overnight, our potential trial participants vanished, and doctors could no longer enroll their patients in our HRG214 Phase 2 trial. The FDA-approved trial was canceled. Virionyx was finished.

Innate Immunotherapeutics

Secondary Progressive Multiple Sclerosis (SPMS)

The failure of a drug development program typically spells disaster for a small biotech company, particularly a single-drug company based in New Zealand.

Virionyx, however, had observed promising results with our adjuvant, MIS416, which had been used in the development of HRG214. It turns out that Dr. Frank Gelder had been treating his autoimmune disease with MIS416 for over a decade, with very positive results.

Secondary Progressive Multiple Sclerosis (SPMS) is one of the most debilitating autoimmune diseases. There is no treatment for SPMS. My uncle suffered from SPMS, and our family witnessed its devastating impact firsthand. SPMS is the end stage of Multiple Sclerosis, occurring after a patient transitions from Relapsing-Remitting Multiple Sclerosis (RRMS).

SPMS disproportionately affects women, who make up about 75 percent of patients. The progression from RRMS to SPMS typically occurs in one's late fifties, after living with RRMS since their early 20s. Most SPMS patients end up in wheelchairs with limited mobility and mental fog. Tragically, suicide is prevalent among patients due to their poor quality of life and the burden they feel they place on their families.

Because SPMS has no treatment options, patients can access experimental treatments under physician supervision. The disease is primarily of European genetic origin, with cases found in the United States, Europe, Canada, Australia, and New Zealand.

Patients in New Zealand were eager to participate in the MIS416 compassionate trial we initiated. MIS416 produced remarkable results, with patients experiencing immediate improvements in physical and mental conditions. Testimonials from patients were published on the Innate website.

FDA Trial

The decision was made to proceed with an official FDA drug trial, including patients from Australia and New Zealand. In 2009, shortly after Virionyx ended the HRG214 FDA trial, the company was renamed Innate Immunotherapeutics. MIS416, an immunotherapeutic drug that stimulated the innate immune system, inspired the new name.

Phase 1A and 1B trials were successfully completed in New Zealand in 2011. Innate then began planning for an FDA Phase 2 trial in the United States—a time-consuming and challenging process.

From 2009 to 2013, I kept Innate alive with several investments.

In December 2013, Innate Immunotherapeutics went public with an IPO in Australia to raise funds for the FDA Phase 2 trial in the United States, Australia, and New Zealand. The stock was listed on the Australian Stock Exchange (ASX). All my stock, along with that of my children, was transferred to Computershare in Australia as part of the IPO. The same was true for all US investors in Virionyx and Innate Immunotherapeutics.

After the public offering, my total investment in Virionyx/Innate Immunotherapeutics was $3.5 million, with my children each investing $600,000.

Significant progress was made during 2014 and 2015 in finding trial sites and recruiting researchers for the Phase 2B SPMS trial. However, nothing moves quickly in the world of FDA trials.

I invested an additional $1.75 million in 2015 and 2016 to keep the company afloat.

The FDA Phase 2 trial was completed in 2017, and we awaited the results. Meanwhile, compassionate trials in New Zealand provided ongoing data. The FDA trial was a double-blinded placebo study, with some patients receiving MIS416 and others a placebo. Based on our compassionate trial results, we "knew" the results would be positive.

FDA Trial Failure

On June 22, 2017, Simon Wilkinson received the MIS416 trial results. I was attending the White House Congressional Picnic when Simon emailed me at 6:55 PM. I was shocked and devastated to learn the trial failed to show significant differences between the MIS416 group and the placebo group. Innate Immunotherapeutics was done.

My total investment in Virionyx and Innate was $5.25 million. My children each invested $600,000. I lost every penny. But I care less about the money and more about the patients who will never access MIS416 to treat their SPMS.

The trial's failure left SPMS patients without a viable treatment. I still cannot reconcile the devastating impact this had on families with mothers and grandmothers condemned to a miserable end-of-life existence.

The trial design excluded our compassionate patients, who showed remarkable improvement with MIS416. These patients, confined to wheelchairs, did not meet the FDA trial's criteria, which required participants to perform tasks such as walking across a room. Consequently, the trial failed to demonstrate efficacy in the early stage SPMS patients, even though compassionate late stage patients in New Zealand demonstrated remarkable efficacy.

SPMS affects individuals differently, with some experiencing rapid health decline and others a slower progression. MIS416 was effective for late-stage SPMS patients, who reported significant improvements in quality of life and mental clarity. Letters from family members of our compassionate patients expressed profound gratitude: "You gave me back my mom. God bless you."

June 22, 2017, remains the saddest day of my life. I know MIS416 works. Yet, the placebo based trial with early stage SPMS patients failed, and there is nothing I can do to change that reality.

If I had one wish, it would be to conduct another MIS416 trial—one that I know would succeed. My legacy of bringing hope to those suffering from SPMS would be fulfilled.

Amplia Therapeutics Ltd.

In April 2018, the decision was made to use the remaining $2 million in cash from the failed MIS416 trial to invest in a struggling cancer development company with potential. This investment aimed to restore some value for Innate Immunotherapeutics' shareholders, who had lost everything.

In May 2018, Innate Immunotherapeutics merged with Amplia Therapeutics, adopting its name. Many executives from Innate transitioned to Amplia.

Amplia has two promising cancer drug candidates: AMP945 and AMP886. These drugs show potential in treating pancreatic cancer and fibrotic cancers. The company trades on the ASX (Australian Securities Exchange) under the symbol ATX.

CHAPTER 17

2007 Erie County Executive Election

Candidate for County Executive

After losing the congressional election in 1998, I never anticipated reentering politics. Losing an election brings a unique kind of disappointment. Unlike other setbacks in life, where new opportunities often emerge quickly, politics offers no clear path forward after a loss. When you're defeated, the race ends abruptly. The phone stops ringing, the press moves on, and your loss has little impact on others. Life simply continues without pause.

My 1998 congressional campaign was a valuable life experience, but after crossing it off my bucket list, I had no intention of looking back. Thankfully, I found renewed purpose in the entrepreneurial world. By chance, I became deeply involved with over a dozen companies, staying as busy as ever. I avoided political events and campaigns entirely. Politics was firmly in my past.

Yet, life has a way of surprising us. On February 7, 2007, Mary and I attended a Buffalo Sabres hockey game, excited about another strong season. The team was on track to win its division and conference for the second consecutive year. Little did I know that Dennis Vacco and his wife were also at the game, seated a few rows above us.

Dennis and I hadn't spoken in nearly nine years since we both lost our elections in 1998. That year, Dennis, the incumbent New York State Attorney General, was defeated by Eliot Spitzer. Dennis and I had crossed paths frequently during that campaign season alongside Governor Pataki, who was running for reelection. At the game, Dennis noticed Mary and me, turned to his wife, and said, "I think I just found the perfect candidate for Erie County executive this year. Look down a few rows to your right—that's Chris Collins and his wife. He's likely the only Republican who can beat Jim Keane in November. His resume will resonate in our bankrupt county, and I know from 1998 that he's capable of running a top-tier campaign."

Unbeknownst to me, Dennis was part of the Erie County Republican Executive Committee, which had spent months searching for a viable candidate. Erie County's political landscape heavily favored Democrats, with a two to one overall voter advantage and an eight to one ratio in Buffalo. The county's financial situation was dire, operating under a New York State-appointed Fiscal Stability Board. Parks were neglected, beaches closed, roads deteriorated, and several bridges were shut down, causing significant traffic issues.

To identify the ideal Republican candidate, the GOP hired the Tarrance Group to conduct a voter survey in early January 2007. Interviews with 300 likely voters revealed the public's sentiments, shaping the committee's search criteria.

After seeing me at the hockey game, Dennis proposed my candidacy to Chris Grant, executive director of the Erie County Republican Party, and Jim Domagalski, the GOP chairman. Though I had been out of politics for nearly a decade, Dennis and Jim vouched for my capabilities, citing my near victory against Congressman John LaFalce in 1998.

Chris Grant was tasked with gauging my interest. On February 12, 2007, he called and spoke to Mary before connecting with me. Chris explained that the Republicans urgently needed a strong candidate to challenge Jim Keane, the Democrats' presumptive nominee. I expressed some interest and agreed to meet Chris and Jim the next morning. During our meeting, I emphasized that if I chose to run, it would be with the intention of winning, not as a symbolic effort.

To explore the possibility further, I reached out to Michael Hook, my 1998 campaign consultant. Michael acknowledged the significant challenges of running as a Republican in a predominantly Democratic county, but believed I had a genuine shot. He agreed to join my campaign, should I decide to proceed. With his encouragement, I informed Chris Grant that I was all in. Together, we began preparations for the race.

Chris invited me to participate in a March 2 meeting with the GOP Executive Committee, where potential candidates would present their cases. *The Buffalo News* picked up the story, running a front-page headline on March 3: "Collins Eyes GOP County Executive Bid." The article described me as the "perfect" Republican candidate, highlighting my business successes and prior congressional campaign. However, it also underscored the daunting voter demographics and the broader challenges facing Republicans.

By March 31, the GOP endorsement process would conclude, determining the party's nominee. While other candidates expressed interest, none had generated the same enthusiasm as my potential candidacy. The stage was set for what would become an intense and closely watched race.

Endorsement

Over the next few weeks, I met with members of the Erie County GOP Executive Committee, attended several local committee meetings, and prepared to launch my campaign. Erie County, home to nearly one million people, comprises forty-four cities, towns, and villages. Each of these municipalities has its own GOP political committee and separately elected mayors or town supervisors.

I earned the support of all the GOP local committees and was confident I would be the endorsed GOP candidate for Erie County executive.

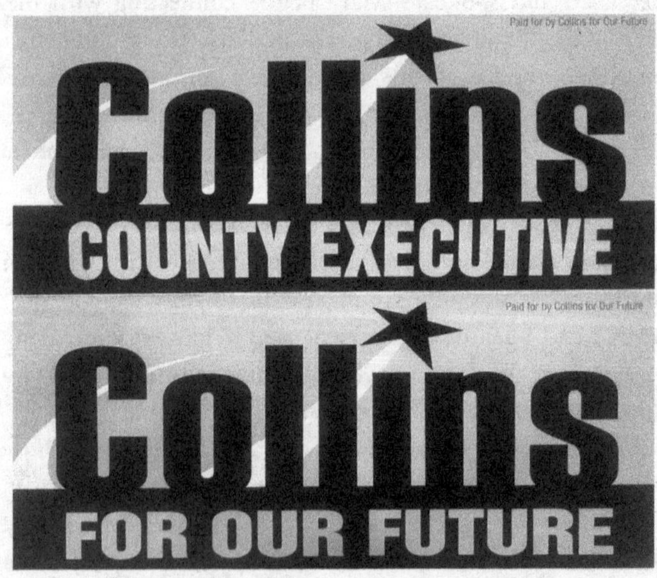

Bumper stickers for Erie County Executive Campaign.

On March 27, 2007, I held a news conference to officially kick off my campaign. The event took place at Volland Electric, a business in my investment portfolio that provided the perfect backdrop to highlight my private-sector experience. My campaign was called "Collins For Our Future." Although the GOP endorsement meeting was scheduled for March 31, it was largely a formality to confirm my endorsement. I was joined at the press conference by Mary and our two children.

The Buffalo News published a favorable story in its City & Region section titled, "Collins enters race with all the trimmings." The article noted that I had all the hallmarks of an official campaign: press releases, bumper stickers, a website, and a team of aides already on board. Bob McCarthy wrote, "The implied message from the new candidate to the Democratic opposition is that money and organization will not be a problem."

I was quoted in the article saying, "Don't worry about 'Collins For Our Future,' we're going to be properly funded. There is no question in my mind about that. As the next county executive, I will put my experience in turning around failed enterprises to work for taxpayers. I will turn around the failed enterprise of county government. I will ensure that taxpayers get value for their tax dollar. I will leverage our community's assets to create economic opportunity. I will say no to bureaucrats, entrenched politicians, and special interests. I will say yes to working families and those who create jobs."

On Saturday, March 31, 2007, I was unanimously endorsed by the sixty-two members of the Erie County GOP Executive Committee. I thanked everyone in attendance and summed up my campaign with the slogan, "Elect a Chief Executive, not a Chief Politician."

Republican Primary

The primary election was scheduled for September 18, 2007. I had one opponent, Bill O'Loughlin, who had qualified to run against me. However, I chose to ignore Bill and focused on traveling through all twenty-six towns, sixteen villages, and two cities in Erie County. I refined my stump speech and printed campaign materials, including palm cards, bumper stickers, and fundraising literature.

The Vision to Build a Bright Future: The Three Rs

- Reform Government
- Rebuild Our Economy
- Reduce Taxes

I introduced Lean Six Sigma to the voters, promising to implement it in Erie County to bring business efficiency to government for the first time in the United States. My training in Lean Six Sigma came from Danaher Corporation after they acquired Nuttall Gear in 1997. Although we had a Total Quality Management system in place, Lean Six Sigma was more detailed and formalized.

I explained the concept of white belts, yellow belts, green belts, black belts, and master black belts working together to improve efficiency in Erie County, reducing costs while improving services. When people joked that it sounded like a group of ninjas, I'd laugh and reply, "Ninjas working for the taxpayer."

Beyond the Three Rs, I crafted a straightforward vision statement for Erie County: "Erie County will be a place where people want to live, businesses want to locate, and tourists want to visit."

I spoke to voters in a language they weren't accustomed to hearing from politicians. As a businessman running for Erie County executive, I emphasized that I was not a politician. I drove this message home in every speech and reinforced it in all campaign materials.

I received positive press coverage after delivering speeches in rural towns, where local weekly newspapers were eager for stories.

Ultimately, Bill O'Loughlin withdrew from the race for Erie County executive and decided to run for Erie County Clerk against incumbent Kathy Hochul. It was a relief not to have to spend money on a primary battle against him.

To broaden my appeal, we created our own minor party, "Taxpayer First," since we were unable to secure a minor party endorsement. This allowed Democrats to vote for me without pulling the Republican lever. Fusion voting in New York permits candidates to run on multiple party lines, with votes from each line contributing to the final total.

Photo of our campaign volunteers working at a parade.

On July 8, 2007, Bob McCarthy published an article titled, "Chris Collins builds his campaign." He summarized my activities and reminded readers of my campaign strategy. He described my campaign as being in a "quiet phase" but noted that I was actively raising the funds necessary to compete in an overwhelmingly Democratic county. McCarthy highlighted my emphasis on running Erie County like a business and tapping into my business contacts to secure the minimum $1 million needed for a county-wide campaign.

He quoted me as saying, "I'm out at the police clambake in Cheektowaga, then to a fundraising lunch, then over to some parade. Practically every night of the week, I'm somewhere."

McCarthy joked that I embraced the campaign with the enthusiasm of a kid at a circus. He noted that I engaged with voters and seemed comfortable in the spotlight. At a Memorial Day parade, a bystander loudly questioned me about the county budget. I shouted back with the businesslike frankness that eludes most politicians, "Reduce it and balance it."

McCarthy ended his story with a warning to Democrats: "Collins' quiet campaign will soon enough become very loud and very serious."

Democrat Primary

Meanwhile, the Democrats were embroiled in a particularly nasty primary fight between James Keane and Paul Clark. Former Mayor of Buffalo Jimmy Griffin added to the chaos, further aiding my campaign. Griffin, who served four terms as Mayor of Buffalo from 1978 to 1993, was known for his colorful personality. He had even mounted a primary challenge against Bill Clinton in the 1996 New Hampshire presidential primary. Nicknamed "Six-Pack Jimmy" for famously advising people to "grab a six-pack and stay home" during the Buffalo blizzard of '85, Griffin's presence in the race was disruptive.

James Keane, who had run for Erie County executive in 1987 but lost in the primary to Dennis Gorski, was a veteran of local politics. Gorski, who served three terms as Erie County executive from 1988 to 1999, had appointed Keane as his deputy county executive after his election in 1987. Paul Clark, an accountant and town supervisor of West Seneca, one of the twenty-six towns in Erie County, was viewed as an outsider by Len Lenihan and the Democratic headquarters.

The animosity between James Keane and Jimmy Griffin was palpable. Their rivalry, steeped in years of political clashes, was fueled by their starkly different backgrounds. Keane, one of sixteen children from a prominent political family, had deep roots in public service—his brother served as commissioner of the Buffalo Fire Department, and his wife, Margaret, was a deputy fire commissioner during her career as a firefighter.

The Democrats dominated Erie County politics, but their party was fractured into two main factions, often clashing over various issues. This internecine conflict was an opportunity for the more unified Republicans to exploit. The grass roots faction of the Democratic Party, led by Buffalo Mayor Byron Brown, was in direct conflict with Erie County Democratic Party Chairman Len Lenihan, whose faction included James Keane. On April 25, 2007, Lenihan and the Erie County Democratic Party endorsed Keane as their candidate for Erie County executive. Keane also secured endorsements from the Working Families Party and the Conservative Party, solidifying his position as the presumptive favorite in a county with a two to one Democratic voter registration advantage.

As Bob McCarthy noted in an April 29, 2007, article, the "Dems will be bruised, battered, and penniless when the Democratic primary is over." The increasingly acrimonious primary between Keane, Clark, and Griffin worked to my advantage, allowing me to focus on retail politics while they exchanged barbs.

The primary received extensive coverage from *The Buffalo News*, chronicling every twist, turn, and attack. While Keane and Clark aired television ads, Griffin ran a low-budget, retail-style campaign. On September 18, 2007, Keane won the Democratic primary with 53 percent of the vote, compared to Clark's 25 percent and Griffin's 22 percent. Griffin spent just $11,000 on his campaign.

Following his victory, Keane criticized me, stating, "Republican Chris Collins tells a good story, but his ideas are wrong. I'm not going to argue with his financial success—his choices have brought him great wealth. But at the expense of too many middle-class dreams."

I responded, "The voters have a real choice in November. They can choose between a career politician who has been around for years and is part of the problem or a chief executive who will finally reform county government and run it like a business. Now is the time to take Erie County from the career politicians who offer nothing more than business as usual—tax increases, wasteful spending, and patronage for their cronies."

Griffin's bitterness towards Keane was evident when asked if he would support him. "No, no. James Keane lied about his service in Vietnam, and I will never support him," Griffin declared. He subsequently endorsed me and campaigned with enthusiasm. Clark endorsed Keane but did so unenthusiastically, rarely appearing with him during the campaign. Clark's Independence Party endorsement ultimately garnered him only 2 percent of the general election vote.

General Election

Conventional wisdom considered James Keane a shoo-in for Erie County executive. He was so confident in his chances that he took a two-week vacation after the primary to recharge for the general election. In his mind, and that of many others, my chances of winning the November 6, 2007 election were nonexistent.

On September 4, 2007, my campaign launched its first television ad. The thirty-second spot featured me at Volland Electric, walking through the aisles and speaking with workers. I emphasized how I would bring the principles that had made me a successful businessman to the Rath County Office Building. I told viewers, "Now I'm ready to fix another failing entity—Erie County government."

This positive introductory ad, released two weeks before the Democratic primary, was a strategic move to introduce me as a businessman, not a politician. While Keane, Clark, and Griffin fought amongst themselves, I presented a vision of reform and professionalism.

The day after Keane won the Democratic primary, we launched our first negative ad targeting the tax increases imposed during the Gorski administration when Keane was deputy county executive. Keane countered with an attack ad branding me as "Republican Chris Collins," linking me to Vice President Dick Cheney and former Defense Secretary Donald Rumsfeld.

The Buffalo News ran a comprehensive, two-page feature on me on September 23, 2007, titled: "Private Sector Savvy—Can Chris Collins' Business Expertise Save Erie County?" The article, accompanied by a large color photo of me on the Volland Electric factory floor, served as an excellent introduction to voters. It highlighted my educational background—a mechanical engineering degree from N.C. State and an MBA from the University of Alabama—and detailed my involvement with eleven companies. The piece underscored my campaign's central theme: running Erie County like a business. Keane, meanwhile, dismissed this approach, claiming, "You can't run government like a business."

Our campaign hired Wilson Research Strategies to conduct a benchmark poll of 400 likely voters from September 26–28, 2007. The survey results were encouraging. Seventy-two percent of respondents believed Erie County was headed in the wrong direction, while only 16 percent felt it was on the right track. This data helped us refine our strategy and focus our media efforts on the issues most important to voters.

The stage was set for a highly competitive general election.

The favorable/unfavorable numbers were also encouraging:

Candidate	Favorable	Unfavorable	No Opinion	Never Heard Of
Chris Collins	42%	8%	29%	21%
James Keane	37%	40%	19%	5%

When asked who they would vote for in the Erie County election, we were surprised:

Candidate	Percentage	Party Affiliation
Chris Collins	39%	Republican, Taxpayer First
James Keane	33%	Democrat, Conservative, Working Families
Paul Clark	12%	Independence Party

When we eliminated Paul Clark from the question, the results were even better for me:

Candidate	Percentage
Chris Collins	46%
James Keane	37%

The results from the push questions, which asked respondents about various issues and how they would affect their vote, confirmed our strategy:

Issue	More Likely to Vote for Collins
Chris Collins has saved eleven businesses and created over 500 jobs in WNY	71%
Chris Collins has pledged to work for one dollar a month until the control board is gone	55%

Issue	**More Likely to Vote for Collins**
Chris Collins has stated he will run Erie County like a business	68%
Chris Collins closed a plant in Mexico and moved the jobs to WNY	68%
Chris Collins has proposed his 3 Rs as his vision: Reform, Rebuild, Reduce	63%

After hearing these push questions, we asked respondents again who they would vote for:

Candidate	**Percentage**
Chris Collins	56%
James Keane	23%

Our poll confirmed our strategy was flawless. We needed to deliver our message effectively to inform voters about the issues and the differences between me and James Keane.

I was frustrated with fundraising. I personally funded the campaign and loaned $300,000 to cover campaign commercials, staff salaries, and materials. Conventional wisdom was that I had no chance of winning, so potential contributors hesitated to be listed as supporters.

On October 2, 2007, everything changed when *The Buffalo News* headline read:

"County executive race called a dead heat

Zogby poll finds Keane and Collins running even with five weeks to go"

The poll revealed Keane and I were statistically tied: Keane at 35 percent, Collins at 34 percent, and Paul Clark at 16 percent, with 15 percent undecided. Additionally, 65 percent of respondents preferred a business background over political experience, and 35 percent believed I was most likely to bring significant improvements to Erie County compared to 30 percent for Keane and 14 percent for Clark.

The day after the poll, Paul Clark endorsed James Keane, attempting to unify Democratic support. Keane's campaign responded with attack ads targeting my business background, falsely claiming I exported jobs overseas. *The Buffalo News* debunked this, confirming my companies export products, not jobs.

Three days after the poll, my mailbox was flooded with contributions. Business leaders who once hesitated now backed my campaign, recognizing my viability as a candidate. This momentum shifted conventional wisdom and solidified my chances.

The Erie County executive holds significant influence, unilaterally issuing contracts for legal, engineering, architectural, and accounting work, as well as emergency road and bridge repairs. Every company reliant on these contracts sought access to the executive.

My campaign gained further traction with two unexpected endorsements.

Jimmy Griffin Endorsement

On October 9, 2007, former Buffalo Mayor Jimmy Griffin endorsed me. Over breakfast at the Lackawanna Old Hotel, he expressed frustration with Paul Clark's endorsement of Keane and pledged to level the playing field by supporting me. Griffin's legendary retail politics came into play as he accompanied me to senior centers and fire stations. His endorsement resonated deeply; people often said, "If Jimmy Griffin supports you, you have my vote."

Griffin's presence and endorsement boosted my credibility. After his passing in 2009, I funded a brass statue of him, now standing proudly in front of Buffalo's downtown baseball stadium.

Alfreda Slominski Endorsement

On October 21, 2007, Alfreda Slominski, the "gold standard" Erie County comptroller from 1974 to 1992, endorsed me. Known for her excellence and independence, Alfreda recorded a powerful radio ad, stating, "No one is more qualified for the job than Chris Collins."

Her endorsement resonated strongly with senior citizens, a reliable voting bloc. Alfreda and I remained close friends until her passing.

These endorsements rattled my opponents, shifting Democrat votes my way and propelling my campaign to victory. Looking back, the support of these influential figures was instrumental in overcoming conventional wisdom and winning the election.

The next *Buffalo News* headline on October 12, 2007, was jolting to everyone:

"Collins Surges Ahead in New Poll

Leads Keane by 9 Points in County Executive Race"

The new poll showed me leading James Keane 38 percent to 29 percent, with Paul Clark receiving 5 percent of the vote. Twenty-eight percent of respondents were undecided, an increase from the poll taken ten days earlier.

The poll also revealed that Keane was supported by only 47 percent of Democrats, while I had secured 22 percent of Democratic support. Interestingly, 38 percent of respondents were still unfamiliar with or unsure about me.

Bob McCarthy humorously addressed this in his weekly opinion column, asking rhetorically about the 38 percent of Erie County voters who didn't recognize my name: "Under what rock do these people live?"

Fundraising Efforts

The Republican establishment organized fundraisers to help me stay on air with my commercials and increase advertising as the general election approached, less than four weeks away. I also loaned my campaign another $200,000 to ensure we had the resources to move forward.

Meanwhile, the Democrats, alarmed by the shift in the polls, grew desperate. Governor Eliot Spitzer came to Buffalo on October 14 to raise funds for James Keane.

Controversy Surrounding Paul Clark

An interesting development emerged regarding Paul Clark, who was accused of receiving bags of cash for his campaign to avoid disclosing donors in his financial reports. After Clark endorsed James Keane, we created a humorous commercial featuring bags of cash, linking Keane to the alleged illegal donations.

On October 16, 2007, the FBI announced an investigation into the cash allegations involving Paul Clark. A key witness testified that he had delivered two bank bags filled with one hundred, twenty, and ten dollar bills, totaling $20,000, to a marketing consultant associated with Clark.

This controversy proved to be ill-timed for James Keane, who had accepted Clark's endorsement.

Campaign Strategy

I filmed an impactful ad at Volland Electric, where I walked toward the camera, pulled a one dollar bill from my pocket, and declared, "As Erie County Executive, I will work for one dollar a month until the Financial Control Board is dismantled." This ad showcased my commitment to restoring financial stability to Erie County government.

Debates

The first debate with James Keane aired live on October 18, 2007. The exchange was professional yet contentious. Keane accused me of conflicts of interest with my private companies, alleging I would steer lucrative contracts to business partners. I countered by labeling Keane a career politician lacking the expertise to bring private-sector jobs to Erie County, saying, "Mr. Keane has never created a job not paid for by the taxpayers."

Keane retorted, "Collins is fond of creating ten-dollar-an-hour jobs that won't sustain the economy or keep local college graduates from leaving the area."

While Keane accused me of initiating negative attack ads, I offered to cease them if he would do the same. Keane declined, insisting he needed to respond to my aired accusations.

A second debate took place on October 25, 2007, at the abandoned Central Terminal in downtown Buffalo—a poignant symbol of the region's decline over the past fifty years. This debate turned sharply personal, with Keane accusing me of being a loan shark and costing the community jobs. I rebutted, "You make this stuff up as you go."

The final debate, on October 28, 2007, shifted focus to substantive issues. We disagreed on the allocation of Erie County's $624 million annual sales tax among cities, towns, and villages. Both of us supported efforts to regionalize the Buffalo Bills fan base, including preseason and regular season games in Toronto, as Erie County owns and maintains the stadium leased to the Bills.

The Final Stretch

With just over a week remaining before the November 6 election, the race reached fever pitch. Both campaigns worked tirelessly to secure votes. *The Buffalo News* extensively covered our campaigns, highlighting Keane's visits to homeless shelters in downtown Buffalo and my meetings in suburban living rooms.

On October 28, *The Buffalo News* endorsed James Keane. They acknowledged the voters faced a tough choice: "Voters can elect a longtime political operative tied to old ways or a businessman with innovative ideas but little understanding of government." They concluded, "In the end, we recommend a vote for Keane. Fixing Erie County starts with fully understanding it, and Keane has the edge in that category."

Despite their endorsement, they recognized my enthusiasm and commitment, noting my potential to disrupt destructive long-standing practices. However, they questioned my political naïveté and ability to navigate a fractured political system.

The Buffalo News continued its in-depth coverage, dedicating significant space to both candidates, including a full-page profile on my background and a four-page feature comparing us.

Election Day

Our campaigns left no stone unturned. We dropped literature, knocked on doors, and ran full-page ads in *The Buffalo News*. The final two headlines from the paper summarized the race:

> "Collins Widens Lead Over Keane to 46% – 33%
>
> 18 Percent Undecided as Election Day Nears"
>
> "Collins Wins in a Landslide
>
> Collins Beats Keane 63% to 35%"

I received 127,007 votes, compared to Keane's 70,816 and Clark's 3,860. I won in forty-three of forty-four cities, towns, and villages in Erie County, losing only in Buffalo, an eight to one Democratic stronghold.

In my victory speech, I declared, "Today, the voters and taxpayers have spoken. On January 2, 2008, Erie County will have a chief executive, not a chief politician."

The Buffalo News reflected on my win, stating, "Chris Collins, smart, driven, and incredibly demanding, is not the first local politician to promise change, reform, and a business approach to government. But he may be the first to actually do it."

James Keane graciously conceded, summarizing his campaign with eight words: "I stepped in front of a freight train."

Despite my victory, the Democrats retained control of the Erie County Legislature with a twelve to three advantage. While this posed challenges, my landslide win gave me a mandate for change that the Legislature would need to respect.

CHAPTER 18

Erie County Executive 2008–2011

Erie County Overview

Erie County is the largest upstate county in New York, home to 954,236 residents. The City of Buffalo, with a population of 267,000, is the largest city in Erie County and serves as the county seat. Erie County covers 1,227 square miles, with more highway lane miles than any other county in New York State. It comprises twenty-six towns, sixteen villages, and two cities.

In 1901, Buffalo was the eighth-largest city in the United States, with a population of 350,000. Over the past 120 years, while the US population grew by over 400 percent (from 77.5 million to 334.2 million), Buffalo lost 25 percent of its population. Once one of the wealthiest cities globally, Buffalo is now the third-poorest large city in the US, following Detroit, MI, and Cleveland, OH.

Lake Erie borders Erie County to the west, with Niagara County and Lake Ontario to the north. The southern part of the county, known as the Southtowns, includes rural farmland, large dairy farms, and towns like Orchard Park and East Aurora. Orchard Park hosts the Buffalo Bills stadium, owned by Erie County, while East Aurora is home to the Roycroft Campus, a National Historic Landmark established in the 1890s by Elbert Hubbard. The campus includes nine of the original fourteen structures that were central to craftsmanship and philosophy in the late nineteenth century.

Erie County is renowned for cultural landmarks such as the Albright-Knox Art Gallery, Burchfield Penney Art Center, Buffalo Zoo, Buffalo History Museum, Buffalo Museum of Science, and Erie County Botanical Gardens. The Erie County Fair, held annually since 1820, is one of the largest county fairs in the US.

Buffalo and Erie County are home to professional sports teams like the Buffalo Bills (NFL), Buffalo Sabres (NHL), Buffalo Bisons (Triple-A baseball), and Buffalo Bandits (lacrosse). Although Buffalo lacks a professional basketball team, the community enthusiastically supports the University at Buffalo's Buffalo Bulls men's basketball team.

The Erie Canal, a historic east-west waterway completed in 1825, connects the Hudson River to Lake Erie. This 363-mile canal reduced transport costs and transit time, transforming Buffalo into the largest inland port in the nation and the unofficial grain capital of North America. It reduced the cost of moving a ton of flour from $120 to six dollars and cut transit time from three weeks to six days. The canal's success helped Buffalo grow into one of the wealthiest cities by the twentieth century.

The Pan-American Exposition of 1901, held in Buffalo, showcased the advent of alternating current (AC) electricity, discovered by Nikola Tesla and promoted by George Westinghouse. The exposition, known as The Rainbow City, featured electric lighting powered by hydroelectric energy from Niagara Falls. Tragically, President William McKinley was assassinated at the exposition, leading to Teddy Roosevelt's inauguration as the youngest president in US history. Roosevelt's swearing-in site is now a Registered National Historic Site.

Erie County maintains numerous parks, including five heritage parks (Chestnut Ridge, Akron Falls, Como Park, Ellicott Creek, and Emery Park) and four special-purpose parks (Elma Meadows Golf Course, Erie County Botanical Gardens, Sprague Brook Park, and Grover Cleveland Golf Course). The county also manages conservation parks, waterfront parks, and thousands of acres of forests planted by the Civilian Conservation Corps in the 1930s.

Transition to Erie County Executive

Following my election on November 6, 2007, I quickly assembled a transition team to prepare for my administration. Erie County was in disarray: parks were neglected, beaches closed, highways deteriorated, and several bridges shut down. Polls revealed that 72 percent of residents believed the county was heading in the wrong direction.

I was elected to enact change and restore fiscal stability to a county on the verge of bankruptcy. During a deep national recession, Erie County faced unique challenges due to years of deficits. These financial issues led to the creation of the Erie County Fiscal Stability Authority (Control Board) by New York State in 2005. By October 2005, the Control Board rejected the county's four-year budget (2006-2009) and assumed control of county finances.

In the fifty-six days between my election and inauguration, *The Buffalo News* published forty-one front-page articles and editorials on my transition. Public interest and optimism were high. I pledged to transform Erie County by implementing Total Quality Management and Lean Six Sigma principles in government—a first in the United States. I promised to run Erie County like a business and accepted a salary of one dollar per month until the Control Board reverted to advisory status.

A November 9 headline in *The Buffalo News* aptly stated, "Broad-based team to get Collins rolling," describing my detailed planning for my first year in office. The newspaper portrayed me as an obsessive statistician, a demanding leader, and a driven executive. Their description emphasized accountability and performance, noting my plans for monthly department head reports and thirty, sixty, and ninety-day goals for all managers.

Transition Team

I selected Phil Ackerman and Phil Corwin to serve as co-chairmen of my transition team. Phil Ackerman was the CEO of National Fuel Gas, and Phil Corwin was the vice president and CFO of the Talking Phone Book, a unit of Hearst Publications. Within two weeks of the election, I completed my transition team executive committee by adding ten prominent executives.

To my knowledge, no government official has ever assembled a transition team of this caliber in less than three weeks following an election. On November 25, I announced the appointment of 186 members to my transition team, each led by a subcommittee chair. These thirty-one subcommittees were each assigned to a specific county department or agency, tasked with identifying potential improvements or operational changes that could help establish policy and legislative goals. Each subcommittee comprised five to six members and was instructed to complete its report by December 20, 2007.

I immediately faced criticism from *Buffalo News* columnist Rod Watson, who would continue to attack me weekly for the next four years. He pointed out that only two of my executive committee and subcommittee chairs, Alphonso O'Neil-White and Al Hammonds, were African American.

Each of the thirty-one transition subcommittees submitted comprehensive reports on their assigned departments and agencies. These reports became invaluable reference materials throughout my administration. The time and effort required to produce such professional reports within such a condensed timeframe were extraordinary.

With approval from the Control Board, I brought Chris Grant, my campaign manager, and Grant Loomis, my campaign spokesperson, onto the Erie County payroll at the end of November 2007. I needed them to manage my schedule and coordinate with the thirty-one transition team subcommittees as we prepared for my December 30, 2007, swearing-in ceremony.

Early Criticism

Erie County Comptroller Mark Poloncarz, who would later become my chief political adversary, wasted no time criticizing my actions. In a *Buffalo News* article about the hiring of Chris Grant and Grant Loomis, Poloncarz stated, "To my knowledge, there has never been an individual put on the county payroll prior to the new county executive coming in. I'm not saying it's wrong. But it would be wrong to put them into a position just to give them a salary when they are not doing the work the position entails."

Community Engagement

On December 2, Mary and I attended a service at True Bethel Baptist Church, a predominantly Black congregation on Buffalo's East Side. The photo accompanying *The Buffalo News* article was priceless, showing me holding a microphone with Mary standing beside me, beaming. Reverend Darius Pridgen, also holding a microphone, was addressing his congregation. The article, titled "Collins Reaches Out at Black Service," noted the robust welcome I received and my invitation to congregants to apply for cabinet positions.

The Buffalo News reported that I had met with members of the Jeremiah Partnership—a collaboration of seven African American churches—to discuss ways to improve social services. Two weeks prior, I had attended the Buffalo Urban League's annual gala, where I met several Black leaders. I also planned to attend the Black Leadership Forum on December 8, 2007.

Focus on the Arts

Before the election, I interviewed with the Erie County Arts Council and later organized a meet-and-greet with cultural leaders in Buffalo and Erie County. During this meeting, I informed them that the arts would be subject to the same rigorous operational scrutiny as all county departments. Many arts organizations depended on Erie County's financial support for their operations.

Transparent Hiring Process

I published a list of thirty-six upper-level "at-will" positions on the Erie County website. Interested applicants were required to submit a resume with four references, a personal qualifications statement, a general qualifications statement matching their education and experience to the job requirements, and an "intentions statement" outlining their goals and motivations. The application deadline was December 21, 2007.

White House Invitation

One highlight of my unexpected landslide victory was an invitation to the White House Christmas party on December 11, 2007. Mary and I attended, had a wonderful time, and took a framed photo with President George W. Bush and First Lady Laura Bush.

Fundraising Efforts

I faced criticism for holding a $150-per-head general reception and a $1,000-per-head VIP fundraiser on December 15, 2007. At the time, my campaign had only $6,700 cash on hand and $350,000 in personal debt owed to me. I raised $150,000 after the election and another $75,000 at the December fundraiser. My goal was to repay my campaign loan quickly and begin building a war chest for the anticipated battle in 2011.

Legislative Strategy

Following the election, four Democrats actively vied for the position of Erie County legislature chair, which held significant power over hiring staff and determining legislative priorities. The contenders included Bob Reynolds, Tom Mazur, Maria Whyte, and incumbent Chair Lynn Marinelli. Marinelli had fallen out of favor with Erie County Democratic Party Chairman Len Lenihan, who wanted her replaced.

In a strategic move, I collaborated with Buffalo Mayor Byron Brown to elect the next chair. We formed an eight-person coalition consisting of five Democrats loyal to Mayor Brown, including Marinelli, and the three Republican legislators. This coalition reelected Marinelli as chair, delivering a shocking blow to the Lenihan faction.

Collaboration with Mayor Brown

This political coup marked the beginning of a strong partnership between Mayor Brown and me. Over the next four years, our administrations collaborated extensively. Our chiefs of staff, Steve Casey and Chris Grant, became close allies, further strengthening the relationship between our offices.

Inauguration

I raised quite a few eyebrows when I announced that my inauguration would be held on December 30, 2007, in Amherst, NY, the largest town in Erie County and home to the sprawling campus of the University at Buffalo (UB).

Seasoned political observers noted that they could not recall any prior inauguration for a county executive held outside downtown Buffalo. We also deviated from tradition by holding the event on December 30 instead of the usual January 1.

The first-ever NHL "Ice Bowl," featuring the Buffalo Sabres and Pittsburgh Penguins, was scheduled for January 1 at Ralph Wilson Stadium. Coupled with New Year's Eve festivities on December 31, our event planners opted for December 30. Mary and I later attended the Ice Bowl, enjoying a phenomenal view of the game from the roof of Ralph Wilson Stadium. Erie County, which owned the stadium and provided security through the Sheriff's Department, permitted us this unique vantage point.

Our ceremony included several musical and dance performances, highlighted by the St. John Baptist Church choir. The UB Center for the Arts was an ideal venue, accommodating up to 2,000 people—and nearly every seat was filled.

Boy Scout Troop 93, where I served as an assistant scoutmaster, led the attendees in the Pledge of Allegiance and coordinated the flag ceremony.

Chris Grant's brother, Thomas Grant, performed "The Star-Spangled Banner" to kick off the event.

Reverend Darius Pridgen opened with a prayer, followed by three lively dance performances. State Supreme Court Justice Frank Caruso presided over the swearing-in ceremony. After taking the oath of office, I delivered my keynote address. The St. John Baptist Church choir returned for a choral performance, and Kristen Luzi concluded the musical segment with a rendition of "God Bless America." Father John Gaglione of Christ the King Church offered the closing prayer.

December 30, 2007 swearing in with Supreme Court Justice Frank Caruso.

Our inauguration was truly a memorable event—unlike anything Erie County or the City of Buffalo had ever seen.

Notably, I had invited Senator Chuck Schumer to deliver the keynote address at my inauguration. He graciously declined due to a prior family commitment but thanked me for the offer. Recognizing the importance of building relationships with New York Democrats, I was determined to approach politics strategically. My detractors would soon discover that underestimating me was a mistake.

Taking Office and Laying the Foundation for Success

With the help of my transition team, I assembled a highly capable group of commissioner-level staff, ready to tackle the challenges ahead. I drew talent from both the private and public sectors, retaining commissioners from the prior administration who were willing to embrace necessary changes. Several deputy commissioners, previously overlooked for promotions due to political reasons, were advanced based on their qualifications and readiness.

I appointed Mark Davis as my deputy county executive. Financially secure after the family sale of The Talking Phone to Hearst Publications, Mark was motivated not by need, but by a desire to help me rescue our bankrupt county. As deputy county executive, he served as Erie County's chief operating officer, overseeing all department heads. His swift reputation as "Mr. No" reflected his firm stance on fiscal discipline—department heads quickly stopped seeking approval for unnecessary spending.

On January 3, 2008, *The Buffalo News* ran a front-page story titled "Collins All Set to Tee Off in New Post." The subtitle, "County Executive's Office Reflects Golfing Interest," highlighted my unique approach to leadership. Reporter Matt Spina wrote, "Chris Collins' new office atop the Rath County Office Building, with its commanding view of Buffalo and Lake Erie, is remarkable for what it does not contain—not one political memento. While other executives fill their offices with photos of presidents, governors, or election night celebrations, Collins displays a framed shot of Billy Casper winning the Masters at Augusta in 1970."

Spina continued, "There's also a framing of Davis Love III as the 1997 PGA champion, Johnny Miller winning the British Open in 1976, and other golf legends in their prime. Collins plans to add an autographed photo of Arnold Palmer."

During my tenure as president and CEO of Nuttall Gear, I had successfully implemented quarterly newsletters to keep employees and customers informed. I replicated this strategy at ZeptoMetrix, with similar success. Recognizing the value of consistent communication, I instructed my communications director, Grant Loomis, to launch a monthly newsletter for Erie County at the start of my administration. *The Erie County Taxpayer Newsletter* was prominently featured on the county website. While we refrained from mailing it to residents to avoid unnecessary expenses, the newsletter became a vital tool for transparency and engagement.

Hitting the Ground Running

First Thirty Days

During the first five months of my administration, *The Buffalo News* published thirty-three front-page stories about the changes I was implementing in Erie County government. The public seemed intrigued that, despite having no prior government experience, I was making a noticeable impact.

As Erie County executive, I was automatically a member of numerous associations and agencies. I also held the responsibility of appointing individuals to over thirty-six nonprofit boards, including the Erie County Medical Center, Erie Community College, Albright-Knox Art Gallery, Buffalo Zoo, Buffalo Science Museum, and the Convention and Visitors Bureau. Additionally, I served on the City of Buffalo Fiscal Stability Authority (Buffalo Control Board). The city's finances were in even worse shape than those of Erie County, and it had been operating under a "hard" control board for several years before my election.

I also joined the Erie County Industrial Development Agency (ECIDA) and appointed Phil Ackerman as chair, alongside Phil Corwin. I maintained a strong influence on the ECIDA, and Mayor Brown, also a member, supported issues that were important to me.

Two weeks into the job, I attended an ECIDA meeting where *The Buffalo News* reported, "New Erie County Executive Chris Collins sent a message Thursday to businesses in the county: If you want a tax break, you'd better justify it." This article covered my stance on a request from Martin's Fantasy Island amusement park for $87,000 in tax incentives for new rides. I argued that denying the tax break would likely not prevent the expansion, as it was necessary for the park to remain competitive. Following the discussion, the tax break proposal was tabled, and the ECIDA adopted a moratorium on approving similar retail or tourism projects. My message was clear—business as usual was over in Erie County. My motto, "In God We Trust; All Others Bring Data," was now public.

Uncovering Waste and Driving Efficiency

Everywhere I looked, I found waste and disregard for taxpayers' money. For instance, I learned of an upcoming auction of surplus office furniture and equipment. On the day before the auction, Mark Davis and I visited the storage building and discovered a mountain of items, including chairs, desks, tables, filing cabinets, computers, TVs, and fax machines. We immediately canceled the auction. Mark then enlisted private sector volunteers to inventory the items, and a computer expert to assess which computers could be recycled or refurbished. *The Buffalo News* covered the story, emphasizing that canceling the auction saved Erie County between $100,000 and $200,000. This sent a clear message that every penny mattered.

A memo was issued to all commissioners requiring them to check the surplus storage room for needed items before purchasing new ones.

Promoting Collaboration

I wanted the community to see that collaboration was a priority. As Erie County executive, I worked to foster cooperation among the forty-four cities, towns, and villages in Erie County. Fortunately, *The Buffalo News* covered these efforts extensively, ensuring that taxpayers were aware of my actions.

On January 23, 2008, the paper reported on an upcoming March 4 meeting I organized with town supervisors, village mayors, and city mayors to address common concerns. Topics included parks, 911 systems, highways, snow plowing, and the impact of the New York State budget. The meeting was an immediate success, leading to quarterly meetings throughout my tenure. This collaboration led to practical solutions, such as shared equipment and coordinated efforts in highway repairs and snow plowing.

Similarly, I convened the five elected Erie County officials for the first of what became monthly meetings. Despite their departmental autonomy, these officials depended on me for their budget allocations. The group included:

- Kathy Hochul, County Clerk (Democrat)
- Frank Clark, District Attorney (Democrat)
- Mark Poloncarz, Comptroller (Democrat)
- Tim Howard, Sheriff (Republican)

I was astounded that such meetings had never occurred before. Common sense practices, like collaboration among leaders, were evidently not standard in Erie County government.

On January 24, 2008, I faced a pivotal vote in the Erie County Legislature. I had been on the job for less than four weeks and was unaware of the critical issue on the agenda. Erie County had the highest sales tax rate in New York at 8.75 percent. An additional 1 percent, or the "extra penny" of sales tax, had been added in 1985 with the approval of the New York State Legislature. This extra penny required reauthorization every two years. The New York State Legislature would only approve it if a super-majority of the Erie County Legislature voted in favor of the extension. The extra penny contributed $135 million annually to Erie County's revenue—a crucial component of a budget for a county teetering on the edge of bankruptcy. Without it, the county's finances would collapse.

Three Democratic legislators attempted to leverage their votes to secure $12.5 million of the extra penny for cultural organizations in the county. To pass the extension, we needed twelve votes. Historically, the three Republican legislators opposed all taxes, whether new or extended. However, their support was critical to passing the measure.

I worked to secure their votes through intensive negotiations, and the extension passed with a twelve to three vote, despite opposition from three Democrats.

Regular Part Time (RPT) Employees

When I assumed office, contracts for both the white-collar and blue-collar unions had expired. Under New York State's Taylor Law, existing union contracts remain in effect until a new agreement is negotiated. While this law prevents unions from striking during expired contracts, it creates a stalemate between management and labor. Management often offers higher wages in exchange for concessions on benefits, but unions are typically unwilling to compromise.

A report prepared by my transition team revealed a contractual clause regarding "Regular Part-Time" (RPT) workers. These employees could work up to thirty-nine hours per week and receive 50 percent of the full-time benefits for holiday pay, vacation, sick leave, and personal time off. They earned the same hourly wage and received identical healthcare benefits as full-time workers.

On January 31, 2008, less than four weeks into my tenure, *The Buffalo News* published an article titled, "Collins Orders More Part-Timers Hired," explaining my directive to fill all job openings with RPT employees. This decision was within my authority as county executive, and since RPT positions were covered under union contracts, union leaders could only voice public complaints. My quoted statement emphasized my commitment to taxpayers: "An RPT employee delivers better value to the taxpayer. It is my intention that the vast majority of our new hires be RPT."

This move challenged union leaders Joan Bender (CSEA, representing 4,200 white-collar workers) and John Orlando (AFSCME, representing 1,800 blue-collar workers). While I expressed willingness to negotiate new contracts, any agreement had to prioritize Erie County taxpayers' interests. My RPT directive marked a significant shift in the county's labor strategy.

Taxpayer Savings

The thirty-one transition team reports prepared before my tenure allowed me to take immediate action. My focus was on identifying taxpayer savings, often ruffling feathers in the process. Mark Davis, Erie County's COO, shared my enthusiasm for uncovering cost-saving measures, making us an effective team.

On February 3, 2008, just days after my RPT announcement, *The Buffalo News* published another article titled, "Need Cell Phone, Car? Collins Wants Proof." The report detailed my initiative requiring county employees to justify their use of take-home vehicles and cell phones. Erie County had 800 cell phones and wireless devices assigned to employees, along with over 100 vehicles for twenty-four-hour use. My policy allowed employees to access pooled cars or department-assigned cell phones as needed.

I also chose not to use county-funded amenities. Instead of a government vehicle and driver, I drove my personal Buick Enclave and used my own cell phone. Previous county executives had received these perks along with a security detail, but I declined them, stating I could handle my own safety. My car was equipped with flashing lights, a siren, and emergency radios, enabling me to respond swiftly if needed.

These early actions defined my approach as county executive: making bold decisions to save taxpayer money, challenging entrenched practices, and setting a precedent for accountability and efficiency in Erie County.

Brighter Future Fund

I pledged to work for one dollar per month until the Erie County Control Board reverted to an "advisory" status. This pledge to the voters and taxpayers of Erie County reflected my confidence in turning the county around and restoring its financial stability.

However, I discovered that I was legally required to take my full county salary of $104,000 per year. To honor my commitment, I established the Brighter Future Fund, a charity to redistribute my salary (after social security taxes) to local non-profit organizations serving the community. A five-member committee was formed to review grant applications and award grants of up to $10,000 to qualifying organizations.

Mark Davis, Erie County deputy county executive, earned a slightly higher salary of $107,000 per year. Since he did not need the income, he generously agreed to donate his salary to the Brighter Future Fund. Together, after social security taxes, we had $180,000 annually to allocate for grants.

The criteria for grant applicants included demonstrating alignment with the Brighter Future Fund's goals:

- Promoting economic self-sufficiency for individuals and families.
- Reducing racial and social disparities among Erie County residents.
- Supporting the county's youth and elderly populations.

Our wives were also included on the five-member committee to review the grant applications.

In the first ten months of 2008, the Brighter Future Fund awarded $138,473 in grants to twenty-one non-profit organizations in Erie County. The first two grants were awarded to the Buffalo Inner City Ballet and the Holy Cross Youth Center, with subsequent grants benefiting additional organizations.

Hepatitis A Outbreak: A Precursor to COVID-19

On Friday, February 8, 2008, a Wegmans grocery store employee in Amherst, NY, was diagnosed with Hepatitis A. After just four weeks on the job, I was notified of the situation by Dr. Anthony Billittier, my health commissioner. The potential exposure of Erie County residents required an urgent and unprecedented response. Dr. Billittier promptly notified the public, urging anyone who shopped at the store to get vaccinated.

We set up an emergency vaccination site at Erie Community College the following morning. The weather was extremely cold, with icy rain pouring down. When I arrived, I found lines wrapped around the building, with over 1,000 elderly individuals in wheelchairs and many others exposed to the harsh elements without adequate clothing. Acting quickly, I coordinated the dispatch of dozens of buses to provide shelter for those waiting. The buses, conveniently available because schools were closed, were numbered and brought to the entrance of the makeshift clinic as needed.

Securing enough vaccines proved challenging. We contacted the CDC for assistance and sourced vaccines from across the country. A significant complication was the shortage of vaccines for children, which required a different formulation. Ultimately, we managed to vaccinate 10,153 people in what became the largest emergency vaccination program in US history. For comparison, the largest previous outbreak was in Pittsburgh, PA, in 2003, where 660 people were infected.

Our response was later studied and used to guide the CDC in planning for future mass vaccination efforts. This experience highlighted how unprepared the US public health system was for a potential flu pandemic, leading to critical improvements in emergency response planning. A *Buffalo*

News article about our efforts presciently titled, "Hepatitis Scare Raises Concerns, Offers Glimpse into Nightmare of a Flu Pandemic," foreshadowed the challenges of COVID-19.

Hepatitis A requires two vaccinations several weeks apart. For the second dose, we developed a drive-through vaccination program, allowing individuals to remain in their vehicles while receiving their shots. This innovative approach proved highly effective and was later adopted by the CDC during the COVID-19 vaccination campaign in 2021.

Lean Six Sigma

Six Sigma was the cornerstone of my campaign to demonstrate to Erie County voters that I had a proven plan to improve business efficiency within the county's bureaucracy. I appointed Al Hammonds as director of Six Sigma. Al, a certified master black belt, had experience working in Lockport, NY, for the Delphi radiator division of General Motors.

Interestingly, *The Buffalo News* overlooked the fact that Al Hammonds was an African American Democrat. His role as my director of Six Sigma, and later as my deputy county executive, was never acknowledged by the publication or by their columnist Rod Watson. Their narrative that painted me as a partisan Republican and racist was contradicted by these facts. Life isn't always fair, and shame on them for this omission.

The 2008 Erie County budget had no funding allocated for a director of Six Sigma, let alone for implementing the program itself. I convinced the Control Board to allocate $200,000 for the first year of Six Sigma.

The program's initial success exceeded expectations. Employee enrollment in training sessions was far higher than anticipated. We updated our proposal and returned to the Control Board, requesting an additional $1 million. Despite skepticism from some members, the board ultimately approved the request.

Over my four-year tenure, Erie County trained twelve black belts, more than one hundred green belts, and several hundred yellow belts. Three black belts even achieved master black belt certification.

Our success with Six Sigma drew attention nationally and internationally. We hosted delegations eager to learn how we implemented Lean Six Sigma in a large municipal government. During my administration, county employment decreased from 6,000 to 4,500 workers. Given the average salary and benefits package of $100,000 per county employee, Lean Six Sigma achieved savings of over $150 million annually.

Collins Sprints Through First 100 Days on the Job

My first one hundred days as county executive were a whirlwind. *The Buffalo News* highlighted my achievements in a detailed two-page article titled "Collins sprints through first 100 days on the job. County executive ruffles feathers but sticks to pledge to streamline government." I appreciated the opening: "If the first 100 days indicate an incumbent's style, they say this about Chris Collins: He will shake the box."

The paper also featured a dedicated column titled "The Collins Update," summarizing key initiatives:

- Run the government like a business: The Lean Six Sigma efficiency program was underway. I also reduced the use of cell phones, cars, and other resources.
- Repair roads, bridges, and parks: I proposed over $50 million in infrastructure spending.
- Promote the economy: I appointed my own team to the ECIDA and CVB and welcomed Seneca Gaming.

They even included lighthearted anecdotes, noting that I often ate grilled cheese sandwiches in the county office building cafeteria and made time to engage with workers who approached me.

One directive I enforced was how county employees answered the phone. I insisted on a standardized greeting, which was printed and distributed:

> "Thank you for calling Erie County. This is [your name]."

This practice, which I also use in my private businesses, ensures callers feel appreciated and improves efficiency. After introducing themselves, callers naturally state their names and reason for calling, streamlining communication. My message to employees was clear: efficiency matters.

Transitioning to Government

Transitioning from the private to the public sector can be challenging due to government bureaucracy, which often presents frustrating roadblocks. Mark Davis, my first deputy county executive, became disillusioned with the unionized county workforce and resigned after six months, on July 9, 2008.

Meanwhile, Six Sigma progressed smoothly. By September, our first class of nine green belts was on track for certification. To underscore the importance of the initiative, I promoted Al Hammonds to deputy county executive shortly after Mark Davis's resignation.

ECMC: Kaleida Merger

One of the most significant and enduring accomplishments of my four-year tenure as Erie County executive was leading and successfully negotiating the merger between the Erie County Medical Center (ECMC) and Kaleida Health, announced on June 24, 2008.

Kaleida Health and ECMC employed over 13,000 workers and accounted for over 40 percent of all hospital care in the eight counties of Western New York. The previous county administration had converted ECMC into a public-benefit corporation and used their control over ECMC in 2004 to borrow $101 million to address a significant gap in the Erie County budget. Because the county government operates on a cash basis, this $101 million ECMC debt obligation was immediately included in the revenue column of the Erie County budget, costing Erie County taxpayers over $25 million annually.

Prior to my tenure as Erie County executive, New York State mandated that ECMC and Kaleida form a unified non-public health entity that included the State University at Buffalo (UB). Legislation required the new non-public health entity to be established by June 30, 2008. However, strong differences of opinion and personality conflicts among the leaders of the three institutions made the consolidation effort an acrimonious and contentious process.

On June 10, I directed my county attorney, Cheryl Green, to file a legal action seeking to compel New York State to close either ECMC or Buffalo General Hospital unless an agreement was reached by the June 30 deadline. This legal move, known as an "Article 78" action, was a bold and unexpected last-minute strategy. Cheryl discovered a provision in the New York State health commission law stating that if Kaleida or ECMC failed to reach a binding agreement by June 30, 2008, the state health commissioner was required to close ECMC or Buffalo General.

State Supreme Court Justice John Curran encouraged mediation to resolve the dispute before the deadline. On June 27, I chaired an intensive negotiation session involving sixty representatives from the three institutions. By the end of the day, we reached an agreement on the structure of the new consolidated organization.

Judge Curran described the process as "the most complex and rewarding thing I've ever been involved with." *The Buffalo News* quoted me in their front-page article about the consolidation, stating: "None of us got everything we wanted. But it's a historic day for health care in Erie County. We reset the table without saddling taxpayers with the bill."

Crash of Flight 3407

Just over a year into my tenure, I faced another major crisis. After successfully handling the Hepatitis A outbreak on February 8, 2008—an event that required vaccinating over 10,000 individuals in five days—I was confronted with a catastrophic airplane crash.

On February 12, 2009, at 10:17 PM, Continental Flight 3407 crashed one mile from my home. All forty-nine people aboard the plane perished, along with one individual in the home destroyed by the crash. The Bombardier Q400, a seventy-four-seat twin-engine turboprop plane operated by Colgan Airways as a feeder airline for Continental, tragically failed to reach its destination.

Upon receiving a phone call from an emergency response coordinator, I rushed to the scene, arriving to find the plane engulfed in flames. Alongside my commissioner of emergency services, Greg Skibitsky, and my health commissioner, Dr. Anthony Billittier, I spearheaded the emergency response, coordinating efforts with the FBI, NTSB, NFTA, and local first responders.

A broken gas line in the house fueled the fire, complicating efforts to extinguish it. The scene was devastating; passenger remains were scattered over a wide area, necessitating prompt site security. Initially, details about the flight and the number of people onboard were unclear. We soon confirmed it was Continental Flight 3407, which had departed Newark, NJ.

The crash was later determined to be entirely due to pilot error. As the plane approached Buffalo Niagara Airport, the autopilot was improperly set, causing the plane to descend too quickly. When a stall warning sounded, the pilot's reaction—raising the nose of the plane—was the opposite of proper training. Trained pilots lower the nose to increase airspeed during a stall. The plane's airspeed dropped, leading to a stall and a fatal nose-down spiral from low altitude.

February 8, 2008 Flight 3407 press briefing.

Families of the victims were desperate for information, but the National Transportation Safety Board (NTSB) and Niagara Frontier Transportation Authority (NFTA) were hesitant to release details. Navigating uncharted territory, I held a press conference as Erie County executive to confirm the deadly crash and provide details, ensuring families were informed.

Over the following weeks, I worked closely with my health commissioner to ensure that every family received the remains of their loved ones for proper burial. I maintained contact with the families after the crash and, as a member of Congress, fought for stringent new safety laws. These laws included increased training hours for pilots and the establishment of a pilot database.

In 2018, I facilitated a meeting between the families and Transportation Secretary Elaine Chao to secure her commitment to maintaining these critical safety measures. The families deeply appreciated her assurances.

Control Board

The Erie County Fiscal Stability Authority (Control Board) was established through New York State legislation signed into law by Governor George Pataki on July 12, 2005. The Control Board was set to operate for thirty-five years, from 2005 to 2039, to enable the issuance of thirty-year revenue bonds on behalf of Erie County.

At the time of its creation, Erie County's finances were in dire straits, plagued by persistent budget deficits that depleted county resources. The Control Board initially functioned as an advisory body, tasked with annually approving the county's four-year budget. However, if the proposed budget was rejected, the board's status would escalate from "advisory" to "control."

On October 6, 2005, the Control Board rejected Erie County's 2006–2009 budget, triggering a "control period" in accordance with the New York Public Authorities Law. This effectively placed the Control Board in complete control of the county's finances.

I found my dealings with the Control Board to be beyond frustrating. I submitted my first four-year budget on October 15, 2008, covering the years 2009–2012. The budget was balanced and, in my view, should have been approved. Had they approved it, the control period would have ended, and the board would have reverted to its advisory status.

However, the Control Board rejected my budget. The six appointed members appeared to relish the power they wielded over Erie County government. I believed their rejection of the 2009–2012 budget stemmed more from ego than fiscal prudence.

Despite this setback, the Control Board was funding my Six Sigma initiative with New York State grant money, so I had to navigate their decisions with a degree of tolerance.

In May 2009, I took the unprecedented step of revising and resubmitting my 2009–2012 budget for approval. I stood firm against the Control Board's plan to issue a thirty-year bond to fund the county government. My refusal to endorse their borrowing plan created significant leverage.

On June 2, 2009, the Erie County Fiscal Stability Authority approved my revised 2009–2012 budget, reverting the board to advisory status. This milestone was achieved just seventeen months into my tenure.

As reported by *The Buffalo News* on June 15, 2009:

> "Collins is known to draw a hard line to get what he wants. Collins refused to let the state-appointed financial control board take out a long-term loan on the government's behalf. Despite his limited leverage, he produced a stalemate. One argument with the control board's usually cordial chairman, Robert Glaser, became so heated that the men talked about stepping outside.
>
> "Finally, with little money to fund summer improvement projects, Collins agreed to let the board secure a one-year loan, and the board approved Collins' four-year plan—the first four-year plan it ever approved."

Turning the Tide

June 2, 2009, marked the fulfillment of a promise I had made to Erie County voters during my campaign. I had aired a television commercial vowing to work for one dollar a month until the Control Board reverted to advisory status.

Few believed I could achieve the results my team delivered in just seventeen months. The headline of *The Buffalo News* article announcing the Control Board's shift to advisory status underscored the transformative impact of my administration.

The article conveyed to Erie County residents that these accomplishments were the result of strategic negotiation and skilled leadership—not mere luck. A photograph accompanying the article captured me seated at my desk in a professional-looking office, symbolizing the determination and effectiveness of my approach.

Adept at Using Political Leverage

Another *Buffalo News* article was titled "Adept at using political chokehold - cutting off money to the other side is how Collins, the negotiator, flexes his muscle."

The article began, "Chris Collins understands the power of money—especially when he threatens to take it away." It quoted me directly: "I do play hardball. I will never apologize for that. I go into negotiations with the endgame in mind. I know my strengths. I know where I want to get to. I want it to be a win-win."

The article accurately highlighted my strategy in dealing with the various external agencies impacting Erie County. It noted my unconventional approach to driving change: "He cuts off their money until he's satisfied with their management or his influence over them."

The Buffalo News provided several examples of this 'chokehold' strategy, including my dealings with the Buffalo Niagara Convention & Visitors Bureau, the Buffalo Zoo, and the Albright-Knox Art Gallery.

The second page of the two-page story featured a headline that encapsulated my approach:

Collins has a knack for getting everything he wants.

The Buffalo News reported that I attribute my greatest achievements to my negotiating style. My chief of staff, Chris Grant, was quoted as saying, "Chris has a fierce sense of urgency and wants to get things done as quickly as possible. One of the things we saw during the county executive's race was fifty years of career politicians holding things back. Chris feels as though he needs to get things done now."

The article cited several instances of me "getting everything I want," including my work with cultural agencies, the Control Board, and the merger of ECMC, Kaleida Health, and the UB Medical School.

A Vision for Erie County

In 2009, I formally introduced my vision for Erie County through a sixteen-page brochure titled "Erie County's Road to a Bright Future."

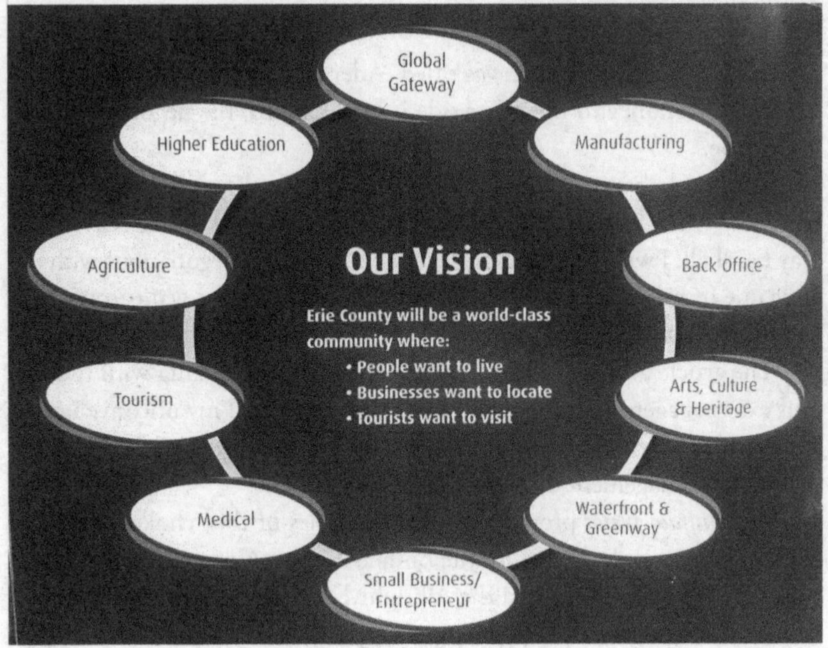

Erie County Executive Road to a Bright Future Brochure.

This comprehensive plan, featuring ten economic initiatives and a vision for the future, became the cornerstone of the remaining two and a half years of my first term as Erie County executive.

In my message to the residents of Erie County, I expanded on my vision and outlined the ten economic initiatives. Here is an excerpt from my message on the second page of the brochure:

- Lean Six Sigma Governance: "We will become the first Lean Six Sigma government in America, sending a message that invites entrepreneurs and businesses to invest and prosper right here in Erie County. We will make our government a partner, not an obstacle, to the business community, helping it flourish and thrive."
- Cultural Heritage: "We will honor our rightful place in history as a critical passageway on the Underground Railroad for enslaved

people seeking freedom in the North. We will maximize our role as a leading cultural destination for tourists worldwide, showcasing world-class attractions and architecture such as Frank Lloyd Wright's Darwin Martin House and Graycliff, the Roycroft Campus, our renowned Olmsted Parks System, the Albright-Knox Art Gallery, and the Burchfield Penney Art Center."

- Economic Growth: "We will position ourselves as a multimodal hub, capitalizing on our geographic location to become an epicenter of trade and jobs in the global economy. We aim to establish Erie County as the back-office capital of America, build upon our manufacturing base, and expand into advanced manufacturing, leveraging cutting-edge innovation and technology."
- Quality of Life: "We will grow by celebrating our world-class people and quality of life. Erie County boasts a skilled, educated workforce with a strong work ethic, affordable housing, short commutes, and world-class attractions."

In conclusion, I emphasized the urgency of our mission: "We must make this vision a reality for our region. We must grow as a community or face stagnation. On the horizon, I see growth and a bright future for our children, grandchildren, and generations yet to come."

DOJ Lawsuit: Erie County Holding Center and Erie County Correctional Facility

In 2007, the Department of Justice (DOJ) Civil Rights Division notified Erie County of its investigation into suicides and allegations of excessive force at the Erie County Holding Center in downtown Buffalo. This occurred before my administration took office.

Cheryl Green, my county attorney, was well aware of the DOJ's investigation upon assuming her role. At the time, Sheriff Tim Howard managed both the Holding Center in Buffalo and the County Jail in Akron, NY.

We collaborated with Sheriff Howard to examine the suicides at the Holding Center and allegations of inmate abuse by guards. Sheriff Howard implemented changes to address these issues and assured us he had the situation under control, negating the need for DOJ interference.

Cheryl conducted an in-depth review of similar DOJ investigations in municipalities nationwide. Her findings revealed that most municipalities cooperated with the DOJ, only to face significant financial burdens later. Under the threat of lawsuits, these municipalities often incurred exorbitant costs to meet what Cheryl described as unreasonable demands from the DOJ.

In August 2008, Cheryl Green prohibited federal investigators from touring the Holding Center or County Jail, unless she could accompany them and participate in interviews with staff or inmates. This unprecedented action was based on Cheryl's discovery that DOJ investigators often misrepresented conversations with jail staff and inmates to support their claims of unacceptable conditions and misconduct. Settlements in such cases frequently led to municipalities constructing new facilities and implementing costly, unnecessary regulations.

To address this potential threat, we preemptively issued a press release to inform Erie County residents that our decision to deny unfettered DOJ access was intended to protect taxpayers. We acknowledged that the DOJ might sue Erie County and pledged to defend our taxpayers vigorously against unnecessary expenditures and property tax increases.

By refusing the DOJ's demands, we disrupted their usual approach of pressuring municipalities into compliance. Our press release signaled that Erie County would not succumb to intimidation.

In July 2009, the DOJ Civil Rights Division released a report citing inhumane and unsafe conditions at both facilities, alleging that Erie County failed to protect inmates' civil rights. The report was compiled without DOJ investigators ever accessing the Holding Center or Jail. The allegations mirrored those made against other municipalities, often resembling a boilerplate document with Erie County's name inserted.

In September 2009, the DOJ filed a federal lawsuit against Erie County officials after we continued to deny access. Around the same time, New York State also filed a lawsuit against Sheriff Howard for refusing to allow state inspectors to interview Holding Center staff without a county attorney or video camera present. Our stance was rooted in safeguarding due process and ensuring transparency during investigations.

The DOJ alleged that conditions at the Erie County Holding Center and County Jail systematically deprived inmates of their constitutional rights. Over the next two years, my staff and I worked with Sheriff Howard to address the primary issue of suicides, which had prompted the DOJ investigation in 2007. It's important to note that there were no suicides at the County Jail.

The Holding Center, housing pretrial detainees, included individuals ranging from serious offenders to college students arrested for minor infractions. Tragically, some college students, especially those detoxing from heroin, committed suicide while in custody. These incidents were particularly difficult to comprehend and explain to the public.

Without waiting for DOJ guidance, my administration implemented practical solutions. We converted the Holding Center's gymnasium into an intake center, where health and mental health professionals assessed new detainees for suicide risk. The gym was renovated to accommodate dormitory-style beds, creating a safer group environment for individuals detoxing from drugs or experiencing other medical issues.

Additionally, we ended an agreement with the City of Buffalo to use the Holding Center as a lockup for newly arrested males. Buffalo established its own lockup in the City Court building, while newly arrested females continued to be housed at the Holding Center.

These changes were driven by our commitment to doing the right thing, not merely to address the DOJ lawsuit. I stated, "The day will come when we ask Federal Judge Skretny to dismiss the DOJ lawsuit. He will evaluate our practices at that time, and everything we are doing now reflects our commitment to continuous improvement."

Our strategy succeeded. On August 18, 2011, the DOJ filed a "Stipulated Order of Dismissal" to resolve its lawsuit. This outcome saved Erie County taxpayers at least $100 million by averting the DOJ's demands for a new facility and excessive staffing increases.

Despite facing intense criticism from *The Buffalo News* for nearly three years, the dismissal validated our approach and highlighted Cheryl Green's exceptional work. The DOJ had never encountered a team as determined and effective as County Executive Chris Collins and County Attorney Cheryl Green.

Gowanda 500-Year Flood

On August 10, 2009, the villages of Gowanda and Silver Creek suffered extensive damage from a 500-year flood. The water supplies of both communities were compromised due to significant damage to village reservoirs and water transmission infrastructures. Residential and commercial properties also experienced severe water and flood damage.

This disaster came on the heels of two other significant events: the February 8, 2008, Hepatitis A vaccination crisis, and the February 12, 2009, crash of Flight 3407. These incidents marked my third monumental challenge in less than two years on the job.

In response, I declared a state of emergency, which led to the area being designated as a Federal Disaster Area. Over $45 million in federal disaster assistance was distributed to more than 1,500 individuals and an estimated 1,100 public projects.

A US Geological Survey recorded over 240 high-water marks, and a subset of these was used to create flood-water surface profiles for four streams. These profiles helped define the extent of flooding in Gowanda and Silver Creek. Remedial measures were implemented to minimize future flooding risks.

My emergency services department worked tirelessly to assist the residents of both communities during this challenging time.

Arts and Cultural Organizations

One of the most contentious issues during my tenure—and likely a factor in my re-election loss—was my approach to funding arts and cultural organizations in Erie County, which received extensive coverage in *The Buffalo News*.

Photo at a typical fundraising dinner for one of the Erie County cultural organizations.

Before even being sworn in, I met with leaders of various arts and cultural organizations in Erie County and informed them that I would require more detailed documentation and justification for any county funding their organizations received.

True to my promise to run Erie County like a business, I scrutinized every dollar in the county budget for potential savings. I discovered that many county legislators had favored arts or cultural organizations to which they allocated taxpayer dollars during the annual budget process.

Although the total amount allocated to these organizations was relatively small, I believed no savings were too insignificant to overlook. For example, I blocked the sale of surplus office equipment within weeks of taking office to explore potential savings through recycling. The taxpayer dollars allocated to arts and cultural organizations seemed, in comparison, a much larger expense.

In my "Erie County Road to a Bright Future" brochure, I identified ten arts and cultural organizations I believed merited taxpayer support as "regional assets" that promoted tourism—one of my key priorities for Erie County's growth and prosperity.

The ten organizations included:

- Zoological Society of Buffalo
- Buffalo Museum of Science
- Buffalo Philharmonic Orchestra
- Albright-Knox Art Gallery
- Penn Dixie Paleontology Site
- Buffalo and Erie County Historical Society
- Theodore Roosevelt Inaugural Site
- Darwin Martin House (Frank Lloyd Wright)
- Burchfield Penney Art Center
- Graycliff Conservancy (Frank Lloyd Wright)

However, I categorized thirty-three smaller, local arts and cultural organizations, such as the Irish Classical Theatre and Shakespeare in the Park, as being unrelated to tourism. These organizations had predominantly local audiences and did not, in my view, attract tourists to Erie County.

Before releasing my four-year budget for 2011–2014, I notified the leaders of these thirty-three organizations to expect significant funding reductions. This announcement sent shockwaves through the arts and cultural community.

When the budget was finalized, I eliminated all county funding for these thirty-three organizations. I encouraged them to seek local support if their offerings were of value. For example, I suggested Shakespeare in the Park pass a collection hat at performances—a suggestion that was not well-received.

The legislature attempted to reinstate funding for these organizations in the 2011–2014 budget. I vetoed their additions, and when they overrode my veto, I declared their actions "null and void," citing violations of the Erie County Charter.

This approach was consistent whenever the twelve to three Democrat legislature passed legislation I opposed. My chief of staff, Chris Grant, would send letters to the legislature declaring their legislation "null and void" due to charter violations. As a result, Chris became known as "Mr. Null and Void."

Four-Year Budget Performance

Erie County finances underwent a fundamental transformation during my four years as Erie County executive. When I was elected, a New York State-appointed Fiscal Stability Authority (Control Board) managed Erie County's finances.

Through the implementation of Lean Six Sigma and other efficiency-related programs, I achieved results that convinced the "hard" Control Board to revert to "advisory" status in June 2009.

My four-year budget mandated that the most current year in the budget be balanced. By law, a forecasted deficit required a property tax increase, while a forecasted surplus necessitated a property tax decrease. Despite this, I ensured the budget remained balanced without resorting to property tax changes. Managing a $1.3 billion annual budget involved forecasting with limited confidence. I explained my assumptions in budget sections and outlined potential actions for revenue shortfalls or unexpected expenses.

When I took office on December 30, 2007, Erie County's finances were the worst among New York's sixty-two counties. By the end of my tenure on December 31, 2011, Erie County was recognized as the county in the best financial shape statewide. Transitioning from "last place" to "first place" remains one of my proudest accomplishments.

We produced actual budget surpluses every year of my administration, despite the 2008–2011 financial meltdown that devastated other counties:

- 2008: $41 million surplus
- 2009: $43 million surplus
- 2010: $23 million surplus
- 2011: $45 million surplus

Additionally, Erie County was the only New York county to pay off all past-due pension obligations. Unlike prior administrations that deferred pension obligations to balance budgets, I paid off these debts and stayed current on all obligations.

I eliminated the practice of selling past-due property tax liens, instead leveraging cash flow to hold these liens and collect accrued high interest. I reduced Erie County's debt by over $100 million and allocated $150 million to an "undesignated" general fund balance, maintaining a reserve for unforeseen expenses or revenue shortfalls. Furthermore, I ceased issuing Revenue Bonds and paid cash for capital projects, road repairs, and bridge repairs.

Summary of Accomplishments

Beyond the financial achievements, I addressed years of neglect preceding my election. When I took office, 72 percent of Erie County residents believed the county was headed in the wrong direction. By the time I left, 74 percent felt the county was headed in the right direction.

During my tenure:

- All county beaches were reopened.
- County park pavilions were rebuilt, playground equipment was installed, and bridges and roads were repaired.
- The Sugar Shack and sawmill were reopened to produce maple syrup and lumber for pavilions and truck beds.

Efficiency improvements enhanced county services, particularly for individuals applying for public assistance. The "One-and-Done" program streamlined enrollment for food stamps, temporary housing, Medicaid, and TANF (Temporary Assistance for Needy Families).

Collaborations with Erie County Clerk Kathy Hochul expanded auto bureaus and introduced a mobile unit serving the county. Major upgrades were made to the Convention Center, and an alliance between Erie County Medical Center and Kaleida Health System created a Center of Excellence for trauma care. Additionally, the 'Visit Buffalo-Niagara' collaboration with Niagara County ended unhealthy competition between the counties.

I prioritized veteran services by elevating the director of veteran affairs to report directly to me. This outreach increased awareness and enrollment in available benefits.

My administration renegotiated county leases and improved employee working conditions. We reorganized the Rath Building, enhancing efficiency and showcasing the benefits of Lean Six Sigma.

Collaborating with Sheriff Tim Howard, we provided new police vehicles and significantly improved the Erie County Holding Center and Jail. Commissioner Pete Vito streamlined the probation department and 911 call center, improving coordination with local police departments.

Waterfront development advanced as I allocated funds to demolish the abandoned "Aud" hockey arena, paving the way for the Erie County waterfront's revival.

By appointing highly qualified commissioners and directors, we maintained a strong focus on constituent service and fiscal responsibility. Despite losing the City of Buffalo with its eight to one Democrat majority, I retained widespread support in surrounding areas, mirroring my 2007 election results.

Erie County hired a Republican entrepreneur/businessman in 2007 to fix its finances, and in 2011, entrusted a Democrat career politician to manage a county that had been restored to fiscal health.

CHAPTER 19

2010 New York Governor Election

THE NATION WAS STUNNED WHEN Governor Eliot Spitzer announced his resignation on March 12, 2008. At a press conference, he apologized to his family and the public for years of sexual misconduct.

The New York Times reported that Spitzer had hired high-priced call girls through an escort service, spending over $80,000 during his tenure as attorney general and governor. The revelations came to light during an FBI investigation into suspicious money transfers, originally suspected to be linked to bribery, which ultimately uncovered the prostitution ring involving Spitzer.

On March 17, 2008, Spitzer resigned, and Lieutenant Governor David Paterson was sworn in as New York's fifty-fifth governor. Paterson became the first legally blind governor of a US state and the first African American Governor of New York. The day after his inauguration, he publicly admitted to having extramarital affairs—a startling revelation so soon after Spitzer's scandal.

This sequence of events was almost surreal, drawing comparisons to implausible movie subplots. But this was real life, showcasing the unpredictability of politics.

Paterson's Challenges

Paterson's governorship began amidst the 2008 financial crisis, which severely impacted New York's economy. The Dow Jones plummeted by 778 points on September 29, 2008—the largest single-day drop until the COVID-19 pandemic in 2020. As the state struggled with mounting deficits, Paterson announced his intent to seek reelection in 2010. This decision surprised many, given his early controversies.

Meanwhile, Attorney General Andrew Cuomo emerged as a potential contender. Popular and well-regarded, Cuomo carried the legacy of his father, Mario Cuomo, who served as New York's governor for three terms. However, Cuomo faced a delicate situation. Running against Paterson, an African American incumbent, could reignite tensions reminiscent of Cuomo's contentious 2002 primary battle with Carl McCall, New York's first African American comptroller. That primary left McCall's campaign weakened and led to accusations of racism within the Democratic National Committee for withholding support. To avoid repeating history, Cuomo appeared hesitant to challenge Paterson directly.

The Republican Landscape

No Republican could win the governorship without securing Erie County, the largest upstate county, with nearly one million residents. Republican George Pataki's victories in 1998 and 2002 relied heavily on his strength in Erie County.

As Erie County executive, I had achieved significant success since my 2007 landslide election victory. With 66 percent of the vote in a predominantly Democratic county, I implemented Lean Six Sigma business efficiencies, rescuing Erie County from near bankruptcy. The New York State Fiscal Stability Board relinquished control of the county's finances just eighteen months into my administration, recognizing Erie County as the state's most financially stable county during the 2008 financial crisis.

Encouraged by this success, I was approached about running for governor. My record as Erie County executive and my transformative use of Lean Six Sigma positioned me as a strong candidate. In April 2009, a statewide poll revealed that 60 percent of New Yorkers disapproved of Paterson's performance—the worst rating ever for a New York governor. This emboldened my quiet exploration of a gubernatorial campaign.

Building Support

Campaign Button promoting my campaign for Governor of New York.

Over nine months, I met with Republican leaders across New York, including county chairs, committees, and influential figures like Ed Cox, the newly elected New York Republican Party chair. I also engaged with groups like The Metropolitan Republican Club, and prominent individuals like billionaire John Catsimatidis and financier Anthony Scaramucci. These efforts helped build momentum for my potential candidacy.

In October 2009, I hosted a successful fundraiser in New York City, further solidifying support. Media interviews, including several with Albany radio host Fred Dicker, raised my profile statewide.

Challenges Ahead

My primary obstacle within the Republican Party was Rick Lazio, who announced his candidacy in September 2009. Lazio, a former congressman, was best known for his unsuccessful 2000 Senate campaign against Hillary Clinton. His debate misstep—placing a campaign finance pledge on Clinton's podium—was widely criticized as chauvinistic and damaged his reputation.

Despite Lazio's candidacy, my strong record and growing support positioned me as a formidable contender. With careful planning and continued outreach, I prepared to take on the challenges of the 2010 gubernatorial race, confident in my ability to bring transformative change to New York State.

There were two incidents that ultimately caused me to withdraw from the gubernatorial race in 2010.

The Antichrist

On October 24, 2009, I served as the keynote speaker at a large GOP fundraiser in Buffalo. Like many speakers, I typically begin my remarks with a humorous comment to put the audience at ease. This time was no different.

The night before the event, I had watched a *History Channel* program about Nostradamus, the 16th-century astrologer who published a book titled *Les Prophéties* in 1555, containing 353 quatrains. The episode, titled "The Third Antichrist," had premiered on September 9, 2009, and explored Nostradamus's prediction of three Antichrists who would bring suffering to humanity. The show posed the question: "Who are they, and when will they come?" It proposed that the first Antichrist was Napoleon, the second was Hitler, and the third is already among us.

During my speech, I recounted the program to lighten the mood and jokingly claimed to know the identity of the third Antichrist: "It's New York State Assembly Speaker Shelly Silver." While the comment drew some laughs, it did not resonate as expected. Unbeknownst to me, many in the audience were aware that Shelly Silver is an Orthodox Jew, making the comparison to Hitler profoundly offensive.

The fallout was swift. The following day, on October 25, 2009, *The New York Daily News* reported my remarks, accusing me of antisemitism and dubbing me "Jew-bashing Chris Collins." *Artvoice*, a Buffalo-based weekly newspaper, featured me on its October 29 front page with a caricature depicting Napoleon, Hitler, and Shelly Silver—horns included—alongside the headline: "Tell us what you really think, CHRIS. Why Collins calling Sheldon Silver the Anti-Christ is no joke."

Despite my apologies, including a personal call to Shelly Silver, where he graciously dismissed the comment, the damage was done. Although I was naive to Silver's religious background and harbor no antisemitic beliefs, this incident became a defining moment in my political career.

Lap Dance

On January 6, 2010, I attended the annual State of the State address delivered by Governor David Paterson in Albany. I wanted to witness his speech in person, expecting him to be my opponent in the 2010 gubernatorial election.

When I arrived at the large auditorium, there were no open seats. My friend and neighbor, Assemblywoman Jane Corwin, had saved me a seat next to her. I had recruited her to run for the Assembly in 2008, and she supported my 2010 gubernatorial bid.

As I took my seat, I noticed frustrated attendees searching for places to sit. A longtime female friend from Buffalo, Laura, spotted me and approached. The three of us were close friends and members of Brookfield Country Club. Laura joked, "I can't find a seat. Can I sit in your lap?"

That was typical banter between us. I laughed and replied, "I don't think this is a good place for a lap dance." The three of us laughed, and Laura moved on to find a seat.

Unbeknownst to me, Assemblyman Joe Errigo, a supporter of Rick Lazio, was nearby and overheard our exchange. Determined to discredit me, Errigo distorted our casual banter and falsely claimed to the press that I suggested Laura could secure a seat in exchange for a lap dance.

Errigo's fabrication was sensationalized in the press.

The media storm grew. My team—particularly Chris Grant and Michael Hook—chastised me but assured me that we could move past it. However, the political fallout was severe.

The Buffalo News ran a front-page story on January 14, 2010, titled, "Collins trips over his tongue again." The article mischaracterized the incident and reignited scrutiny over my earlier comment about Shelly Silver.

The End of the Campaign

I was in New York City when *The Buffalo News* article was published. Michael Hook called the next day with a clear directive: I needed to withdraw from the gubernatorial race. He argued that the series of controversies had rendered me unelectable statewide. He suggested I issue a simple statement citing the state's unfavorable political demographics for Republicans in 2010 as the reason for my decision.

On January 15, 2010, I officially ended my unofficial candidacy for governor with a press release. Rick Lazio had won. His supporters' underhanded tactics had effectively ended my campaign.

Ironically, just weeks later, on February 26, 2010, Governor David Paterson announced he would not seek reelection. Andrew Cuomo declared his candidacy and became the Democratic frontrunner. Running against Cuomo in 2010 would have been an insurmountable challenge, so in hindsight, the controversies spared me from a futile campaign.

Serendipity

The "lap dance" debacle, while devastating at the time, turned out to be a blessing in disguise. It saved me the embarrassment of continuing an official gubernatorial campaign doomed to fail against Andrew Cuomo, who was unbeatable in 2010.

Life's ironies continued. Andrew Cuomo later resigned as governor in 2021 amidst a sexual harassment scandal. His successor, Kathy Hochul, had lost her 2012 congressional reelection bid to me. If she had won that election, she might never have become lieutenant governor or risen to the governorship.

On June 2, 2010, the New York State GOP officially endorsed Rick Lazio. After my withdrawal, I encouraged my friend Carl Paladino to run for governor. With Tea Party support, he defeated Lazio in the primary but lost to Cuomo in the general election.

History's twists and turns remind us that what seems like a defeat can sometimes be a disguised victory.

CHAPTER 20

2011 Erie County Executive Reelection

Mark Poloncarz

From the day I was elected Erie County executive in 2007, I anticipated that my reelection opponent in 2011 would be Erie County Comptroller Mark Poloncarz. He began attacking me immediately after my election, even before I was sworn into office.

Mark Poloncarz is a political animal with a singular focus on himself. He used his position as Erie County comptroller to manipulate budget projections and assumptions, aiming to discredit my administration at every opportunity. He publicly opposed 90 percent of my decisions but never offered explanations or justifications for his disagreements.

While I focused on taxpayers and the challenges of operating under the oversight of a Control Board for Erie County finances, Poloncarz criticized decisions without having to grapple with the budget constraints that informed them.

As a liberal Democrat, Poloncarz was a favorite of *The Buffalo News*. His focus was on the City of Buffalo, often ignoring the suburbs. Buffalo represents one-third of Erie County's population and has an eight to one Democrat advantage. Despite his role as Erie County comptroller, he demonstrated a surprising lack of fiscal discipline. His department paid bills, but that was the extent of his responsibilities.

In contrast, as county executive, I served as the CEO, COO, and CFO of Erie County. My Budget Director, Greg Gach, was responsible for county finances. We prepared the four-year budget annually, without input from Poloncarz. His title might as well have been "Erie County Bill Payer."

Key functions such as property tax collection, sales tax receipts, Medicaid expenses, and pension payments were managed by other departments or New York State. The role of comptroller seemed redundant and wasteful, and much of Poloncarz's office could have been eliminated without impacting county operations.

With minimal responsibility for county finances, Poloncarz had the freedom to criticize my decisions without accountability. *The Buffalo News* consistently supported his critiques, often aligning with his narrative. At times, it felt as though Poloncarz was collaborating with *The Buffalo News* editorial board.

Poloncarz's Positions and Criticisms

Poloncarz's public positions during my first term often highlighted his incompetence:

- He opposed my Lean Six Sigma initiative and stated he would terminate it if elected.
- He criticized my cuts to arts and cultural organizations and promised to increase funding beyond my budgets.
- He disagreed with my efforts to consolidate Erie County's excessive number of libraries.
- He opposed my decision to challenge the DOJ's demand to build a new Holding Center and hire additional staff.
- He rejected my cost-saving measures for hiring Regular Part-Time (RPT) employees.
- He promised to negotiate union contracts with significant wage increases without reducing costly benefits.
- Despite increased spending on roads and bridges, Poloncarz frequently claimed my administration neglected infrastructure.

Additionally, Poloncarz supported projects like a new Erie County Community College campus in downtown Buffalo and opposed my decision to prevent the Control Board from issuing thirty-year revenue bonds, which would have prolonged its authority indefinitely.

Preparing for Reelection

As 2011 approached, I anticipated a challenging reelection in a county with a two to one Democrat voter advantage. I had $1.2 million in my campaign account by the end of 2010 and had repaid my personal loan from the 2007 election. Confident in my track record, I was ready for a tough race.

My campaign launched on March 26, 2011, emphasizing my accomplishments and efficient governance.

Kathy Hochul, another potential Democrat challenger, shifted her focus to the special election for NY-26 after Congressman Chris Lee's resignation. With Hochul out, Poloncarz officially became my opponent in May 2011.

Campaign Developments

Throughout the campaign, I highlighted Erie County's fiscal stability. By April 2011, the county surplus was $23 million, and I proposed using it for infrastructure improvements and other critical projects. Despite these successes, Poloncarz attacked my administration's priorities, often misrepresenting the facts—such as promising to fix roads not under county jurisdiction.

On July 19, 2011, I announced a midyear budget surplus of $13 million, reinforcing my administration's fiscal discipline. My campaign's financial advantage was significant, with $1.6 million cash-on-hand compared to Poloncarz's $154,363.

The Election

Despite my administration's accomplishments, the October 2011 *Buffalo News* poll showed a tight race, with me leading 49 percent to 46 percent. The poll reflected the challenges of running in a heavily Democrat county and the sustained negative coverage from *The Buffalo News*.

Poloncarz and I debated twice in October 2011, with both performances exposing voters to our contrasting styles and platforms. *The Buffalo News* endorsed Poloncarz, citing a desire for a candidate who balanced financial realities with civic priorities.

On November 8, 2011, I lost reelection 53 percent to 47 percent. I won decisively in the suburbs but lost heavily in the City of Buffalo. The two to one Democrat voter advantage in Erie County proved insurmountable.

In conceding, I expressed pride in the fiscal stability I brought to Erie County, stating, "The county is better today than it was four years ago. The public has spoken. This is a democracy. I'm returning to the private sector where I know how to create jobs."

CHAPTER 21

2012 Congressional Election

Background

I never expected to lose my reelection as Erie County executive on November 8, 2011. However, I accepted my defeat and ensured a smooth transition of power to my opponent, Mark Poloncarz.

Mary and I flew to Marco Island, FL, on January 16, 2012, to relax and unwind after my loss. We had purchased a house there in November of 2011, and there were many things that needed our attention at the new house. Meanwhile, my partner at ZeptoMetrix was dealing with the unexpected death of his wife on January 20. The funeral for Karen Hengst was set for January 25, so we flew back to Buffalo on January 23.

I had no idea what my future would look like. I had private investments in ZeptoMetrix, Bloch Industries, Audubon Machinery, Niagara Ceramics, Easom Automation, and Volland Electric. I could restart my weekly visits to each company and provide input as I had done before being elected Erie County executive, but I wasn't sure what I wanted to do.

Life became a day-to-day routine. We drove to Boston for my daughter's dance recital at Boston College, spent a couple of days visiting friends, and returned to Florida on February 4.

I still wasn't sure what I wanted to do and felt a little empty after unexpectedly losing my reelection. I started to consider challenging Rep. Kathy Hochul in the upcoming congressional election on November 6, 2012.

Reflecting on Kathy Hochul

Kathy Hochul was Erie County clerk while I was Erie County executive. She was a separately elected county official. While I controlled the budget as the CEO of Erie County, Hochul ran the Clerk's office and DMV. Though I didn't particularly like her, I supported her department with the funds needed to deliver quality services to Erie County residents.

When Rep. Tom Reynolds decided not to seek reelection in 2008, I was approached to run for his seat in Congress but declined. The GOP chose Chris Lee, a local businessman, who was easily elected in 2008 and reelected in 2010. However, Rep. Lee resigned on February 9, 2011, after a scandal involving flirtatious emails and a shirtless photo surfaced.

Kathy Hochul ran for his seat in a special election on May 24, 2011. I was approached to run as well but declined, believing my skills were better suited for executive roles than legislative ones. Instead, I recruited Jane Corwin, a New York Assembly member, to run against Hochul. Jane agreed, and with NY-26 being a strong Republican district, we were confident in her chances. However, Jack Davis, a businessman opposed to free trade, entered the race as an Independent, splitting the Republican vote. Kathy Hochul won the election with 47.2 percent of the vote.

The Decision to Run

I invited Chris Grant and Michael Hook to Marco Island to discuss the possibility of challenging Kathy Hochul in the 2012 general election. At that time, congressional districts were being redrawn following the 2010 census. The Hochul seat, previously designated as NY-26, was redesignated as NY-27. The new district boundaries were finalized on March 19, 2012, encompassing parts of eight counties and requiring campaigning across both the Buffalo and Rochester media markets. This doubled the cost of an already expensive race.

Both Chris and Michael warned that defeating Hochul would be challenging. As an incumbent and a Democrat who had flipped a traditionally Republican district, she would have access to significant resources. Hochul had a reputation as a hardworking, retail politician which further complicated the race. She visited every diner and event in the district, shaking hands and building goodwill. She also positioned herself as a moderate, distancing herself from traditional Democratic policies that didn't resonate in NY-27.

Despite these challenges, I decided to run. I believed I could expose the Hochul hypocrisy and capitalize on her alignment with President Barack Obama and Nancy Pelosi, both unpopular in NY-27. Chris Grant agreed to be my campaign manager, and Michael Hook signed on as my consultant.

Primary Race Against David Bellavia

I announced my decision to run for Congress against Rep. Kathy Hochul on March 23, 2012, during an interview with *The Buffalo News*. The newspaper featured my decision as its top story in the Sunday, March 25 edition, with the bold headline: "Collins launches campaign for Congress in 27th District." Bob McCarthy, the political reporter, gave me the perfect introduction to inform voters of my determination to defeat liberal Congresswoman Kathy Hochul in the November general election.

Initially, I did not expect to face a primary opponent in the June 26, 2012, primary election. David Bellavia had already announced his candidacy against Hochul, but we anticipated he might withdraw once I entered the race. Bellavia had been a candidate in the 2011 special election but withdrew to endorse Jack Davis. Ultimately, David Bellavia did not withdraw and I ran against him in the June primary.

David Bellavia is a bona fide war hero. He was awarded the Silver Star for valor during the Iraq War for his courageous actions in the Second Battle of Fallujah on November 10, 2004. His Silver Star citation details an extraordinary account of bravery: clearing a block of insurgent-occupied buildings, engaging in multiple close-combat encounters, and neutralizing insurgents, including one through hand-to-hand combat.

Jumping ahead, on June 7, 2019, it was revealed that the Silver Star Bellavia was awarded would be upgraded to the Medal of Honor. The ceremony, held at the White House on June 25, 2019, was presided over by President Donald Trump, making Bellavia the only living Medal of Honor recipient from the Iraq War.

I had tremendous respect for the service David Bellavia provided to the nation, but I needed to defeat David Bellavia in the primary before focusing on the general election against Kathy Hochul. David Bellavia had secured endorsements from six of the eight counties in NY-27, most of which were rural areas where he had deep roots. Many rural county chairmen resented Erie County's dominance in nominations, given its significantly larger population.

I secured endorsements from Erie and Niagara counties, the two largest in the district, as well as from the New York State Conservative Party. This guaranteed me a spot on the November 6 general election ballot, even if I lost the Republican primary. New York's electoral fusion voting allowed candidates to appear on multiple party lines and combine votes for the final tally.

My campaign strategy against Bellavia was straightforward and positive. I avoided fundraisers, choosing instead to use my own funds for the primary. My efforts centered on direct mail, social media, and tele-town halls. I refrained from negative campaigning, frequently stating, "David Bellavia is a war hero. I thank him for his service to our country. I simply offer voters a different resume for consideration."

I declined to debate Bellavia, fearing it would boost his name recognition in Erie County, where he was largely unknown. His campaign manager, Michael Caputo, humorously hired someone to dress in a chicken suit to mock my refusal, standing outside my neighborhood with a sign challenging me to debate.

In the June 26 primary, I won decisively, garnering 59.9 percent of the vote (11,677 to 7,830). While Bellavia dominated the rural counties, I overwhelmingly carried Erie and Niagara counties. The low voter turnout—just 11 percent of registered Republicans—highlighted the challenges of primary elections in New York.

After the primary, I became close friends with both David Bellavia and Michael Caputo. Politics is best approached without personal grudges. Both men endorsed and campaigned for me in the general election against Kathy Hochul.

Bellavia raised $100,000 for his campaign, which I matched with personal funds.

General Election—November 6, 2012

Winning the primary was a relief, but I knew defeating Kathy Hochul would require a focused strategy. Hochul, was running on the Democrat and Working Families Party lines, and was backed by the Democratic Congressional Campaign Committee, which prioritized defending her seat.

The Buffalo News extensively covered our race, which it deemed the marquee contest of 2012. The newspaper dominated five of the district's eight counties, representing 80 percent of voters, while *The Democrat and Chronicle* in Rochester served the remaining three rural counties.

The key to my strategy was tying Hochul to President Barack Obama, who was deeply unpopular in the district. In 2008, Obama lost the area to John McCain 45 percent to 55 percent. By 2012, his support further eroded, losing to Mitt Romney 43 percent to 57 percent.

Palm Card for 2012 congressional campaign.

We allocated 75 percent of our $1 million campaign budget to television, with $750,000 committed to ads. Additional funds were directed to radio, direct mail, polling, and campaign overhead. Despite this, we knew Hochul would outspend us significantly, relying on potential Super PAC support.

My campaign's media efforts were managed by Chris Grant (direct mail) and Michael Hook (television ads). I was well-known in Erie and Niagara counties, thanks to Buffalo-based television, but remained relatively unknown in the three Rochester-area counties.

We faced a tough decision on allocating ad spending between the Buffalo and Rochester markets. Ultimately, we devoted 70 percent of our TV budget to Erie and Niagara counties, which represented 80 percent of the vote, while the remainder targeted the Rochester market to increase name recognition in the outer counties.

Hochul, as the incumbent, spent significant time in these rural areas, understanding they were crucial for her reelection. Meanwhile, we relied on tying her to Obama and House Speaker Nancy Pelosi to sway conservative voters.

A photograph of Hochul walking with Obama at the White House became a pivotal piece of campaign material. In it, she wore a white blazer and skirt, a blue blouse, and her congressional pin while smiling starstruck at the president. This image perfectly illustrated our message about her alignment with the Obama administration.

That photo became the centerpiece of our negative campaign advertising and direct mail. The main piece of negative mail featured the Obama/Hochul photo on the front of a six-inch by eleven-inch postcard. On the right side of the front of the mail piece, it read: "We need someone in Congress who will stand up to Barack Obama, not follow him...."

Our entire campaign focused on Republican, Conservative, and Independent voters who disliked Barack Obama. We didn't need or expect a single Democrat to vote for me. We couldn't care less if our mail and television ads infuriated the Democrats.

NY-27 was overwhelmingly conservative, pro-Second Amendment, pro-life, and Christian. The district was rural, with more dairy cows than people. It was 98 percent white and only 2 percent minority.

We began airing television commercials on August 17, 2012. We committed to three straight months of television, targeting the 6:00 PM, 10:00 PM, and 11:00 PM news slots. These programs attracted reliable voters. With a tight budget, we couldn't afford to advertise on shows that catered to kids or people less likely to vote.

Hochul allowed us to run negative commercials tying her to Barack Obama for two weeks before she went on the air. When she finally did, her commercials were ineffective and didn't mention me at all. It was apparent she wasn't receiving good advice. I had the "A" team; Kathy Hochul had a "C" team.

I traveled throughout the district, concentrating on the outer rural areas where I wasn't well-known. I attended county fairs, marched in parades, visited dozens of dairy farms, and shook hands in restaurants and diners (a task I didn't particularly enjoy).

Kathy Hochul and I debated four times. Our first debate was on October 17. I was prepared to answer every question in a way that tied Kathy Hochul to Barack Obama. Regardless of the question, I would start my answer by saying, "I'm glad you asked me that question. It reminds me of how Kathy Hochul and Barack Obama are destroying our country, killing jobs, and making it difficult for our hardworking farmers to provide for their families."

I was a broken record. I got under Kathy's skin by repeatedly asking if she would vote for Barack Obama in the election. She refused to answer directly, often pivoting to other topics. Frustrated, she would reply, "You are running against me, not President Obama."

I would counter with, "You fully support Barack Obama and vote with Nancy Pelosi over 80 percent of the time to support the liberal tax-and-spend policies that are destroying our country. Why don't you just confirm the obvious: that you will be voting for Barack Obama in the election?"

I've been told I clearly outperformed Kathy Hochul in all our debates. The debates garnered significant media coverage, and I knew everyone watching was likely to vote.

The most helpless feeling came from watching my opponent outspend me four to one, with significantly more television and direct mail, in addition to outside groups and PACs airing their commercials. I felt abandoned until the Credit Unions, of all organizations, came to my rescue near the end of the campaign. I was out of money, polls showed Kathy Hochul and me in a dead heat, and outside groups were hammering me with negative ads.

PACs can't legally coordinate with a campaign, so you never know if or when they'll support you. The day I saw an attack ad targeting Kathy Hochul that we didn't produce was a very good day for my campaign. I remain forever indebted to the Credit Unions for their support as the election approached.

When all the dust settled, I had spent over $1.3 million on the 2012 election. Kathy Hochul spent $4.9 million, with PACs supporting her spending another $4.0 million on negative ads. That's politics; don't play the game if you can't handle the pressure.

On November 4, 2012, a *Buffalo News* poll showed me with a narrow lead: 48 percent to 47 percent, with 5 percent undecided. Despite enduring over $8 million in negative ads, I was still ahead.

Election Day arrived on November 6, 2012. *The Buffalo News* headline summed it up: "Hochul, Collins Await What May Be a Long Night."

At midnight on November 6, I held a slight lead:

County	Collins Votes	Hochul Votes
Erie County	61,193	59,353
Orleans County	6,874	6,248
Genesee County	11,508	10,755
Monroe County	6,232	5,954
Wyoming County	8,203	6,603
Livingston County	11,792	12,181
Niagara County	11,646	12,256
Ontario County	13,044	13,406

In raw numbers, I was leading 149,360 to 144,800 with 99 percent of the vote counted.

There were still 12,721 absentee ballots to be counted, along with a few election districts in rural counties. Absentee ballots typically trend similarly to general election results. Kathy Hochul would need to win 70 percent of these to make up my 4,560-vote lead. When all votes were counted, I won by 5,001 votes, or 1.57 percent. Our race was the twelfth closest in the United States.

I received 161,220 votes to Kathy Hochul's 156,219, securing 50.8 percent to her 49.2 percent.

I won the election and was headed to Congress.

Headlines:

- "Collins Claims Victory Over Hochul" (November 7)
- "Rising Again, Collins Heads for Capitol Hill" (November 8)
- "Collins Bounces Back, Ready to Take on Washington" (November 9)

Chris Collins: (November 8): "This win is the best because many people said we were down and out—in fact, dead on arrival."

Kathy Hochul: (November 8): "Democracy worked. This is how we choose our leaders. I walk away with pride."

CHAPTER 22

Congress 2013–2014

I WON MY ELECTION TO Congress representing NY-27 on November 6, 2012, defeating incumbent Rep. Kathy Hochul by 1.57 percent. My win was the twelfth closest race among the 435 Members elected in 2012.

Kathy Hochul was one of only five incumbent Democrats to lose her reelection in 2012. Now Governor of New York, her loss to me in 2012 remains the only election she has ever lost.

President Barack Obama and Vice President Joe Biden defeated the Mitt Romney/Paul Ryan ticket with a popular vote of 51.1 percent to 47.2 percent.

Paul Ryan returned to Congress as chairman of the Budget Committee. Republican leadership remained consistent with John Boehner as speaker of the House, Eric Cantor as majority leader, Kevin McCarthy as whip, Steve Scalise as deputy whip, and Cathy McMorris-Rogers as conference chair.

The Republicans lost a net eight seats in the 2012 election, reducing their majority from 242 members to 234 members. Despite this, John Boehner continued as speaker of the House, while Nancy Pelosi remained the minority leader for the Democrats.

I had significant work ahead after the election. I needed to hire staff for my district and Washington offices, and secure housing in Washington. Shifting from a chief executive role to that of a legislator required a fundamental change in approach.

Orientation

The new members of Congress elected in 2012 are referred to as the 2012 Freshman Class, which included thirty-seven new Republican members and forty-eight new Democrats. Orientation for new members, organized by the House Administration Committee, aimed to prepare lawmakers for their roles before being sworn in on January 3, 2013.

Mary and I arrived in Washington three days before orientation to search for housing. I purchased a two-bedroom condo near the Capitol. *The Buffalo News* noted this purchase in an article. "For Lawmakers in DC, a lifestyle divide. As Collins buys a condo, colleagues sleep in their offices," highlighting the differences in housing choices among lawmakers.

Over one hundred members of Congress opt to sleep in their offices due to the lack of government reimbursement for housing, relying on inflatable mattresses or pull-out sofas. They shower in the House gym and transport their clothes from their office to the gym.

Office Staff

Members of Congress receive a budget to pay staff and manage district offices. The House covers the pay for the member of Congress and also pays for all the fringe benefits for staff.

I benefited from affordable airfare and inexpensive rent for my district offices. Members flying to the West Coast, or members with offices in major cities, had to be very frugal in other areas to stay within their budgets.

My district covered eight counties in Western New York, and I established offices in Clarence and Geneseo to provide convenient access for constituents. My staff included six employees in Washington, DC, and six employees in my district offices.

Swearing-In

The 113th Congress convened on January 3, 2013. Mary and our two children joined me to celebrate my achievement of being elected to Congress. I hosted a reception in my new office in the Longworth House Office Building, where donors and supporters offered their congratulations.

Official Congressional Photo.

113th Congress

Congress is in session three weeks a month, with Members in Washington for four days and three nights each week. The House recesses for the entire month of August every year and also recesses for the entire month of October during election years.

Committee Assignments

Every member serves on one or more of the twenty committees in Congress. I secured spots on the Agriculture and Small Business Committees, and was surprised to receive an invitation to join the Science, Space, and Technology Committee by Chairman Lamar Smith. As one of the few engineers in Congress, Chairman Smith wanted my expertise and background to help on his committee. I was the only freshman member of Congress to serve on three committees.

I was honored to be appointed as the chairman of the Small Business Committee's Subcommittee on Healthcare and Technology, with oversight on the implementation of President Obama's healthcare law and how it affected small business. In addition to oversight of the health care law, my subcommittee also had jurisdiction over technology, telecommunications and intellectual property issues as they pertained to small businesses. I was the only freshman member of Congress to chair a subcommittee.

Serving on the Agriculture Committee put me in a critical position to advocate for the reauthorization of The Farm Bill, which had expired in 2012. My work on The Farm Bill resulted in it being successfully reauthorized in 2013, providing stability for farmers in NY-27.

Fundraising

Fundraising is a challenging aspect of politics. Members must raise funds for reelection and meet "dues" assessments for their party. During my tenure, I exceeded my Republican Party dues by over 150 percent.

Legislation

My Legislative Director, Jeff Freeland, played a pivotal role in reviewing and analyzing legislation. My voting record demonstrated a moderate conservative stance. I was a member of both the House Republican Study Committee Caucus and the moderate Tuesday Group Main Street Caucus, bridging ideological divides within the party.

Notably, I was one of only twenty-eight Republicans who voted to keep the government running during a potential shutdown in 2013. I consistently aligned with committee chair recommendations, earning goodwill within Republican leadership.

Constituent Service

Members spend more time in their districts than in Washington. My district staff managed my schedule carefully to avoid burnout. I focused on agriculture, the primary economic activity in my district, through farm tours and community events.

I frequently spoke at schools, enjoying the interaction with students and their candid questions. Mary and I also attended numerous district events, from galas to volunteer fire company fundraisers. These gatherings provided valuable connections and insights into the community's needs.

Through these efforts, I navigated the complexities of congressional service while remaining accessible and responsive to my constituents.

Each year, my staff coordinated an art competition with all the high schools located in NY-27. The winning piece of artwork would be displayed for one year in the hallway tunnel connecting the Capitol to the House office buildings. Each member of Congress placed one piece of artwork on the walls in the tunnel for everyone walking through to observe and enjoy.

Another activity I always looked forward to was selecting students who applied to various service academies: West Point, the Naval Academy, the Air Force Academy, and the Merchant Marine Academy. Each student chosen for these United States Service Academies needed a recommendation from their member of Congress. I assembled a committee of volunteers to interview the students who requested a nomination to one or more of the academies.

I honored veterans every chance I could. Whenever there was a Veterans of Foreign Wars (VFW) event anywhere in the district, I'd be there.

I am a lifelong Scout, recipient of the National Distinguished Eagle Scout Award, and served as chairman of the Scout Caucus in Congress. I hosted the National Chief Scout Executive on his yearly trek to Washington to present his annual Report to the Nation.

Israel

Members of Congress are often given opportunities to travel to gain knowledge and study issues firsthand. All freshmen are encouraged to travel to Israel to meet with the president and prime minister of Israel. In 2013, the 2012 Republican Freshman Class was offered a trip to Israel from August 10–17, hosted by Majority Leader Eric Cantor. Twenty-five members of Congress and their spouses flew business class from Washington, DC to Israel.

The Israel–Palestine–Syria conflict was raging at the time of our scheduled trip. My wife was unwilling to travel to a war-ravaged part of the world. I received permission to have my son accompany me as my family member guest. He was twenty years old at the time and a sophomore at Villanova University, and joined me with Mary's approval. Although intellectually Mary knew we would be safe, emotionally, she couldn't handle the trip.

Our seven-day congressional trip to Israel was educational, sobering, and fun. It is hard to imagine the isolated and fragile state of Israel without actually spending time there. The historic ruins and biblical connections to everything we saw were truly awe-inspiring.

We never had a dull moment or any downtime during the entire trip. Security was provided throughout and served as a constant reminder of the dangers Israelis face daily.

Our briefings were thorough and detailed. We met with all the key leaders in Israel, who were emphatic about their dedication to Israel's survival amidst threats from various Islamic factions in the Middle East.

Touring historic sites, swimming in the Sea of Galilee, and taking a mud bath in the Dead Sea were wonderful experiences.

My son was the only participant who wasn't a member, spouse, or staff member. Every speaker noticed him and went out of their way to make him feel welcome. This was especially true for Prime Minister Benjamin Netanyahu and President Shimon Peres.

Antarctica

The Science, Space, and Technology Committee planned a trip to Antarctica with the director of the National Science Foundation, who oversees the United States Antarctic Program. The eight-day trip took place from December 13–21, 2014.

December 15, 2014 Congressional trip to Antarctica.

Ten members of Congress (six Republicans and four Democrats) and eight staff members flew commercially to Christchurch, New Zealand. From there, we boarded a military C-130 transport ski plane to fly to McMurdo Station, Antarctica. Tourists cannot visit Antarctica in the same way we did during our trip.

We flew helicopters into the Dry Valley, just south of the actual South Pole. Outfitted with gear for the subzero environment, we wore bright red thermal jackets that were very distinctive. We were allowed to take home smooth, wind-blown stone artifacts from the Dry Valley. Only the director of the National Science Foundation has the authority to approve the removal of these artifacts.

We flew helicopters onto glaciers and visited with curious penguins. Penguins in Antarctica face no natural threats, so they had no fear of twenty humans in bright red thermal coats lined up in a row. The penguins marched up to study the strange humans staring at them.

We toured the science station and received a briefing on the research conducted at McMurdo Station.

The highlight of the trip was flying on the C-130 transport ski plane and landing on the ice at Amundsen-Scott South Pole Station. Tourists have no way to travel to the South Pole. The geographic South Pole shifts each year due to ice movement, with brass markers driven into the ice to mark its location. Nearby, a ceremonial South Pole is lined with the flags of the various nations conducting research in Antarctica.

The engines on the C-130 transport plane could not be shut down during our visit to the South Pole. The temperatures were too cold to restart the engines if shut down. Our time at the South Pole was limited by the plane's fuel consumption while waiting on the ice for our return to McMurdo Station.

2014 Reelection

Having defeated incumbent Rep. Kathy Hochul, who spent $4,858,496 in her losing reelection campaign, no Democrat wanted to run against me in the 2014 election. The Democrats recruited a sacrificial lamb, Jim O'Donnell, whom I defeated on November 4, 2014, by a margin of 71 percent to 29 percent.

What a difference two years made between 2012 and 2014. I was on a roll, having fun, and enjoying Congress with a good balance in life. I was in Washington for only ninety-four nights in 2013 and eighty-six nights in 2014. Most women would love the balance Mary and I had. I was gone just enough for Mary to have the perfect amount of free time to socialize with her friends.

I never enjoyed a "job" more than my position as a member of Congress. I was proud to represent my district and worked hard to fight for my constituents on issues important to them. My future goal during my tenure was to chair the influential Energy and Commerce Committee.

I was on track to achieve that goal until my world collapsed on August 8, 2018, when I was indicted for insider trading and ultimately resigned from Congress on September 30, 2019.

CHAPTER 23

Congress 2015–2016

AFTER WINNING MY 2014 REELECTION in a landslide on November 4, 2014, defeating Jim O'Donnell by forty-two points (71 to 29 percent), I was ready to return to Washington to pursue my goal of being appointed to the Energy and Commerce (E&C) Committee.

Energy and Commerce Committee

During the 2014 elections, I actively campaigned for fellow Republicans in New York, contributing to the New York delegation's growth from six to nine members. All incumbents were reelected, and we welcomed Elise Stefanik, John Katko, and Lee Zeldin as new freshmen members.

2015 brochure promoting my qualifications to be appointed to the Energy & Commerce Committee.

My staff prepared a first-class marketing brochure highlighting my credentials to present to the Steering Committee, aiming to secure a spot on E&C. The presentation, possibly the most professional the Steering Committee had ever seen, included a comprehensive letter signed by all eight New York members of Congress. The letter endorsed my qualifications and reinforced the points detailed in the brochure.

John Boehner informed me that competition for the five openings on E&C was fierce. He was impressed with my background and credited himself for securing my spot on the committee.

Being selected for E&C was a significant achievement. Chairman Fred Upton assigned me to three of the most prestigious subcommittees: Health, Telecommunications, and Oversight. I was thrilled with these appointments, as they aligned with my legislative priorities.

The Buffalo News celebrated my appointment with a front-page story titled, "Collins wins seat on major House panel," and a sub-title, "Energy post a forum to promote fracking." The article emphasized that my position gave Western New York a voice on a committee central to American economic policy, from energy to telecommunications.

Legislative Contributions

In my role on the health subcommittee, I contributed to the 21st Century Cures legislation. This bill addressed healthcare advancements and included provisions I drafted to expedite FDA drug trials and improve orphan drug approvals. By consulting with FDA officials, I secured language enabling the agency to hire experienced PhD researchers with competitive salaries.

On the telecommunications subcommittee, I tackled the issue of pirate radio operators disrupting emergency broadcasts in urban areas. My advocacy prompted the FCC to prioritize shutting down these illegal operations, enhancing public safety.

A Strong Team and New Challenges

Congressional Staff gathering in Washington.

My office staff was regarded as one of the best in Washington, functioning like a well-oiled machine. With my new E&C assignment, their workload increased significantly. Chris Grant, my chief of staff since my time as Erie County executive, reorganized our team and hired a healthcare policy expert to support our work on the health subcommittee.

My seating arrangement in the House changed with the addition of three New York Republicans. Sitting with Elise Stefanik and John Katko, we quickly developed a close friendship. Their loyalty was a blessing during the challenges I later faced.

2015 Highlights

In early 2015, I opposed efforts to defund the Department of Homeland Security, a move driven by Republican frustration with President Obama's immigration policies. On March 4, 2015, I was one of seventy-five Republicans who voted to fund the DHS, earning praise from *The Buffalo News* for my responsible governance.

My most notable accomplishment in 2015 was reviving the Export-Import Bank. Initially defunded in 2014 due to Tea Party opposition, I worked with bipartisan colleagues to gather enough signatures for a discharge petition, forcing a vote. On October 29, 2015, the House voted 313–118 to restore the bank. *The Buffalo News* commended my leadership, noting my business background was instrumental in the fight.

Global Insights: Tanzania

As a member of the Aspen Institute, a nonpartisan organization promoting dialogue and action on global issues, my wife Mary and I attended a conference in Tanzania from August 8–18, 2015. We visited sites like Arusha National Park, the Masaai Women's Workshop, and local farms, gaining firsthand insights into the challenges faced by African communities.

Following the conference, Mary and I joined colleagues on a three-day safari in the Serengeti. This unforgettable experience brought us close to wildlife, including elephants, lions, and giraffes, while staying in luxury tents and traveling through the wilderness.

Looking Ahead

My tenure during this period was marked by meaningful legislative achievements, strong relationships, and unique experiences. These moments not only defined my career but also shaped my perspective as a public servant.

Pearl Harbor

A large group of members traveled as a Congressional Delegation (codel) to Pearl Harbor to commemorate the seventieth anniversary of the end of

World War II. A "codel" refers to a group of members traveling together on official government business.

The ceremony took place aboard the *Battleship Missouri* Memorial on September 2, 2015. Mary accompanied me on the trip. Members charged the cost of the trip to their government budget accounts.

We flew to Hawaii on September 1 and returned to Washington on September 4. We had free time to enjoy Hawaii before and after the commemoration on September 2.

The ceremony was somber, featuring a Surrender Ceremony in remembrance of the Japanese surrender on September 2, 1945. Various dignitaries, including Admiral Scott Swift, commander of the US Pacific Fleet, gave speeches. The Pacific Fleet Band played "God Bless America," followed by a flag-folding ceremony and a rifle salute from the Pacific Fleet firing detail. The ceremony concluded with bagpipes playing "Amazing Grace" and the Pacific Fleet Band performing "Taps."

2016

Over Christmas break, from December 18, 2015, to January 2, 2016, our family traveled to our vacation home on Marco Island, FL. We had purchased the house in 2011 at the bottom of the market—timing is everything.

My chief of staff, Chris Grant, resigned to form a political consulting firm. Big Dog Strategies has since become one of the premier political consulting firms, recognized for its exceptional direct mail services to campaigns nationwide. Chris had managed my campaign for Erie County executive and served as my chief of staff after I was elected in 2007. He also managed my campaign against Representative Kathy Hochul in 2012 and transitioned with me to Washington as my congressional chief of staff. Although I hated to lose Chris from my team, I fully understood and supported his entrepreneurial move to start his own firm.

Michael Hook joined as my new chief of staff. Michael had previously served as chief of staff to Representative Bill Paxon before co-founding a political consulting firm with Bill Greener in 1998. Michael directed my 1998 campaign against Representative John LaFalce. He and Bill Greener parted ways in 2013. When Michael learned of Chris Grant's departure, he expressed interest in returning to politics and offered to serve as my chief of staff. For me, it was a no-brainer; I immediately hired Michael.

This transition marked a flip-flop; when Chris Grant was my chief, we hired Michael Hook as our political consultant. Now, with Michael as my chief, we hired Chris as our consultant.

Returning to Congress on January 3, 2016, I felt renewed and eager to start my fourth year. However, I was frustrated by my lack of appearances on national cable TV during my first three years in office. Although I had occasional TV appearances in Buffalo, I challenged my communications director to secure three national TV spots for me in 2016. In retrospect, it was a modest goal.

Presidential Election

The 2016 presidential election intensified as the year began, with seventeen major Republican candidates vying for the nomination. I endorsed Jeb Bush on April 15, 2015, believing he would secure the Republican candidacy. However, Jeb struggled in the debates, and Donald Trump labeled him "Low Energy Jeb."

Jeb Bush formally exited the race on February 20, 2016, after Trump's South Carolina primary victory. Trump went on to win the Nevada primary on February 23. On February 24, 2016, at 8:00 AM, I decided to endorse Donald J. Trump for president. After notifying Trump's campaign, Donald Trump called to thank me and encouraged me to engage actively with the media.

I issued a press release emphasizing the need for a chief executive, not a chief politician, in the White House—a slogan I had previously used in my successful 2007 Erie County executive campaign. Unbeknownst to me, I was the first sitting member of Congress to endorse Trump. My communications director far exceeded his goal of three national TV appearances during the year, on just that one day.

I'll delve into my time campaigning with Donald Trump in another chapter.

Colgan Flight 3407

As Erie County executive, I faced the tragic aftermath of a commercial plane crash. On February 12, 2009, Colgan Flight 3407 crashed one mile from my home in Clarence, NY, killing all forty-nine passengers and crew, along with one resident of the home it struck.

The crash was caused by pilot error stemming from inexperience and insufficient training. Following the tragedy, Congress passed legislation requiring additional pilot training and creating a database to document pilot experience and any prior issues. Before this, records of the pilot's failures were unavailable to Colgan during the hiring process. The new 1,500-hour rule for first officers, adopted despite opposition from major airlines, aimed to enhance safety standards.

I led efforts in Congress to protect the integrity of this legislation, resisting annual attempts by major airlines to weaken their provisions. Every February 12, we held a press conference with the victims' families to reaffirm our commitment to aviation safety. Additionally, I delivered a one-minute speech on the House floor to honor the crash victims.

Congressional Memberships and Events

I participated in the moderate Tuesday Group caucus, established in 1995 by Amo Houghton, which supported centrist policy positions often opposed by the Freedom Caucus. As its most conservative member, I also belonged to the Republican Study Committee (RSC), which leaned more conservative than the Tuesday Group but remained moderate compared to the Freedom Caucus.

To support fundraising, I hosted events in Buffalo, inviting House leadership to meet constituents in a social setting. These events featured prominent figures such as Chairman Fred Upton, Representative Peter King, and former Speaker John Boehner.

Mary and our daughter attended the First Ladies Lunch on May 12, 2016, an annual White House event featuring prominent musicians and entertainers. Mary's lifetime membership in the Spousal Congressional Club ensures her attendance at future events.

On June 9–10, 2016, I held my Collins Congressional Caucus fly-in, organizing meetings with key figures such as Speaker Paul Ryan and Majority Leader Kevin McCarthy. These events provided invaluable networking opportunities for donors, solidifying their continued support.

I also formed the Trump Congressional Caucus, recruiting ten members for weekly lunch meetings with Trump's campaign staff. Despite my active role as a Trump surrogate, I remained committed to my congressional responsibilities.

2016 Reelection

Having won with 71 percent of the vote in 2014, I faced a weaker Democratic challenger in 2016. With minimal campaign spending, I defeated Diana Kastenbaum on November 8, securing 67.2 percent of the vote.

Donald J. Trump's election as president marked the beginning of a transformative era. As Trump's surrogate, I was appointed congressional liaison to the White House by Speaker Paul Ryan. My third term, serving in the 115th Congress, promised to be both eventful and exciting.

CHAPTER 24

Trump Election 2016

THE 2016 PRESIDENTIAL ELECTION WAS heating up as we headed into 2016. Originally, seventeen major candidates were vying for the Republican nomination. I believe if you are going to do something, be bold and be first. Consistent with that philosophy, I jumped on board the Jeb Bush bandwagon. On April 15, 2015, my campaign wrote a $25,000 check to Jeb Bush's Right to Rise Presidential PAC. I attended a couple of major Right to Rise political events. Jeb Bush formally announced his candidacy for president on June 15, 2015. I hosted a fundraiser for Jeb Bush in Buffalo on June 30, 2015. By the time Jeb Bush announced, I had already been part of his campaign for two months.

Donald Trump formally announced his candidacy for president on June 16, 2015.

I had met Donald Trump when he was considering a run for governor of New York in 2014. He came to Buffalo to meet with Republican leaders in Erie County. As the largest upstate county in New York, no Republican had any chance of being elected governor without winning in Erie County. It was a pleasant meeting, but by the end, it was clear Donald Trump was not going to pursue the governor's race. He sounded as though he was considering the difficult challenge of running for president in 2016. I don't think anyone in that conference room in 2014 thought he had any chance of being elected president.

In the first Republican debate on August 6, 2015, televised on Fox News, no one knew what to expect. Donald Trump was not the focus for the other nine candidates invited to participate in the debate. Ted Cruz focused on Jeb Bush. Jeb Bush focused on Marco Rubio. Chris Christie was focused on himself. Ben Carson had trouble getting anyone to ask him a question. Donald Trump was entertaining in a way unique to his personality. After the debate was over, Trump being Trump totally controlled the narrative.

Jeb Bush floundered as a presidential candidate. One by one, Republican candidates started withdrawing from consideration for the presidential nomination.

By the February 20, 2016, South Carolina primary, six Republicans were left in the race: Donald Trump, Jeb Bush, Ted Cruz, Marco Rubio, John Kasich, and Ben Carson.

I knew Jeb Bush was not going to continue his candidacy after his disastrous debate performance in New Hampshire on February 9, 2016. Donald Trump won the New Hampshire Primary and followed it with a win in South Carolina on February 20.

Jeb Bush formally dropped out of the presidential race on February 20, following Trump's victory in South Carolina. I told Michael Hook, my chief of staff, that I was ready to switch my support from Jeb Bush to Donald Trump. He asked me to wait until after the Nevada caucus on February 23 to see if Trump could win out west. Trump prevailed again and won the Nevada caucus.

Trump Endorsement

At 8:00 AM on Wednesday, February 24, 2016, I formally announced my endorsement of Donald J. Trump for president of the United States.

I wasn't sure if Donald Trump wanted my endorsement. I didn't know if he wanted *any* endorsements. His message was that he was an outsider, not a Washington insider. I'm an outsider as well, but I was a member of Congress.

I called his campaign and told them I was going to endorse Donald Trump. I said that if they wanted me to fly under the radar, simply issue a press release, ignore phone calls, and not do any interviews, that would be fine.

Donald Trump called me back, thanked me for endorsing him, and encouraged me to do as much press as I could.

I sent out a press release stating that our nation needed a chief executive, not a chief politician, in the White House. That was my campaign slogan when I beat James Keane for Erie County executive in 2007.

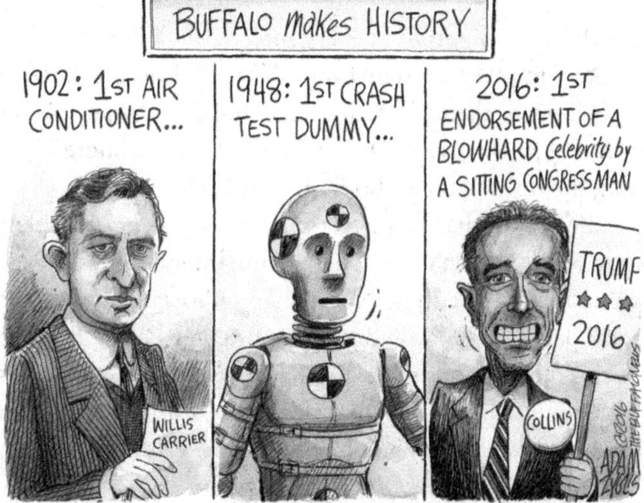

I didn't know at the time that I was the first sitting member of Congress to endorse Donald Trump for president. With all the momentum behind his candidacy, I assumed several members of the House and several senators had already endorsed him.

On February 28, 2016, Senator Jeff Sessions endorsed Donald Trump. It made perfect sense that Trump chose Jeff Sessions to officially nominate him for president on July 19, 2016, at the Republican convention in Cleveland. It also made perfect sense that I was chosen to second his nomination for president. I was the first member of the House to endorse him, and Jeff Sessions was the first senator to do so.

Starting on February 24, 2016, my life changed forever.

In the days following my endorsement, I was interviewed on Fox News, CNN, MSNBC, Fox Business, ABC News, and NPR. Local Western New York radio stations WHAM and WBEN also interviewed me, as did *The New York Times*, *The Buffalo News*, *The Hill*, *The Atlantic*, *USA Today*, *Roll Call*, *Washington Examiner*, and *RealClearPolitics*.

Trump Surrogate

I was asked the same question in every interview: "Why Trump?" For me, the answer was simple. As I stated on CNN, "We need a chief executive, not a chief politician. Donald Trump is the individual as president who can lead this country and provide a bright future for our children. Trump has been signing the front of a paycheck, not the back."

I learned early on that you need to have several "go-to statements" in your "happy place" as a fallback when giving interviews. I had coined the phrase "Elect a chief executive, Not a chief politician" during my county executive campaign in 2007. I created the Brighter Future Fund to handle my charitable contributions when I donated my county executive salary to charity. My political message had always been to focus on providing our children and grandchildren a bright future. These messages aptly applied to Donald Trump's candidacy.

CNN interview at the Presidential Convention on July 21, 2016 at 7:20 AM.

I became a major surrogate for Donald Trump on cable news. Over the next eight months leading up to the presidential election on November 8, 2016, I did eighty-seven interviews. There are only 173 weekdays in that time span. I was doing interviews nearly every other day for eight months.

Between the election and the end of the year, I did another twenty-five interviews over seven weeks. In total, I conducted 112 interviews over 208 days, not counting weekends.

Ben Carson withdrew on March 4, Marco Rubio on March 15, Ted Cruz on May 3, and John Kasich on May 4. Donald Trump was the last man standing, securing the Republican presidential nomination.

Trump is the Candidate

I became a regular guest with Chris Cuomo and Wolf Blitzer on CNN, Stuart Varney and Charles Payne on Fox Business, Chuck Todd and Steve Kornacki on MSNBC, and Neil Cavuto on Fox News.

Whenever I least expected it, I'd get a call from Donald Trump thanking me for an interview. You never knew when he might be watching. I'd see "blocked call" on my phone and pretty much knew it would be Donald Trump on the line.

I formed the Trump Congressional Leadership Caucus. We met weekly for lunch at the Capitol Hill Club, just down the street from the Cannon House Office Building. Our first meeting was on April 14, 2016. We met with Paul Manafort (campaign chairman), Cory Lewandowski (campaign manager), and Rick Dearborn (Jeff Sessions' chief of staff), who updated us on the campaign. The eleven members of the Trump Caucus were:

- Chris Collins—chair (NY)
- Duncan Hunter (CA)
- Billy Long (MO)
- Marsha Blackburn (TN)
- Lou Barletta (PA)
- Mike Kelly (PA)
- Tom Marino (PA)
- Bill Shuster (PA)
- Scott DesJarlais (TN)

- Tom Reed (NY)
- Kevin Cramer (ND)

We received considerable ridicule from other Republican members, who did not respect Trump and thought we were foolish to be such visible supporters.

I was named honorary co-chair of Trump's New York campaign committee. On April 18, 2016, I hosted Donald Trump to speak to a massive crowd at Key Bank Center in Buffalo, the home arena of the Buffalo Sabres hockey team. The crowd was rowdy, loud, and boisterous. Before I took the podium to introduce Trump, we gathered in a room just off the main floor, where Trump took photos with supporters.

On April 19, 2016, Donald Trump swept the New York Primary. My popularity in my congressional district soared when Trump won. I had received a great deal of criticism after endorsing Trump on February 24. Some of his subsequent statements and positions were not well received, leading certain local GOP leaders to vote against renominating me for Congress. However, once Trump resoundingly won the primary vote on April 19, I was hailed as a "hero" for supporting him.

Some of Trump's comments—on immigration, deporting twelve million illegal immigrants, building the wall, releasing his tax returns, and gun control—made for interesting interviews, especially on networks like CNN and MSNBC. I held my own during discussions with Chris Cuomo, Wolf Blitzer, Chuck Todd, Andrea Mitchell, and Steve Kornacki.

The Buffalo News attacked me weekly with front-page stories. They had been doing so ever since I was elected Erie County executive in 2007, so this wasn't new to me. Adam Zyglis, a Pulitzer Prize-winning political cartoonist, frequently had fun at my expense. After my endorsement of Trump and some of Trump's more controversial comments, I'd often wake up to find myself caricatured in *The Buffalo News*.

Trump secured the Republican nomination on May 26 with 1,237 pledged delegates, the number required to clinch the 2016 Republican presidential nomination. On July 15, 2016, Trump announced that Governor Mike Pence would be his vice-presidential running mate.

Republican National Convention

Typical press gaggle

The Republican National Convention was held from July 18 to July 21 in Cleveland. My role to second Trump's nomination was scheduled for 6:00 PM on July 19. *The Buffalo News* ran a front-page story on July 15 titled, "Collins To Speak at GOP Convention." I was quoted as saying, "I am proud to carry Western New York's message on behalf of Donald Trump. That message is loud and clear: folks in our community want Mr. Trump to secure our borders, stand up to our enemies, and take back the jobs stolen by Mexico and China. I am glad to be part of the growing movement behind Donald Trump and making America great for all Americans."

I had a busy schedule at the convention. All the TV personalities were present, seeking interviews. I was happy to oblige, as I knew many of them personally. I delivered a rousing breakfast speech to the New York delegation, earning a standing ovation. Later, I delivered another speech to thousands at Quicken Loans Arena and received yet another standing ovation.

The New York delegation was seated directly in front of the stage where I would second Trump's nomination. Knowing I had a friendly audience bolstered my confidence as I addressed millions of TV viewers. I wasn't the least bit nervous. People often forgot that I had a speaking role at the 2008 Republican National Convention in St. Paul, Minnesota, following Hurricane Gustav, where John McCain was nominated for president with Sarah Palin as his running mate.

Jeff Sessions and I arrived at 5:45 PM and had makeup applied. We believed we had ample time to walk over to the stage and wait for our turn to speak. Paul Ryan was on stage introducing speakers. Jeff appeared a bit confused about where to go, and I kept nudging him along. Suddenly, I realized the program was ahead of schedule. It wasn't quite 6:00 PM, yet it was apparent that Jeff Sessions was about to be introduced to nominate Donald Trump.

I hurried Jeff along. He seemed baffled and unprepared to speak before millions of viewers. Paul Ryan finished his introduction, and I pushed Jeff Sessions onto the stage. Jeff stumbled out to the podium and delivered his five-minute nomination speech.

After Jeff's speech, I was introduced to give my three-minute seconding speech. Feeling completely at ease, I looked down at the New York delegation, pointed to them, and gave a thumbs up. They stood and cheered.

Comfortable with the teleprompter and drawing on my extensive TV interview experience, I thoroughly enjoyed my moment. I delivered a rousing speech and received a standing ovation as I exited the stage.

The Buffalo News ran a front-page story on July 20 with the headline: "Collins' Early Loyalty to Trump Prompts Talk of 'Mr. Secretary.'" The article quoted my speech: "We in Western New York know Donald Trump is not merely a candidate. Donald Trump is a movement." They also published a photo of me at the podium, smiling broadly and giving two thumbs up.

The next morning, I conducted more interviews than ever following Trump's official nomination. I appeared on CNN, Fox News, and MSNBC prior to my speech on the 19th. The morning after, I followed up with additional interviews on CNN, Fox News, Fox Business, and MSNBC. I capped off the day with interviews with CNN's Wolf Blitzer and Fox Business' Lou Dobbs.

Aspen Institute Symposium: London

Mary and I traveled to London, England, from August 10 to 16 for the Aspen Institute's annual August symposium for members of Congress. While in London, my staff received a call from Trump's team requesting my attendance at an important meeting at Trump Tower on August 17. My staff rerouted my flight from London to JFK, instead of BWI, and booked a flight for Mary from JFK to Buffalo.

Trump Campaign Organization

Upon landing at JFK, I was met by a car that took me to Trump Tower. There, I joined a conference room filled with notable figures, including General Michael Flynn, Rep. Peter King, Rudy Giuliani, and Paul Manafort, who had replaced Cory Lewandowski as campaign manager on June 20. It was also the first day on the campaign for Kellyanne Conway and Steve Bannon, and the last day for Paul Manafort.

Kellyanne Conway replaced Paul Manafort as campaign manager, while Steve Bannon became campaign chief executive.

As chair of the Trump Congressional Leadership Caucus, I was present to observe. One remarkable moment during the meeting stood out. The discussion turned to Syria and ISIS; specifically, how strong a stance Trump should take on ISIS. Someone suggested Trump declare war on ISIS, sparking a debate about whether ISIS could be considered a state and whether the term "war" was too harsh.

Amid the debate, Trump turned to Kellyanne Conway, asking, "Kellyanne, how will this play? How will the women of America respond if I use that language?" Without hesitation, Kellyanne responded, "Mr. Trump, I think around 72.6 percent of American women will want you to use that kind of language. You will not lose support. That's exactly what the soccer moms of this country want to hear."

Trump nodded and said emphatically, "That's what we are going to do." From that moment, it was clear that Kellyanne's insights and advice, particularly on women's issues, were invaluable. The team's chemistry and resolve seemed to solidify, propelling the campaign forward.

Steve Bannon didn't say a word during the meeting. It was obvious that he and Trump had a long, established history. He observed intently, listening and watching the dynamics unfold.

I flew back to Buffalo after the Trump meeting. This was during the August recess, and I had a busy schedule waiting for me in the district.

Trump Debates

The first presidential debate was held on September 26 at Hofstra University in Hempstead, NY. No one knew what to expect. I attended the debate as part of the Trump delegation.

Before the debate, I interviewed with CNN, MSNBC, Fox News, and Channel 10 in Rochester.

The debate was certainly interesting. Hillary Clinton is a skilled debater. She expertly got under Donald Trump's skin, raising issues that exacerbated tensions and disrupted his focus. She controlled the dynamic, steering Trump off his "Make America Great Again" message. Instead of pivoting, he often directly answered her provocations, losing opportunities to redirect the conversation.

September 26, 2016 First Trump debate at Hofstra University.

The debate didn't go well for Trump. But then again, it was Hillary Clinton. While she doesn't exactly warm people's hearts, her experience shone through. Despite the setback, the Trump campaign team remained optimistic that the second and third debates would yield better outcomes. It was preferable for mistakes to occur during the first debate rather than the final one.

After the debate, I served as a spokesperson for the press. Holding a large red poster with my name displayed vertically, one of my staff members ensured it was visible to attract media attention. Runners from various TV stations approached, and I conducted interviews with all the major networks.

The following day, I was back on CNN, Fox Business, and MSNBC discussing the debate.

The second debate occurred on October 9 in St. Louis, MO, at Washington University, and the third on October 19 in Las Vegas, NV, at the University of Nevada. Most observers considered the last two debates to be draws, though some media outlets gave Hillary Clinton a slight edge. Within the Trump camp, we were relieved the debates were over and satisfied that Trump held his ground in the final two.

October Surprise

On October 7, 2016, the "October surprise" dropped: the infamous *Access Hollywood* tapes. Recorded in 2005, the tapes captured Trump making lewd comments about women, including, "And when you're a star, they let you do it. You can do anything. " This revelation emerged just two days before the second debate with Hillary Clinton.

Trump quickly issued a statement apologizing but attempted to deflect criticism by referencing Bill Clinton's past behavior, claiming, "Bill Clinton has said far worse than me on the golf course."

Support for Trump plummeted. High-profile Republicans, including Mitt Romney, Reince Priebus, Jeb Bush, John Kasich, and John McCain, publicly condemned him. Several called on Trump to withdraw from the race in favor of Mike Pence. Paul Ryan stated he was "sickened" and would no longer support or defend Trump's campaign. Billy Bush, who was part of the tape, lost his job on the *Today Show*.

Many believed Trump's chances of winning the election were over. Critics seized the moment to further denounce him. It was a grim time for the campaign. I told my colleagues, "I'm going to do my best to defend Donald Trump. It doesn't look good, but remember, we're running against Hillary Clinton."

I received numerous calls to appear on cable news to respond to the *Access Hollywood* scandal. I was one of the few Trump supporters willing to address the controversy directly, appearing on CNN, Fox News, Fox Business, and MSNBC.

I publicly stated, "The comments made by Mr. Trump were disappointing. There is no room in our society for comments like these. Mr. Trump has apologized. These are his words, but let's remember Bill Clinton's actions. And let's remember that Hillary is a phony feminist who destroyed the lives of the very women Bill Clinton preyed upon. My support for Mr. Trump remains unchanged because he is the only candidate who will bring jobs back, secure our borders, and stand up to our enemies."

In other interviews, I said, "In this case, we have words; in Bill Clinton's case, we have actions. We need to keep perspective and focus on making America great again, ensuring a bright future for our children and grandchildren."

Trump Election

During an election year, Congress recesses in August and October, resuming only after the election. I wouldn't return to Washington until November 14, 2016.

In the district, I was busy campaigning for reelection against Diana Kastenbaum. She wasn't a strong challenger, so my spending was limited to lawn signs. However, I made sure to visit farms and small businesses—never taking anything for granted in politics.

Mary and I voted at 9:00 AM on Election Day. As usual, I brought donuts to the polling station. The press was eager to interview me, and I confidently stated that I felt optimistic about both my reelection and Trump's chances of becoming president.

As results trickled in, nerves were high. My election was called in my favor within thirty minutes of polls closing. While I wasn't worried about my race, it was a relief to have it finalized.

The presidential race was a rollercoaster, with many states too close to call as the night stretched on. I stayed up until 2:29 AM when the race was finally called for Donald Trump. Hillary Clinton conceded, and Donald Trump was officially declared the forty-fifth president of the United States. I went to bed.

November 9, 2016 celebrating Trump's victory at 2:45 AM after the election was called.

Donald Trump is Elected President of the United States

At 9:00 AM the next morning, I received a call from a Trump staffer. They informed me that President-elect Trump wanted to speak with me. Seeing a blocked call that showed up soon after, as likely from Trump, I answered, "Mr. President-elect, how good does that sound?"

On speakerphone with Ivanka present, Trump expressed gratitude. He asked, "Did you really think we were going to get it done?"

I replied, "Yes, sir. I always believed we could, despite a few concerns along the way. Your resilience made the difference."

Trump acknowledged my support, saying, "You defended me during some very tough times, especially after the *Access Hollywood* tapes. You stood by me when almost everyone else turned away. I'll never forget that."

We spoke for about twenty minutes. It struck me that, as the president-elect, he could have been speaking to world leaders. Instead, he took the time to thank me. It was a testament to his appreciation of loyalty. I was honored by the call, which reflected his genuine gratitude and character.

I knew the rumors circulating about me joining the administration. In Congress, my friends had been calling me "Mr. Secretary" for months. I told President-elect Trump that I didn't want to join his administration—not to be presumptuous or anything. I explained that I enjoyed my role in Congress and wanted to continue supporting him from there. I suggested it might make sense for me to serve as the congressional liaison to the White House so I could watch his back.

Trump assured me he would consider my request and said it made perfect sense since I had been watching his back for the past eight months.

Three hours after speaking with President-elect Trump, I received a call from Speaker Paul Ryan. He told me Trump had just called him, and during their brief ten-minute conversation, the president-elect expressed his interest in having me serve as the liaison between Congress and the White House.

Paul Ryan said he agreed with Trump's suggestion and planned to announce to the Republican Conference that I would be the congressional liaison to the White House. He explained that I would oversee a system to help Trump fill 4,000 political positions throughout the executive branch. Specifically, he told me that any member of Congress wishing to recommend themselves or someone else for a position in the Trump administration would have to go through me.

Paul Ryan then asked me for a favor: to second his nomination as speaker of the House after we were sworn in on January 3, 2017. He acknowledged making a mistake in distancing himself from Trump after the release of the *Access Hollywood* tapes and knew he wasn't seen as a Trump ally. He believed that if I seconded his nomination, it would signal to our Conference that Trump was okay with him. After all, if Collins, Trump's guy in Congress, endorsed Paul Ryan, it must mean Trump supported him too.

I agreed to second Paul Ryan's nomination, and he was elected speaker of the 116th Congress.

After the Election

Over the next few months, *The Buffalo News* published glowing articles about me. It certainly pays to be on a winning team. On December 4, 2016, the Sunday edition featured a half-page photo of me on the front page with the headline, "Collins Emerging as a Power Broker." The subtitle read, "Vocal supporter of Trump is helping fill 4,000 positions."

The article stated, "The election of Donald J. Trump as president turned Rep. Chris Collins from back-bencher to power broker. After three relatively low-key years in Congress followed by a year as one of Trump's most outspoken supporters, the Republican from Clarence now finds himself as the point person for recommending a new US Attorney for Western New York, as well as most likely a new federal judge. He finds himself in charge of a system for helping Trump fill 4,000 political positions throughout the executive branch."

It continued, "Collins' influence increased not only because of his willingness to appear on television repeatedly as a Trump advocate but also due to longstanding traditions. When the President and the senior Senator of a state are from the same party, the senior Senator traditionally recommends candidates for federal posts. However, when the senior Senator and President are from different parties, that responsibility shifts to House Members who belong to the President's party."

Trump appointed me to the sixteen-member executive committee of his Transition Team. This select group included key Trump insiders such as:

- Vice President Mike Pence
- Donald Trump, Jr.
- Ivanka Trump
- Eric Trump
- Rudy Giuliani
- Newt Gingrich
- Steve Bannon
- Reince Priebus

- Peter Thiel
- Ben Carson
- Chris Christie
- Senator Jeff Sessions
- Tom Reed
- Michael Flynn
- Kellyanne Conway

Trump also assembled an advisory staff to handle the day-to-day tasks of setting up a new administration, which included:

- Kellyanne Conway—Senior Advisor
- Rudy Giuliani—Senior Advisor
- Ben Carson—VP Selection Committee
- Hope Hicks—Press Secretary
- Chris Christie—Senior Advisor
- Michael Cohen—Special Counsel
- Michael Flynn—Military Advisor
- Anthony Scaramucci—Finance Chairman
- George Papadopoulos—Foreign Policy Advisor
- Omarosa Manigault—African American Outreach
- Jeff Sessions—Chair of National Security
- Steve Bannon—Senior Advisor

The 115th Congress was shaping up to be a wild ride, though at the time, I had no idea just how wild it would become. For the moment, I was on cloud nine, with the brightest future imaginable ahead of me. Nothing, I thought, could stand in the way of achieving my ultimate goal: becoming chairman of the House Energy and Commerce Committee.

I never anticipated the challenges that would arise, particularly from someone, who, in my opinion, is as unprofessional, deceitful, and self-serving as US Attorney Geoffrey Berman, who would later come after me and my son.

CHAPTER 25

Congress 2017–2018

I WAS SWORN IN AS the Member of Congress for NY-27 on January 3, 2017. This marked the start of my third term in Congress. I was reelected with 67.2 percent of the vote, holding what was considered a very safe Republican seat.

For the first time since 2005, Republicans had complete control in Washington. The House, Senate, and Presidency were all under Republican leadership, with President Donald Trump, House Speaker Paul Ryan, and Senate Majority Leader Mitch McConnell at the helm.

115th Congress

The 115th Congress was notably different from the 113th and 114th Congresses, during which Barack Obama was president. Divided government is historically more common, as the public often prefers this arrangement over single-party rule. However, for at least the next two years, Republicans enjoyed full control of government, while Democrats, relegated to minority status, faced a period of diminished influence.

My third term was set to be very different from my first. As a freshman in the 113th Congress, I served on three relatively unimportant committees, was largely unknown in Washington, and did not engage with national press or cable television. All of that changed when I endorsed Donald Trump on February 24, 2016. A quote in one newspaper captured this shift: "Before Trump, he was kind of a back-bench Republican—solid but not noteworthy. Now he is a partner to the President."

The headlines reflected my rising prominence:

- "Lawmaker is Talent Scout for Trump"
- "Donald Trump Taps Little-Known Lawmaker to Be 'Eyes and Ears' in Congress"

- "Rep. Chris Collins: I could be 'go-between' between Trump and Ryan"
- "Trump Appoints Collins to His Transition Team"
- "Once-Obscure Rep. Chris Collins Sees His Star Rise with Trump"
- "Want a Job in Trump's Administration? Get on Chris Collins's Spreadsheet"

During 2016, I conducted 216 interviews with national and local press, as well as cable television anchors. In 2017, I was interviewed 161 times. I became a regular guest on CNN with Chris Cuomo and Wolf Blitzer; Fox Business with Stuart Varney, Maria Bartiromo, Lou Dobbs, Neil Cavuto, and Charles Payne; and MSNBC with Chuck Todd, Kate Snow, and Steve Kornacki. Additionally, I engaged with six local TV stations in Buffalo and Rochester, NY, and was interviewed by prominent outlets including *The New York Times*, *The Wall Street Journal*, *The Washington Post*, *Politico*, *The Hill*, *USA Today*, *Bloomberg*, *The Buffalo News*, and *The* (Rochester) *Democrat and Chronicle*.

As I began my third term, I was a seasoned veteran on the prestigious House Energy and Commerce Committee, continuing to serve on the Health, Telecommunications, and Oversight subcommittees. My campaign account was well-funded, and I had repaid the $500,000 loan from my challenging 2012 election. Most importantly, I was recognized as President Trump's key surrogate in Congress, serving as the congressional liaison to the White House and as a member of the sixteen-member executive committee of his Transition Team.

Routine in Congress

My routine in the 115th Congress was similar to previous terms. I flew to Washington on Mondays or Tuesdays, spending three nights and four days there. I typically spent three weeks in Washington per month, with August recess dedicated to district work. My district offices remained busy with constituent services, handling veterans' benefits, passports, Medicaid, and other issues. My district director represented me at official events, local Republican meetings, and managed my schedule when I was home.

My Washington staff faced a heavier workload in the 115th Congress. With Trump in the White House, there was greater potential for our legislation to become law. My communications director managed an increased media presence, while my legislative director focused on committee activities.

I continued to chair House floor sessions, especially on fly-in days when I arrived before noon. Committee hearings occupied most afternoons, and I remained active in the conservative Republican Study Committee and the moderate Tuesday Group. I chaired the Scouting Caucus and participated in numerous other caucuses to support various causes, foster PAC fundraising, and meet influential figures.

Lunch with Bo Derek on April 2, 2014.

One memorable event was a lunch with Bo Derek, a passionate horse enthusiast and advocate against horse slaughter. As a member of the Animal Welfare Institute Caucus, I supported the SAFE Act, which sought to ban horse slaughter in the United States. During the lunch, Bo Derek graciously posed for a photo with me. While my friends and peers recognized her from the iconic 1979 movie *10*, my children humorously asked who she was.

Fundraising remained a significant focus. Serving on the Energy and Commerce Committee meant higher dues to support the NRCC. I also contributed to colleagues facing competitive reelections, fostering goodwill and bolstering the party's efforts. My safe district allowed me to direct funds to these endeavors.

I hosted breakfast, lunch, and dinner fundraisers in Washington, with lobbyists contributing $500 for breakfast, $500 to $1,000 for lunch, and $1,500 to $2,500 for dinner. Breakfasts were held at the Capitol Hill Club, lunches at local restaurants, and dinners at the Trump International Hotel, where I reserved a private dining space overlooking the lobby. Each dinner raised $10,000 to $15,000.

In this chapter, I'll delve into the key events, accomplishments, and challenges I faced during the 115th Congress.

President Donald J. Trump

Transition

Between Donald Trump's election on November 8, 2016, and his inauguration on January 20, 2017, there was much to accomplish. Trump needed to select his cabinet members, hire his White House staff, and initiate the legislative processes necessary to achieve his vision of "Making America Great Again." He also had to engage with Congress to build support for his priorities, including working with members who had distanced themselves during his campaign following the *Access Hollywood* incident.

A significant aspect of the transition was hiring and finding staff. The president-elect must personally cover staff expenses before the swearing-in ceremony on January 20. To address this, Trump established the "Trump For America" presidential transition committee, successfully raising $5.4 million from lobbyists, corporations, and private citizens. I was asked to assist with fundraising and readily agreed. On January 5, 2017, I hosted a $5,000-a-head fundraising luncheon featuring Kellyanne Conway in

Buffalo. The event was highly successful, raising over $100,000 for the transition.

Media coverage of my role during this period varied. One newspaper described me as a conduit for lawmakers to share concerns or proposals for legislation and staffing with the transition team. Another analyst found my role unusual, noting, "A new president generally relies on leadership. Collins has been in Congress less than four years, holds no leadership role, and chairs no committees. However, he was the first lawmaker on Capitol Hill to endorse Trump's presidential bid and chaired Trump's US House Leadership Committee during the campaign."

As a result of my involvement, I was inundated with requests from congressional colleagues seeking positions in the administration or advocating for friends and constituents. To manage these inquiries, I created a spreadsheet tracking each request, along with remarks and endorsements. I met regularly with the transition team to share and review this list with the appropriate staff responsible for department staffing.

Inauguration

Donald Trump's inauguration took place on January 20, 2017, with celebratory events beginning the day before. Mary and I attended several formal gatherings on January 19, including a black-tie celebration at the Library of Congress and a candlelit dinner at Union Station with House leadership and the Trumps.

The inauguration ceremony itself began at 10:30 AM on January 20 at the US Capitol. The architect of the Capitol constructed the inaugural platform on the west front of the Capitol, with seating and fencing arranged across the grounds. Facing the National Mall, with its iconic Washington Monument and Lincoln Memorial, the ceremony drew approximately 160,000 spectators in person, with an additional 30.6 million watching on television.

Seated on the platform alongside President Trump were former presidents, Supreme Court justices, Medal of Honor recipients, members of Congress, and the president's family. I was the only rank-and-file member of Congress assigned a seat on the platform, while others sat in bleachers.

Mary and the spouses of other members were seated on the lawn in front of the Capitol.

Chief Justice John Roberts administered the presidential oath of office. Following the brief ceremony, President Trump delivered a speech broadcast worldwide.

January 20, 2017 Mary and President Trump at lunch following the inauguration.

After the ceremony, a private lunch was held in Statuary Hall in the Capitol. I was the only rank-and-file member invited to this event. Mary and I were seated with Rudy Giuliani and his wife, among other dignitaries. Following the meal, I arranged for Mary to take a photo with President Trump, a moment we cherish and have prominently displayed in our home.

That evening, we attended several black-tie galas hosted by various organizations across Washington. Accompanied by friends from Buffalo, we managed to attend four galas before calling it a night, exhausted but exhilarated by the two-day inaugural festivities.

Meetings and Events at the White House

On February 9, 2017, while I was in Buffalo for an eye exam, I received a phone call from President Trump. He wanted me to organize a meeting of the Trump Congressional Caucus at the White House to celebrate his victory. We scheduled the meeting for February 16.

On that day, the eleven members of the Trump Congressional Caucus gathered at the White House for a 10:30 AM meeting. After clearing security, we were ushered into the Roosevelt Room in the West Wing. President Trump and Vice President Pence joined us, and after some casual conversation, President Trump invited us to tour the Oval Office.

Trump sat at his desk with the eleven of us and Vice President Pence standing behind him for a photo. The White House photographer, always a step behind the president, was ready for a group photo. I was positioned in the back of the group, which was fine.

There were only twelve of us, so it would be a great photo regardless of placement. Before the photographer could take the shot, Trump looked back and shouted, "Where's Collins? Get up here."

The group around the desk made room for me to stand directly to the president's right. We all posed with our thumbs up as the photo was taken. I have two framed copies of those photos displayed in our home.

Trump is always conscious of his surroundings and aware of who's in the room. In several meetings with the president in the Roosevelt Room, my place card was always positioned so I would sit directly to his left.

He included me in meetings where my presence was more symbolic than necessary. I didn't mind. I always enjoyed visiting the White House and made a habit of taking a few small boxes of M&Ms, adorned with the presidential seal and Trump's autograph. Back at my office, my staff eagerly claimed them. I have similar M&M boxes from Presidents George Bush, Barack Obama, and Donald Trump displayed on a shelf in my home office.

February 16, 2017 meeting of Trump Caucus in the Oval Office.

After White House meetings, we often encountered reporters outside for Q&A sessions. More often than not, my colleagues motioned for me to summarize the meeting before the questioning began.

Official White House announcements were held in the Rose Garden, directly behind the Oval Office. Staff would arrange seating and set up teleprompters on either side of the podium. Reading naturally from teleprompters requires practice. You need to glance at the audience and alternate between the teleprompters while maintaining a steady rhythm.

Sometimes, members of Congress were seated in front of the podium; other times, we stood on the marble steps leading into the White House.

On those occasions, I was usually in the first three rows, often standing near Rep. Billy Long (R-MO), who liked being front and center in every photo.

Air Force One

There is nothing quite as special as flying on *Air Force One*. My first invitation came on July 28, 2017, when the president was traveling to New York City to address law enforcement about the MS-13 threat. Rep. Peter King, whose district included the speech venue at Suffolk County Community College, joined the trip. I wasn't sure why I was invited, but I have a feeling President Trump never forgot my early endorsement.

At Andrews Air Force Base, I joined members of the press and White House staff to board *Air Force One*. My assigned seat near the front of the passenger section had my name on it. Shortly after I sat down, an Air Force flight attendant asked if I needed anything.

After takeoff, I was invited to the conference room, which featured a large table and two big-screen televisions. Peter King accompanied me, and soon Trump joined us to discuss his speech and reflect on his first six months in office.

The trip to Long Island was short. After landing, we traveled in a motorcade to the college for the speech. Before speaking, Trump scanned the room and called out, "Collins, where are you?" I waved, and he pointed at me, saying, "That's my guy." His recognition always made me feel special and drew curious stares from those around me.

The speech Trump delivered that day is considered one of the most chilling of his presidency. He graphically described the MS-13 threat, declaring, "Together we are going to restore safety to our streets and peace to our communities. We're going to destroy the vile, criminal cartel MS-13. They kidnap, extort, rape, and rob. They turn peaceful neighborhoods into bloodstained killing fields. They're animals."

After the speech, we returned to *Air Force One*. Once airborne, Trump invited Peter King and me to his office, where a White House photographer captured a photo of us with the president. That photo hangs in a special place alongside the one taken in the Oval Office.

When we landed, Trump invited us to disembark via the front steps of *Air Force One*, a rare privilege captured by news cameras. The day was unforgettable, despite coming just a month after I received devastating news about the failure of Innate Immunotherapeutics' multiple sclerosis drug trial. I will cover that event in a later chapter.

July 28, 2017 in Trump's private office on Air Force One.

White House Christmas Party

The Congressional White House Christmas Party on December 20, 2017, was a black-tie event similar to the annual Congressional Picnic held in June. Members of Congress and their families were the only attendees. Mary flew to Washington to join me for President Trump's first Christmas party.

December 5, 2017 White House Christmas party.

We arrived as the event began, giving us the opportunity to tour the White House and take photos before it became crowded. Members could access all the rooms and even sit on the furniture, unlike during public tours when areas are roped off.

Everyone wanted a photo with the president and first lady. We were given a red card and instructed to watch for a Marine carrying a matching placard. When we saw it, we headed to a room set up for photos. Following instructions, we had a beautiful picture taken with President Trump and First Lady Melania Trump in front of a fireplace.

We also have similar photos with President George Bush and First Lady Laura Bush from 2008, and with President Barack Obama and First Lady Michelle Obama from 2016. Each holds a special place in our collection of cherished memories.

Mike Pence Visit to Buffalo

On October 17, 2017, I hosted Vice President Mike Pence at a fundraising event I organized in Buffalo. *Air Force Two* landed at the Buffalo Niagara International Airport, where an enthusiastic crowd of over 200 people gathered to cheer his arrival. It was one of the largest airport crowds ever assembled to greet Vice President Pence.

We held a small business-focused meeting at Performance Advantage Company, owned by Dick Young, one of my most loyal supporters. The primary topic of discussion was tax reform, which was at the forefront of Congress' agenda as we approached a crucial period to pass and enact HR-1, the Tax Cuts and Jobs Act. The press followed us closely since national politicians rarely visit Buffalo, and Western New Yorkers were eager to hear about Vice President Pence's trip.

Previously, I had hosted then-candidate Donald Trump at a spirited campaign event in Buffalo on April 18, 2016. Earlier in 2017, on January 5, I hosted Kellyanne Conway to raise funds for Trump for America, which needed support for the transition. Having Mike Pence visit Buffalo felt like achieving a political trifecta.

Everyone knew I was close to Trump and his team, but the vice president's participation in a business forum and fundraiser I hosted reinforced that perception. The fundraiser that evening, following the small business forum, raised over $400,000—an extraordinary amount for a single event in Buffalo on a Tuesday night.

Arctic Circle

On May 8, 2017, the House Science Committee organized a Congressional Delegation (Codel) with nine members of Congress and their spouses traveling to the North Pole. Although I was no longer serving on the science committee, I was invited to participate as a past member. My wife, Mary, was not interested in traveling to Greenland, so I received permission for my son to accompany me. This trip mirrored my 2013 visit to Israel, where my son had also joined me.

My journey to the Arctic Circle, combined with my 2013 trip to Antarctica, makes me one of the few individuals who have visited both the South Pole and the North Pole. A group of five colleagues and I, who traveled together to Antarctica, jokingly called ourselves the "Bi-Polar six." As I've previously noted, tourists cannot visit the South Pole unless they are research scientists or members of Congress traveling with the National Science Foundation.

The purpose of our Arctic Circle trip was to gain insight into the significant US investments in Arctic data collection and scientific research. The Arctic Circle encompasses areas between sixty-six degrees north and ninety degrees north latitude, including parts of Alaska, Greenland, Canada, Russia, Norway, Sweden, Finland, and Iceland. The National Science Foundation (NSF) funds much of this research, and our delegation visited four NSF facilities.

We departed Andrews Air Force Base on a C40C luxury military plane with a dedicated Air Force crew. On May 8, we flew directly to Barrow, Alaska (seventy-one degrees north), the northernmost point in the US within the Arctic Circle. The 7.5-hour flight took us to a location four hours behind Eastern Standard Time, where daylight persists twenty-four/seven during the spring, summer, and fall months.

In Barrow, we toured the Barrow Arctic Research Center (BARC), ventured onto the sea ice, and visited I⊠isa⊠vik College. On May 9, we explored additional Barrow research facilities before flying to Fairbanks, Alaska. The following day, May 10, included a scenic river rafting trip to view the Alaskan wilderness, followed by a meeting with Secretary of State Rex Tillerson at the Arctic Council's twentieth-anniversary celebration.

On May 11, we flew to Thule, Greenland, where we engaged with leadership at Thule Air Base, located at seventy-six degrees north. Greenland, three times the size of Texas, is covered by sea ice two miles thick and over 250,000 years old. The next day, we toured Thule's facilities, including science labs and the assembly of a new Smithsonian Astrophysical Observatory 12m Radio Telescope. Later, we boarded a NASA P3 aircraft for a two-hour research flight over the sea ice as part of Operation Ice Bridge (OIB).

On May 13, members of Congress traveled to Summit Station aboard a 1941 Douglas DC3 twin-engine aircraft. Located at the highest point above Greenland's ice sheet (10,551 feet), Summit Station required landing on skis on an ice runway in temperatures of negative fifteen degrees

Fahrenheit. While Members visited the station, family members explored the Russell Glacier.

We returned to Washington, DC, on May 14 aboard the C40C luxury aircraft that had brought us to Barrow six days earlier.

Oslo, Norway

In August 2017, Mary and I traveled to Oslo, Norway, for the Aspen Institute's annual summit, held during Congress' summer recess. The summit, which ran from August 9 to 15, focused on energy issues, particularly oil exploration and drilling.

We participated in numerous discussions with Norwegian energy executives. Norway is a progressive country and takes pride in generating 99 percent of its electricity from hydropower plants supplemented by wind turbines. However, Norwegian officials displayed a hypocritical attitude toward oil usage. Despite boasting about their renewable energy achievements, Norway remains one of the world's largest oil exporters, producing two million barrels of oil daily and actively exploring for more.

During our time in Oslo, we visited the Viking Ship Museum, which features ninth-century Viking ships, and enjoyed shopping on Karl Johans Street in downtown Oslo, where the summit took place.

2017 Legislation in the 115th Congress

HR-1: Tax Cuts and Jobs Act

With Republicans holding total control of the government in the 115th Congress, expectations were high for conservative legislation to undo much of Barack Obama's liberal agenda. However, achieving these goals proved more complicated than the public anticipated.

The Senate's filibuster rule required sixty votes to pass most legislation, but Republicans held only fifty seats. This allowed Minority Leader Chuck Schumer to block conservative bills. Meanwhile, the Republican House majority of 241–194 faced internal divisions among the ultra-conservative Freedom Caucus, moderate Tuesday Group, and Republican Study

Committee, making consensus challenging. Democrats, led by Nancy Pelosi, uniformly opposed Republican-led legislation.

Despite these hurdles, the top priority for President Trump and congressional Republicans was passing meaningful tax reform. The designation of HR-1 as the Tax Cuts and Jobs Act signaled its importance as the primary focus of the 115th Congress.

The only viable path to passing HR-1 was through budget reconciliation, a process allowing budget-related legislation to pass the Senate with a simple majority. The parliamentarian ensures reconciliation bills address only budgetary matters, excluding social, educational, or other non-budgetary issues.

HR-1 underwent extensive committee debates, focusing on tax code changes to provide relief for small businesses and overtaxed individuals. Republicans championed lower taxes and spending, while Democrats advocated for higher taxes on businesses and wealthy individuals to fund increased spending.

The bill proposed several controversial changes:

- State and Local Tax (SALT) Deduction Cap: Limited to $10,000, this cap significantly impacted high-tax states like New York and California. For example, my property taxes in New York were $25,000 annually, and my state income taxes exceeded $100,000, yet I could only deduct $10,000 under HR-1.
- Standard Deduction Increase: Raised from $12,700 to $24,000 for married couples, effectively eliminating the need for many taxpayers in high-tax states to itemize deductions.
- Estate Tax Deduction: Increased from $5.7 million to $11.2 million per couple, though the 40 percent tax on estates exceeding this amount remained unchanged. While many Republicans supported eliminating the estate tax entirely, budgetary constraints required compromises.
- Top Marginal Tax Rate: Reduced from 39.6 percent to 37 percent.

HR-1 passed on December 22, 2017, under reconciliation for the 2018 fiscal year budget. I proudly voted in favor of this landmark legislation.

HR: 931 Firefighters Cancer Registry Act

People often overlook the fact that most members of Congress never sponsor legislation under their name that gets passed and signed into law. Individual bills are frequently combined with other legislation submitted by leadership for a House vote. Committee chairpersons also often move individual pieces of legislation under their name and sponsorship. It is not unusual for challengers in congressional races to exploit this fact, running commercials or producing direct mail pieces that criticize incumbents for never authoring legislation that was signed into law. These efforts aim to label the incumbent as ineffective.

June 26, 2018, celebrating the Firefighters Cancer Registry Bill with Speaker Paul Ryan.

I sponsored HR-931 on February 7, 2017, shortly after the 115th Congress convened. Serving as a majority member of the Energy and Commerce Committee and a member of its Health Subcommittee, I introduced HR-931, also known as the Firefighters Cancer Registry Act. My district primarily consisted of volunteer fire companies, as rural NY-27 lacked paid fire departments. During my travels in the district, I frequently met with firefighters, attended firefighter banquets, and engaged with their leadership.

HR-931 required the Centers for Disease Control and Prevention (CDC) to develop and maintain a voluntary registry of firefighters to collect occupational history, and other relevant data for studying cancer incidence among firefighters.

Specifically:

The registry was intended to improve cancer monitoring among firefighters and publish epidemiological information.

The CDC was tasked with including specific details in the registry, such as the number and type of fire incidents attended by an individual.

- The registry would connect with state-based cancer registries to gather data.
- The CDC would also:
  - Develop strategies to encourage participation,
  - Provide guidance for states and firefighting agencies, and
  - Seek feedback from non-federal experts.
- The CDC had to ensure that registry data would be publicly available while complying with privacy laws.

HR-931 passed out of the Energy and Commerce Committee by unanimous voice vote on July 27, 2017. It was approved by the House on September 12, 2017, again by unanimous voice vote, and sent to the Senate. On May 10, 2018, the Senate passed HR-931 by unanimous consent. President Trump signed it into law on July 7, 2018. Despite being uncontroversial and widely supported, it took seventeen months to navigate the legislative process.

By July 7, 2018, I had my own sponsored legislation, HR-931, signed into law. A framed original copy of HR-931 now hangs on my office wall at home.

Federal Judge John Sinatra

As the Republican Member of Congress for Western New York, I was approached by Don McGahn, the White House counsel, to recommend a candidate for the US District Court for the Western District of New York.

Typically, recommendations for federal judge appointments come from the senior senator of the state where the vacancy exists. However, in New York, both Senators—Schumer and Gillibrand—were Democrats, serving under a Republican president. Thus, the recommendation fell to me. President Trump and Don McGahn also wanted to afford me the prestige of making the nomination.

I recommended John Sinatra, a highly qualified attorney and brother of my business partner, Nick Sinatra—a fact noted by the press. At forty-six, John was relatively young, which made him an ideal candidate for a lifetime appointment. President Trump nominated John Sinatra for the federal judgeship on May 15, 2018.

Government processes move slowly. Although John's nomination gained reluctant support from Senator Schumer and passed out of the Senate Judiciary Committee on September 13, 2018, the Senate did not confirm it before the year ended. President Trump resubmitted the nomination on April 8, 2019. Over a year had passed since John's initial nomination, and I grew concerned about his confirmation prospects. However, on June 20, 2019, the Judiciary Committee approved his nomination again, and the Senate confirmed him on December 4, 2019, by a 75–18 vote. John Sinatra received his lifetime commission on December 5, 2019. I take great pride in having played a pivotal role in confirming a conservative judge for a lifetime appointment.

International Joint Commission

The International Joint Commission (IJC) is a bi-national organization established by the US and Canada under the Boundary Waters Treaty of 1909. Comprising three US commissioners and three Canadian commissioners, the IJC addresses waterway issues along the US-Canada border.

My congressional district bordered Lake Ontario: a major Great Lake shared with Canada. The St. Lawrence River, which flows from Lake

Ontario to the Atlantic Ocean, serves as a boundary between the two nations. Constituents along Lake Ontario's southern shore often expressed frustration over water levels and a perceived lack of representation. No New Yorker was serving on the IJC, which oversees waterways from Washington state to New York.

I successfully advocated for President Trump to appoint Jane Corwin, a friend and neighbor, as a US commissioner on the IJC. Jane's designation as US chair further delighted my constituents, who felt their voices were finally being heard regarding Lake Ontario's water levels. Jane's appointment significantly bolstered support from my district's northernmost county.

Other Noteworthy Events During the 115th Congress

Rep. Tom Price, my friend and an investor in Innate Immunotherapeutics, was confirmed as secretary of health and human services on February 10, 2017. Senator Schumer drew attention to Tom's investment in the company, leading to a temporary spike in its stock price. Tom sold his shares before the company's drug trial failed in June 2017. He resigned on September 29, 2017, over travel-related controversies.

General Michael Flynn resigned as national security advisor on February 13, 2017, after serving only twenty-two days in Donald Trump's administration.

Mary and I attended the yearly Tuesday Group/Main Street Partnership annual conference held from May 5 to May 7, 2017, at Amelia Island, Florida. The conference always occurs at the same time of year and generally coincides with Mary's birthday on May 6.

On June 14, 2017, Majority Whip Steve Scalise was shot during a baseball practice in Alexandria, Virginia. Representative Brad Wenstrup (R-OH), a surgeon who served in Iraq, saved Steve's life by using a tourniquet to stop the bleeding. Steve was rushed to the hospital with only minutes to spare. Two brave capitol police officers were injured while rushing at the gunman but survived. They shot and killed the deranged assailant.

The White House Congressional Picnic took place on June 22, 2017, the day of my fateful call to my son.

From July 21 to July 23, 2017, I led a delegation of members to the Boy Scout National Jamboree in Beckley, West Virginia. As chair of the Congressional Scout Caucus, I joined fellow lifetime Scouters in making presentations and answering attendees' questions about Congress. We also met with top Scout executives from headquarters in Irving, Texas.

On April 24, 2018, the FBI knocked on my door, and my nightmare began.

2018: Indictment and Reelection Campaign

All my success in Congress, my ties to President Trump, and my sky-high approval in NY-27 came crashing down on August 8, 2018, when the Southern District of New York indicted me on eleven felony counts of securities fraud and conspiracy to commit securities fraud. My son and six others with ties to him had sold stock in Innate Immunotherapeutics on June 23, 2017, after I made a fateful call to him during the Congressional White House Picnic on June 22, 2017. I shared the negative FDA drug trial results for our drug to treat secondary multiple sclerosis with my son, believing no one could sell the stock due to a trading halt in Australia, where the company and stock were registered.

Before my indictment, I faced a weak challenger. Nate McMurray seemed like the Democrats' sacrificial lamb for the 2018 election.

I completely ignored Nate McMurray initially, as is standard strategy for strong incumbents. I refused to debate him, knowing a debate would boost his name recognition.

After my indictment, everything changed. I was devastated and uncertain about my next steps. On August 11, 2018, I issued a press release suspending my campaign and announced I would not seek reelection, believing the Republicans could replace me with another candidate.

Over the next month, Republicans struggled to agree on my replacement. The language used to describe me during these discussions was disheartening. I was a mental wreck and resented the disparaging comments from some county chairmen.

By September 19, 2018, I regained my resolve. At a press conference, I shocked everyone—county chairs and US Attorney Geoffrey Berman included—by announcing I would restart my campaign.

I informed my staff of my decision and committed to spend all of the $1.3 million in my campaign account to defeat Nate McMurray.

TV commercial attacking Nate McMurray.

My campaign consultant, Chris Grant, devised a scorched-earth strategy. On September 21, we launched a devastating negative ad against Nate McMurray. The ad featured a video of Nate speaking fluent Korean, bowing at the beginning and end. Though he deleted the video, we obtained a copy. The ad superimposed an image of Kim Jong Un over Nate's shoulder, with subtitles claiming:

"Nate McMurray wants to be your next Congressman. Worked to send jobs to China & Korea. Helped American companies hire foreign workers. Fewer jobs for us…more jobs for China & Korea. You can take Nate McMurray at his word."

Over the next seven weeks, I spent $1.3 million to defeat Nate McMurray, allocating over $1 million for television ads and $250,000 for negative direct mail. We did not spend a single penny on positive ads or mailers.

Nate McMurray benefited from my legal troubles, raising over $1.3 million after my indictment. However, he spent his funds poorly, ending his campaign with only $23,543 in cash-on-hand. He spent $922,702 on television and direct mail, with more than half on positive ads instead of attacking me.

Democratic consultants capitalized on Nate's inexperience, charging over $350,000 in fees and providing ineffective campaign advice. Despite being indicted on eleven felony counts and given no chance of winning, I prevailed.

I won the election by 1,087 votes out of 279,205 cast in NY-27—a margin of only 0.00389 percent. My reelection was the fourth closest congressional race in the country. The counting of military and absentee ballots dragged on for over a week, causing immense anxiety for my team and me.

Finances and Fundraising

I ended 2016 with $699,177 in cash-on-hand and no debt. During 2017 and 2018, I raised $1,321,298—$605,222 from individuals and $716,076 from PACs. My support for Trump and my Energy and Commerce committee assignment fueled robust fundraising.

After my indictment on August 8, 2018, fundraising ceased. I had expected an easy reelection and anticipated ending 2018 with over $1.5 million in cash-on-hand. When I resumed my campaign on September 19, I spent $1,138,849 in the final seven weeks to secure a narrow victory of 1,087 votes. By year's end, I had $204,416 in cash-on-hand.

I WON my reelection. Margin of victory: 1,087 votes—0.00389 percent. I WON my reelection.

Return to Congress

Congress was in recess for the entire month of October leading up to the election. During an election year, this is standard practice to allow members to campaign in their districts.

When I returned to Congress on November 13, 2018, my confidence had been restored. I felt somewhat vindicated by my victory over Nate McMurray on November 6. Most of my colleagues in Congress were unaware of my win. Members typically focus on their own reelection campaigns and other races within their states, but they don't necessarily follow contests in other parts of the country.

I lost count of how many members approached me, expressing that they would miss me in the next Congress. Their assumption was that I had lost my reelection bid. After all, it seemed unimaginable that a member facing eleven felony charges could win reelection. When I smiled and told them I had been reelected and would be serving with them in the next Congress, they congratulated me enthusiastically, shaking my hand with vigor. I had accomplished the impossible.

I arranged a meeting with Kevin McCarthy, then the majority leader of the Republican Conference. Speaker Paul Ryan, who removed me from the Energy and Commerce Committee following my indictment, did not run for reelection in the 2018 midterm elections. I was eager to have my committee assignment on Energy and Commerce reinstated. I explained to Kevin that the rule Paul Ryan had invoked to remove me from the committee did not apply to rank-and-file members. The rule stated that a committee chair who was indicted must step down as chair but could remain on the committee.

Kevin was seeking my support for his bid to continue as majority leader of the Republican Conference. I assured him of my support and expressed my hope that he would reinstate my committee assignment. He seemed unaware that the rule Paul Ryan had applied only pertained to committee chairs. Kevin said he would have his staff review the rule and follow up with me.

I acknowledged to Kevin that I understood why Paul Ryan had removed me from the committee, even though he had improperly invoked a rule that did not apply to my case. In the United States, a person is presumed innocent until proven guilty, but an indicted member inevitably suffers a tarnished reputation. I reminded Kevin that my constituents, fully aware of my indictment, had reelected me to represent them. They deserved to have their representative serve on a committee, just as other members of Congress do.

I thought my meeting with Kevin McCarthy had gone well. His body language suggested he agreed with my reasoning and recognized that Paul Ryan had acted improperly in removing me from Energy and Commerce.

The next day, however, I was blindsided when Kevin McCarthy introduced a new rule for the 116th Congress. The rule explicitly stated that any member indicted on felony charges could not serve on a committee. This was a direct slap in the face and a clear show of disrespect for my constituents who had reelected me.

The bottom line was that I would not be reinstated to the Energy and Commerce Committee or any other committee. My afternoons in Washington, when committees held their hearings and markups, would now be unoccupied.

I had hoped that my hard work on Energy and Commerce would be recognized. As an effective member of Congress, I believed I deserved to continue serving on the committee.

I had been a key co-sponsor of legislation to assist Vietnam veterans exposed to Agent Orange, who did not qualify for disability or healthcare benefits because they served in the Navy and remained aboard ship. This legislation, known as the Blue Water Navy Vietnam Veterans Act, was signed into law in 2019, rectifying a travesty that had persisted for fifty years.

I also played a significant role in the Choice Act, which allowed veterans to access medical care outside the VA when faced with long delays or when living far from VA facilities.

In addition, I worked closely with the Army Corps of Engineers to secure funding for critical projects in Western New York, including prioritizing Mount Morris Dam.

Volunteer fire departments often lack sufficient funding to stay properly equipped. I had been effective in securing critical government grants for many fire departments in Western New York to purchase protective safety gear, air packs, and emergency response equipment.

The saving grace for not serving on a committee was that the Democrats regained control of the House in the midterm elections, and Nancy Pelosi was elected speaker. With Democrats in control of all committees, Republicans were marginalized and sidelined. As a result, Republican members on committees had little to no influence on legislation or hearings. Their attendance at committee meetings became virtually meaningless.

CHAPTER 26

Congress 2019

I WON MY REELECTION ON November 6, 2018, by the slimmest of margins against Nate McMurray. My 1,087-vote differential was the fourth-closest victory in the entire country. I had to wait an agonizing week after the election to confirm my victory as absentee and military ballots were tallied. Each new count brought a smaller margin of victory. I vividly recall sitting outside my house in Marco Island, smoking cigars, as the results came in. When the final count was completed, despite the closeness, I won. In politics, a win is all that matters.

Returning to Washington for the swearing-in on January 4, 2019, was bittersweet. The 2018 midterm elections had been devastating for Republicans. As is typical in midterms, the president's party suffered significant losses. The "blue wave" delivered the Democrats forty-one seats in the House, flipping control back to them and installing Nancy Pelosi as speaker.

My life had dramatically changed since my indictment on August 8, 2018, on eleven felony counts. I was stripped of my committee assignment on Energy and Commerce and forced to relinquish my position as chair of the Scout Caucus. Fundraising dried up, and invitations to prominent events vanished. My political career was no longer recognizable.

The only consolation in my grim situation was that Democrats, not Republicans, now held the majority. From 2010 to 2018, Republicans had controlled the House, but the pendulum swung in 2018. Being in the minority in Congress is a bleak experience. The majority party controls all committees, decides what legislation comes to a vote, and renders the minority's role virtually irrelevant. Even if I had retained my committee assignments, I would have had little influence. Ironically, I felt I was better off without them. At least I didn't have to endure the frustration of powerless committee meetings.

With the Democrats in charge, Republicans defaulted to voting "Nay" on nearly every bill. Votes were no longer whipped, and there was little need for strategy. As a minority member, showing up often felt like a formality. Having spent my first six years in the majority, I saw the stark difference and knew my current situation was not unique to me—it was simply the reality of being a Republican in a Democratic-controlled House.

I went through the motions of my job. I commuted to Washington three weeks a month, attended votes, and spent time in my congressional office with my staff. Many staff members left for other positions, and I couldn't fault them. Constituent visits for Capitol or White House tours continued, though less frequently. I enjoyed escorting constituents to the White House for impromptu tours, a privilege reserved for members of Congress. These moments provided a rare sense of connection and normalcy.

Back home in the district, life was equally unfulfilling. Invitations to farms, businesses, and schools ceased. "Innocent until proven guilty" did not seem to apply. In the public eye, I was guilty until proven otherwise.

On the House floor, I found comfort in the company of fellow New York Republicans Elise Stefanik, John Katko, and Claudia Tenney. Claudia, the newest Republican from New York, had been elected in 2016. They were genuinely concerned about my mental health, especially Elise, who often checked in to see if I was okay. Her kindness was a balm during difficult days.

Privately, I was a wreck. Winning reelection provided structure to my life, forcing me to continue my duties and preventing me from wallowing in despair. If I had lost, I feared I would have spent my days in Marco Island, smoking cigars and obsessing over my misfortunes. That would not have been healthy.

Meanwhile, my legal troubles loomed. US Attorney Geoffrey Berman pursued my case with relentless determination. I worried constantly about my children, and my wife Mary, whose social life in Buffalo had evaporated. Brookfield Country Club asked me to transfer my membership to Mary to avoid associating with me. I had been a member for thirty-eight years. I also was forced to resign from the board of directors of the Greater Niagara Frontier Boy Scout Council.

When I agreed to a plea deal on September 20, 2019, the reality of my situation came crashing down. Congress was in session until September 27, after which it would recess until October 15. Knowing my resignation was imminent, I began packing my condo and put it up for sale as a turn-key property.

During my final week in Washington, I felt like a ghost. I cast my votes, wandered the Capitol to admire its beauty one last time, and thanked my colleagues for their friendship. Many sensed something was amiss but refrained from prying.

After my staff left on Friday, September 27, I packed up my personal belongings and prepared to leave my office for good. House Administration would take over the operation of my offices following my resignation.

On September 30, 2019, I submitted my resignation to Speaker Pelosi and Governor Andrew Cuomo. I flew to Marco Island and obtained a Florida driver's license and voter registration. This small administrative task was significant. On that day, I could truthfully answer "no" to the question of whether I had ever been convicted of a felony. By the next day, the answer would change to "yes," and I would lose my voting rights. I became a full-fledged Florida resident on September 30.

The next day, October 1, I pled guilty in a New York City courtroom to one count of Conspiracy to Commit Securities Fraud and one count of Making a False Statement to Law Enforcement. My son and his future father-in-law, Steve—also pled guilty to one count of Conspiracy to Commit Securities Fraud. Sentencing for me was scheduled for January 17, 2020 and January 23, 2020 for my son.

I returned to Marco Island, feeling a profound sense of shame and uncertainty. The media headlines were brutal. My legacy was reduced to a single word: felon. My family life was in disarray, and everything I had built over seventy years seemed meaningless.

Despite my despair, I focused on preparing for sentencing. I compiled lists of friends and colleagues who might write letters of support to Judge Broderick. To my surprise, 137 individuals—including family, business partners, and members of Congress—sent letters on my behalf. Their words were a source of solace and a testament to the relationships I had built over the years.

However, the media seized on this effort. *The New York Post* published a sensational story with the headline "Chris Collins Begs Friends to Write Letters in Bid for Leniency." Opponents mobilized, flooding the court with negative letters. Groups like "Citizens Against Collins," led by local activist Michelle Schoeneman, launched campaigns urging maximum punishment. Judge Broderick received sixty-five negative letters alongside the 137 positive ones.

Ultimately, the probation department recommended a relatively lenient sentence of one year and a day.

On January 16, 2020, I traveled to New York City for my sentencing. The following day, my fate was sealed.

Judge Broderick disregarded the probation department recommendation and sentenced me to twenty-six months in prison. His decision felt politically motivated and deeply unfair, but it was final.

CHAPTER 27

Legal Saga

Innate Immunotherapeutics

My investment in Innate Immunotherapeutics began in 2005. Over the years, I invested $5,250,000 and acquired 37,899,139 shares of the company. Innate, originally named Virionyx, was a private entity before going public on the Australian Stock Exchange (ASX) in 2013.

I held a 38 percent ownership stake in Innate, while my children each owned 5 percent, having paid $600,000 each for their 5,200,000 shares.

When I first invested in Virionyx in 2005, the company was in the early stages of developing HRG214, a drug aimed at treating HIV/AIDS patients. However, the HRG214 drug trial was abandoned in 2008 when two new antiretroviral drugs received accelerated approval from the FDA. These newly approved drugs were far less expensive to produce than HRG214.

Under normal circumstances, the failure of a drug development program would spell doom for a small biotech company, especially one reliant on a single drug and based in New Zealand. However, Virionyx had observed promising results from the adjuvant (MIS416) used during the development of HRG214. (An adjuvant is a substance that enhances the body's immune response to an antigen or virus.)

In 2009, the company rebranded itself as Innate Immunotherapeutics and shifted its focus toward developing MIS416, a drug to treat secondary progressive multiple sclerosis (SPMS)—a debilitating autoimmune disease. I became the lead investor in a $2 million fundraising round that closed on December 28, 2009, providing the resources needed for Innate to advance its work on MIS416.

Between 2009 and 2016, MIS416 development progressed positively. In October 2014, approval was granted to conduct a Phase 2B clinical trial for the drug. This trial, expected to conclude in June 2017, was double-blind and placebo-controlled, designed to ensure results reflected real-life outcomes and confirmed MIS416s clinical efficacy in treating SPMS. Everyone involved with Innate was highly optimistic, confident the trial results would be favorable and pave the way for FDA accelerated approval of MIS416 as a treatment for secondary progressive multiple sclerosis.

White House Congressional Picnic

The 2017 White House Congressional Picnic was held on June 22, 2017. Attendance was restricted to members of Congress and their staff or guests. I invited two of my supporters, Chris Graham, the president of Volland Electric, and Gerry Buchheit, a long-time supporter of my political career, to join me. My chief of staff, Michael Hook, also attended the picnic with me. The event began at 6:00 PM.

All three of my guests were investors in Innate Immunotherapeutics. Over the years, dozens of my friends, business associates, and other members of Congress had invested in Innate. I believed Innate would become the first company in the world to receive FDA approval for a drug to treat SPMS, a debilitating autoimmune disease. I shared my enthusiasm about MIS416 with everyone I knew.

Simon Wilkinson, the CEO of Innate, had informed the company's directors that the top-line results of the Phase 2B trial would be received on Friday, June 23, 2017 (Australian time). Australia is fourteen hours ahead of the United States, meaning 9:00 AM Friday in Australia corresponded to 7:00 PM Thursday in the United States.

There were no confidentiality restrictions on communicating with investors about the expected timing of the Phase 2B trial results in June 2017.

The board of Innate had previously implemented a "closed period" for all employees and board members from June 5 to July 11, 2017. During this period, employees and board members were prohibited from trading Innate shares. This restriction aimed to prevent the misuse of confidential trial results for insider trading.

Additionally, the Board decided that a "trading halt" would be issued on the Australian Stock Exchange (ASX) as soon as the trial results were received. Innate stock was officially registered and traded in Australia and not regulated by the US Securities and Exchange Commission (SEC).

The trading halt for Innate Immunotherapeutics stock went into effect at 10:53 PM Thursday (US time), which was 12:53 PM Friday (Australian time). However, inexplicably, NASDAQ did not honor the trading halt, and trading of Innate shares continued on Friday morning on NASDAQ's over-the-counter (OTC) market in the US. The OTC listings, also known as "Pink Sheets," typically feature low-priced, unlisted penny stocks. At the time, Innate stock traded on NASDAQ for approximately fifty cents per share.

The White House Picnic was an enjoyable event. I introduced my three guests to several members of Congress and members of President Trump's administration, including Ivanka Trump, who attended with her children. At 6:45 PM, I noticed Vice President Pence standing off to the side with his wife. I seized the opportunity to introduce my guests to the vice president and took photos of them shaking hands. We chatted with Mike and Karen Pence for about five minutes.

President Trump was scheduled to address the crowd at 7:30 PM. A roped-off area had been set up for his speech. At 6:55 PM, I received an email from Simon Wilkinson. I mentioned to my guests that Simon, the CEO of Innate, had emailed me. As we walked away from our conversation with the vice president, I excused myself to a private spot to read the email.

At 7:10 PM, I opened the email and read, with disbelief, that the Phase 2B trial for MIS416 had failed. Simon's email stated: "I have bad news to report that the top-line analysis of the twelve-month trial indicates clinical failure, showing no clinically meaningful or statistically significant differences between MIS416 and placebo. No doubt this is considered extremely bad news."

The news hit me like a tsunami. My brain shut down. I stared blankly into the crowd, disoriented. Although I don't remember replying to Simon, records show I responded at 7:10 PM, stating: "Wow. Makes no sense. How are these results even possible???"

I have no memory of what happened between 7:00 PM Thursday and Friday morning. I have since learned about "dissociative amnesia," a rare condition stemming from emotional shock or trauma, which can cause memory loss for brief periods. This describes my mental state after reading Simon's email.

Through records and conversations, I pieced together the events that followed. After reading Simon's email, I returned to my guests, visibly shaken. Records show I called my son at 7:16 PM for six minutes, and Mary at 7:23 PM for another six minutes. I have a vague memory of making these calls but cannot recall the content of the conversations.

President Trump addressed the crowd at 7:27 PM. According to photos on my phone, I arranged for my guests to take pictures with President Trump and Melania Trump at 7:54 and 7:55 PM. Few people have had the opportunity to be photographed with Melania Trump.

Chris Graham recounted that after President Trump's speech, he and Melania greeted attendees along a rope line. President Trump recognized me, shook my hand, and allowed my group to step inside the rope line. I took several photos of Chris Graham with the president, Chris Graham with both the president and Melania, and similar photos for Michael Hook and Gerry Buchheit.

Chris Graham also recalled that we went to dinner at 8:30 PM at the Trump International Hotel on Pennsylvania Avenue, a few blocks from the White House. While I vaguely remember going to dinner, I cannot recall any details of the meal. Chris said the dinner was pleasant but noted that I seemed distracted. He confirmed I did not share the trial results with them.

After dinner, I drove back to my condo. I had parked my car at the Trump International Hotel before walking to the White House for the Congressional Picnic.

Friday Morning Phone Call with My Son

I woke up on Friday morning, June 23, 2017, feeling groggy and disoriented. I vaguely remembered receiving bad news about the Innate Phase 2B trial but had little recollection of the prior night. I thought Simon Wilkinson had called me during the White House Picnic to deliver the devastating news that the MIS416 trial had failed. Simon and I always communicated by phone, so this assumption felt natural.

However, I later discovered through my attorneys during the discovery process that Simon had actually sent me an email, not made a phone call. At the time, I wasn't aware of this detail.

I did vaguely remember calling Mary and my son but had no memory of what was said during those conversations.

A trading halt on Innate Immunotherapeutics stock was issued in Australia, effective at 10:53 PM Thursday night (EST). Based on this halt, and assuming NASDAQ would honor it, no one should have been able to sell Innate Immunotherapeutics stock.

At 9:41 AM on Friday morning, I received a phone call from my son. We spoke for nine minutes. During the call, my son informed me that I had shared the negative trial results with him when I called him at 7:10 PM on Thursday night.

Michael Quinn, chairman of the board of Innate Immunotherapeutics, later wrote a letter to Judge Broderick prior to my sentencing. In the letter, he stated:

"The trial failure surprised and devastated everyone associated with the company. We were all shocked. Many Innate Board members shared the negative trial results with family members. With a trading halt in place, there was no ability for anyone to trade on the ASX, so there was no risk of insider trading. It is tragic that there was unsanctioned and unofficial trading of Innate stock in the United States on NASDAQ, over which the company had no control. The Board failed to circumvent all possible trading."

During our nine-minute phone conversation at 9:41 AM on Friday morning, my son informed me of shocking news: Innate stock was trading on NASDAQ, and he had sold some of his shares. He told me that his fiancée had also sold shares. I didn't know she even owned any shares. He also told me his future father-in-law sold shares.

I initially thought this was impossible due to the trading halt. However, it turned out that NASDAQ did not honor the trading halt, leading to a surge in Innate stock trading. This trading activity was fueled by public knowledge that Innate had received the MIS416 trial results, and that there was a trading halt on the Australian Stock Exchange.

Our family held our Innate stock on the electronic Computershare exchange in Australia, as did most US-based Innate investors. Only a few investors, who had not participated in the various Innate private placements, purchased their shares on NASDAQ over-the-counter. I didn't know that my son had moved his stock from Australia to the United States two weeks prior to the release of the trail results.

What happened on Friday morning at 9:30 AM when NASDAQ opened could not be undone. Despite extensive investigations, early morning FBI home raids, and high-pressure interviews, no criminal charges were ever filed against others who sold Innate Immunotherapeutics stock that Friday morning. No one ever told the FBI that I shared trial results with them.

What I know for sure is this:

- I did not sell any Innate stock prior to the public release of the negative trial results.
- I did not anticipate that my son could sell any shares of Innate, as I believed his shares were held at Computershare in Australia. I also knew there was a trading halt on Innate stock as of 10:53 PM Thursday night.

April 25, 2018 FBI Raids

Following the public release of the failed MIS416 drug trial results on June 27, 2017, my son and I never spoke again about his Innate stock sales. What was done, was done.

My son and his fiancée were engaged, but no marriage date had been set. He had purchased her a beautiful diamond ring, and together they bought a lovely townhouse in Asbury Park, New Jersey, near the Jersey Shore.

In February 2018, they both quit their jobs. ZeptoMetrix, the company where my son held a 16 percent stake, was doing exceptionally well. He had been working as an electrical engineer for AT&T, while she was employed as a CPA at PricewaterhouseCoopers. Both had stable, well-paying jobs, but with my son's substantial distributions from ZeptoMetrix they decided to leave their careers behind. Their plan was to travel and enjoy life, free from the constraints of traditional employment—a mindset often associated with millennials, quite different from that of baby boomers.

On Wednesday, April 25, 2018, everything changed. At 6:00 AM, thirty FBI agents conducted coordinated raids across six states, targeting twelve homes with search warrants related to the sale of Innate Immunotherapeutics stock on June 23, 2017. The FBI's objective was to gather computers and cell phones containing evidence of insider trading. They focused on anyone connected to me, even tangentially, who had sold Innate stock on that day.

Geoffrey Berman, US Attorney for the Southern District of New York (SDNY), led the investigation into the unusually high volume of Innate stock trades on NASDAQ on June 23, 2017. The Securities and Exchange Commission (SEC) was also scrutinizing this trading activity. Berman's interest intensified when he discovered a potential link to me, Congressman Christopher Collins, a prominent supporter of President Donald Trump. Berman's reputation for seeking high-profile cases and media attention added fuel to his determination.

For ten months, from June 2017 to April 2018, the DOJ, FBI, and SEC conducted an exhaustive investigation, uncovering every possible connection between the individuals who sold Innate stock and myself. The raids, meticulously planned, involved collaboration among multiple US Attorneys and FBI Special Agents across jurisdictions. Agents had surveilled their targets—including my son and his fiancée, who were scheduled to leave for Australia on April 26, 2018. The raid was scheduled for April 25 to ensure they were at home.

At 6:00 AM, I was asleep in my Washington, DC condo on 215 I Street, NE. Congress was in session. Loud banging on my front door woke me. Initially, I ignored it, assuming it was a mistake. The banging persisted for five minutes before my phone rang. The caller identified himself as an FBI agent and requested that I open the door.

Surprised, I dressed quickly and answered. Two agents—one male and one female—stood outside. They wanted to discuss my involvement with Innate Immunotherapeutics. They noted that I was represented by Baker Hostetler for an issue related to the House of Representatives and asked if the firm represented me in any other matters. I confirmed they represented me for the one issue but not for anything else.

I made the mistake of inviting the agents inside. Looking back, I advise anyone in a similar situation to insist they contact your attorney instead. Their sole objective was to entrap me into making a false statement, a felony that would exacerbate my legal challenges. Initially, their questioning was general and non-threatening, but it became clear they were experienced in manipulation.

After thirty minutes of discussing my thirteen-year involvement with Innate, the agents revealed their true purpose: they asked if I had shared negative drug trial results with my son to help him avoid losses by selling stock. Alarmed, I told them to leave, asserting that they should not be speaking with me without my attorney present. As they departed, one agent smugly claimed they knew I had shared the trial results with my son so he could sell stock and avoid losses. Angry, I shouted back at the agent that I did not share trial results with my son so he could sell stock and avoid losses. That was a true statement. I didn't know my son had moved his stock to the US and thought his stock was still in Australia where it couldn't be traded.

Disturbed by the FBI visit to my condo, I called my son but couldn't reach him. I then called Mary, who mentioned receiving a voicemail from the FBI but hadn't returned the call. Finally, my son called me back using his fiancée's phone; his own phone and computer had been seized during the raid. Six agents had entered their townhouse, terrifying them. His fiancée had mistaken the agents for robbers and thrown her engagement ring across the room to protect it—a moment that, in hindsight, was almost comic.

The agents interrogated my son and his fiancée separately. My son explained that he had sold 25 percent of his Innate stock as a hedge against potential bad news following a trading halt on the stock—a common strategy. This was truthful; he had only sold a portion of his shares. He also told the FBI that I hadn't shared trial results with him.

Similar raids occurred at Steve's home, where he also faced identical tactics. Two agents interrogated him and his wife while two others searched their house. Like my son, they denied any wrongdoing and cited the trading halt as their reason for selling stock.

Interestingly, my position as a congressman appeared to afford me some protection. The FBI agents at my door lacked a search warrant and didn't seize my devices, unlike the others targeted that morning. Still, the simultaneous raids made it clear this was a nationwide operation.

Later that day, I met Michael Hook at my congressional office to discuss the situation. He contacted my attorney at Baker Hostetler, who promptly arrived to confer with us. Mark Braden, while skilled, did not practice criminal law. He referred me to Jon Barr, a criminal defense attorney at the firm.

The events of April 25, 2018, marked the beginning of a harrowing journey—one that would forever alter our lives.

April 25, 2018–August 8, 2018

The next three and a half months were awful. I couldn't tell anyone except my family and Michael Hook that I was under investigation by the DOJ, FBI, SEC, and SDNY for alleged insider trading and tipping.

My son and his fiancée were completely shaken. This situation was unimaginable and unexpected. In hindsight, everyone acknowledged it was a mistake to sell the Innate stock. But that decision had been made during a single day filled with emotion and despair over the failed drug trial. It couldn't be reversed.

I hired Jon Barr from the Baker Hostetler office in Washington, DC, and his partner Jon New from their New York City office. Both had experience as assistant US attorneys and were well-versed in the inner workings of a US Attorney's office.

They recommended separate legal representation for my son, his fiancée, and Steve.

Our attorneys worked hard to prevent criminal charges. They submitted memos and letters to various agencies, arguing our case. They pointed out that I hadn't sold any stock and emphasized the trading halt on Innate stock on the ASX.

The main challenge for the SDNY prosecutors was that they had no recording of my phone call with my son. Despite their aggressive and inappropriate tactics, they eventually realized I hadn't shared trial results with anyone—except perhaps my son, who sold Innate stock on June 23, 2017.

After a thorough review of my electronic devices, investigators found no texts or emails between me and anyone who sold stock. There were no communications between me and my son or Steve—no texts, emails, or phone calls.

Both my son and Steve denied that I had shared the trial results with them.

Geoffrey Berman, however, seemed determined to pursue me and refused to settle with charges solely against my son and Steve.

The case SDNY and the FBI were building against me was entirely circumstantial. They had a stronger case against my son and Steve, since they both sold stock and contacted others who also sold. Against me, all they had was the fact that I called my son a few minutes after receiving the trial results and spoke with him for six minutes. They couldn't prove what was said during that call, and both of us denied I had shared the trial results.

Despite our attorneys' efforts, the SDNY showed no willingness to treat the matter as a civil issue rather than a criminal one. It became evident that my son and I would be arrested and charged with criminal counts of insider trading.

Jon Barr tried to confirm with Geoffrey Berman whether I would be allowed to self-surrender if indicted. Berman was evasive, saying only that he would "take it under advisement."

On Friday, August 3, 2018, I received a call from an anonymous individual. He didn't give his name but mentioned he knew me from my time as Erie County executive. He expressed admiration for my dedication to Erie County and my success in implementing Lean Six Sigma in government operations.

The caller disclosed that the FBI office in Buffalo was working with SDNY to arrest me at home in a dramatic early-morning raid, complete with TV cameras. He said he was personally upset and angry about this planned spectacle.

While shocked, I wasn't entirely surprised. Geoffrey Berman appeared eager to make a public display of me being arrested and dragged out of my house in my underwear.

I quickly packed a bag, and Mary drove me to the Hertz car rental office at the airport. I rented a car under Mary's name, used her credit card, and drove to New York City. To avoid detection, I turned off my cell phone, removed the SIM card, and paid cash for everything. After dropping off the rental car in New York, I took a taxi to my daughter's apartment in Manhattan.

My daughter greeted me with a big hug. I explained everything: that I was going to be arrested and indicted on felony counts of insider trading, that her brother and Steve would also be arrested, and about the planned spectacle I had learned about from the anonymous caller, who obviously worked in the FBI office in Buffalo.

As an attorney, she was horrified by the apparent malice in the justice system.

The FBI searched for me but couldn't find me. Geoffrey Berman didn't get his show. Instead, he called my attorney and, acting as if nothing had happened, accepted the proposal for a self-surrender. It was scheduled for the next day—Wednesday, August 8, 2018.

August 8, 2018: Arrest and Indictment

We scheduled a meeting at Baker Hostetler the following morning to initiate the arrest and arraignment process. I had to purchase a pair of loafers since my shoes had laces, which were not permitted, and I was informed that belts were also prohibited.

We were told that my son and I would be transported separately to the FBI office. Two FBI agents met each of us in the Baker Hostetler lobby, and they had three vehicles prepared for our trip. Our attorneys planned to meet us at the federal courthouse, where Judge Broderick would oversee our arraignment. I knew this day would be dreadful.

To manage the anticipated media frenzy over a sitting member of Congress facing indictment, combined with the looming November 6, 2018, election, my team chartered a private jet to take Mary and me directly to Buffalo after the indictment. We also scheduled a press conference at a local hotel to address my constituents in NY-27.

At the FBI office, the processing went smoothly. Everyone acted professionally and treated all three of us respectfully. We had mugshots and fingerprints taken and filled out various questionnaires. The grim reality of the situation loomed over us. The entire process lasted about two hours.

We were then driven to the courthouse for arraignment. The FBI cars entered the garage. My son and Steve had arrived before me. I was stunned and mortified to see them standing at the basement entrance to the courthouse, handcuffed with their hands behind their backs. I thought, *WTF? That's my Eagle Scout son. This is wrong.*

When I got out of the car with the agents escorting me, one agent noticed the same scene I did. He gestured to the agents standing with my son and Steve with a throat-cutting motion. The agents immediately removed the handcuffs. I felt a sense of relief seeing that.

We were escorted into the basement and led to an area with actual jail cells. We were placed in a cell, and the door was locked. *Holy shit,* I thought. We were prisoners—locked in jail.

After waiting two hours, we were escorted into a courtroom filled with people. Mary, my son's fiancée, and Steve's wife sat among the spectators. Our attorneys occupied a table opposite the prosecutors. My son, Steve, and I each sat beside our respective lawyers. Each of us had two attorneys representing us at the arraignment.

The hearing proceeded quickly. When the judge entered the room, everyone stood. After he was seated, we followed suit. Following some preliminary statements and introductions, Judge Broderick addressed each of us individually. When our names were called, we stood, the charges were read aloud, and we each pleaded, "Not guilty."

I was indicted on eleven felony counts: one count of Conspiracy to Commit Securities Fraud, seven counts of Securities Fraud, one count of Conspiracy to Commit Wire Fraud, one count of Wire Fraud, and one count of Making a False Statement to Law Enforcement.

We were released on $500,000 bond each. The paperwork had been completed prior to the hearing, and the bond amounts were prearranged. My son and I had sufficient assets to secure our bonds, while Mary co-signed for Steve's bond.

Indicted and Uncertain Future

After leaving the courtroom, we faced a swarm of reporters shouting questions. My son and Steve departed in cars with their attorneys. I approached the reporters, raised my hand to silence them, and promised to answer their questions one at a time.

I told them I was not guilty and intended to fight the charges in court, confident that I would be exonerated. When asked about my reelection in ninety days, I admitted uncertainty about running again.

Once the questions were answered, I joined Mary and our attorneys in a car to the Westchester County Airport. A private jet awaited us, and we flew back to Buffalo.

At the Prior Aviation terminal in Buffalo, my congressional staff greeted us. We drove downtown for a press conference at the Hyatt Hotel.

The conference room was packed. The number of TV cameras present exceeded anything I'd ever seen in Buffalo, reminiscent of the night I seconded Donald Trump's nomination for president.

Standing at the podium with Mary at my side, I commanded the room's attention. I began by stating that I would not take questions, emphasizing there would be future opportunities for discussion. In a firm, authoritative voice, I declared my innocence, criticized the charges from the Southern District of New York as meritless, and promised to fight them in court, expecting vindication from a jury of my peers.

After my statement, Mary and I exited as reporters shouted questions. Surrounded by staff, we left the venue and drove home to Clarence.

Exhausted, we collapsed on the sofa. It had been the longest day of my life. My future seemed uncertain—whether to withdraw from reelection or face voters while under indictment for eleven felonies.

That evening, I addressed a necessary task: surrendering my five handguns and pistol permit, as required by the indictment. Having anticipated this, I had prepared the firearms in a box. My friend, Sheriff Tim Howard, agreed to store them safely until I could reclaim them. I also mailed my Pistol Carry Permit to the supervisor of the Pistol Permit Department at Erie County Hall.

US Attorney Geoffrey Berman

Geoffrey Berman, US Attorney in the Southern District of New York, knew my indictment would significantly impact my reelection. He discusses his decision to indict me less than ninety days before the election in his book *Holding the Line,* published on September 13, 2022.

Berman's team of prosecutors presented him with the dilemma surrounding the timing of my indictment. There is an unwritten rule in the DOJ that they avoid indicting a case that could materially affect an election, absent exigent circumstances. My case was ready to be filed, but there was no urgency—I wasn't going anywhere. More than a year had already passed since I called my son from the White House lawn on June 22, 2017. The election was less than ninety days away. Delaying the indictment by ninety days would have had no impact on the case or its prosecution.

To quote Berman's book: "Do we indict Collins before the election - which would have a significant negative impact on his chances for reelection - or wait to indict him right after the election? After all, an indictment contains only allegations, and Collins is entitled to a presumption of innocence. Indicting the case before the election could be perceived as an inappropriate political act on the part of our office. In making the decision to move forward, I thought Collins' constituents deserved to know about our charges, and he had over sixty days to present his side of the story."

Berman consciously chose to indict me with the deliberate and inappropriate expectation that it would significantly harm my reelection prospects.

Continuing from his book: "After first saying after the indictment that he would not seek reelection; he reversed course and reentered the race. The team and I watched his news conference live from my office and learned his plans along with the rest of the general public. He ended up winning a fourth term in New York's Twenty-seventh Congressional District."

Following my Indictment

When I returned to Congress after my indictment, I didn't know how I would be received. Congress was in August recess, giving me a few weeks to collect myself. This was a "guess what, now what" moment if there ever was one.

Over the next few days, I met with my staff and advisors to discuss whether I should withdraw from the election. I had been reelected with almost 70 percent of the vote in 2014 and 2016 and was favored to achieve a similar result in 2018 before the indictment. However, my advisors were realistic: with eleven felony charges against me, they believed my chances of reelection were zero. In the court of public opinion, "innocent until proven guilty" does not apply; voters think "Guilty until proven innocent." I decided not to run and announced my decision in a written statement on August 11, 2018.

I didn't fully understand New York election law. Since the primary had passed, there were only two ways to withdraw: death, which was not an option, or running for another office and withdrawing from the congressional race. While technically possible, the Democrats would fight this strategy tooth and nail, as they wanted to run against me, knowing I likely wouldn't win.

After a month of reflection, I regained my determination. When I returned to Buffalo after the indictment, I felt beaten. My world had collapsed; I was embarrassed, my family was humiliated, and I had let down my constituents. My reputation was in shambles. But I decided to fight back.

I called Chris Grant, my political advisor, and Michael Hook, my chief of staff, to tell them I was reentering the race. I said we needed a scorched-earth campaign. I would not win by being Mr. Nice Guy, and I would spend every dollar in my campaign account to secure victory. There was no tomorrow if I lost.

On September 19, 2018, I held a press conference to announce my decision to resume my reelection campaign.

Returning to Congress

Before returning to Congress on September 4, 2018, I emailed my Republican colleagues, explaining my situation and asserting my innocence. I informed them of my plans to run for reelection and win. They treated me as if nothing had happened. A few close friends expressed their support, inquiring about my well-being and offering help.

Paul Ryan called me to a meeting where he informed me that I would be stripped of my assignment on the Energy and Commerce Committee due to rules barring indicted members from serving on committees. I accepted my fate. Little did I know that the rule that Paul Ryan quoted didn't exist.

I covered that detail of my reelection campaign in another chapter but, suffice it to say: *I WON.* It was a narrow victory—less than one point—and we waited almost a week for it to be confirmed. But in politics, a win is a win, whether by thirty points or one point.

After the election, I returned to Congress on November 13, 2018. Many colleagues approached me, expecting me to be leaving. Their faces reflected surprise when I told them, "I won my reelection. I'll be back next Congress."

The 2018 midterms were disastrous for Paul Ryan and the Republicans. Democrats gained forty-one seats, and Nancy Pelosi became speaker. My win, despite eleven felony counts hanging over my head, was even more remarkable given the Republicans' poor performance overall.

I hoped to regain my seat on the Energy and Commerce Committee. My constituents reelected me despite the indictment, and they deserved full representation. Kevin McCarthy, seeking votes to become Republican leader, heard my case. I explained that Paul Ryan's rule barring indicted members from committees was fabricated. I pledged my support for McCarthy, hoping he'd restore my position.

McCarthy was elected minority leader, but instead of returning me to the EC&C Committee, he crafted a new rule explicitly preventing indicted members of Congress from serving on committees. I began my term in the 116th Congress without any committee assignment.

Life isn't fair, but no one ever said it would be.

Fighting the DOJ and SDNY

We pulled out all the stops. I knew I was fighting for my life and my son's life. We hired private investigators to interview everyone involved in any way with the prosecution's case. We needed firsthand information on the strength of the case against the three of us.

My defense cost $3,200,000. My son's defense cost $2,000,000. Steve's defense cost $800,000. I paid the legal bills for all three of us. Not many people can afford to spend over $6 million to fight the DOJ once they sink their teeth into you.

Over the six months following our indictment on August 8, 2018, we set our strategy. We were going to hit the SDNY on several fronts.

On February 8, 2019, we filed three motions with the court:

1. A Motion for a Bill of Particulars: We sought detailed information about:
    - All interstate wires the government intended to rely upon at trial.
    - Every act that took place in the Southern District of New York.
    - The scope of the charged conspiracy and personal benefits that flowed to the defendants.

2. A Motion to Compel the Government: This motion asked the court to order the Government to:
    - Review documents in the sole possession of the United States Securities and Exchange Commission (SEC) for possible Brady material.
    - Review, for Brady and Rule 16 material, documents obtained pursuant to search warrants that the government determined were non-responsive.
    - Produce, one year in advance of trial, the full notes of interviews with two witnesses.

3. A Motion Citing the Speech or Debate Clause: Relying on the constitutional Speech or Debate Clause, we sought an order directing the government to produce:
    - The complete contents of electronically stored information obtained via search warrants for personal accounts, and devices belonging to current and former congressional staffers.
    - Reports of statements made by staffers interviewed during the investigation.

On March 8, 2019, the Government filed a forty-two-page memorandum of law opposing our pretrial motions. The document strongly objected to our arguments, addressing each motion as follows:

- "The Defendants Are Not Entitled to a Bill of Particulars":
    - The government's voluntary disclosures rendered our motion unnecessary.
- "The Court Should Deny the Defendant's Disclosure Motion":
    - It argued against the applicability of Brady and Rule 16 to the requested materials.
- "Congressman Collins's Allegations of a Speech or Debate Violation Are Meritless":
    - It claimed the searches and interviews did not violate the constitutional protections afforded by the Speech or Debate Clause.

In conclusion, the government respectfully submitted that the court should deny our motions in their entirety.

On March 22, 2019, we filed a twenty-page memorandum of law in support of our motion for a bill of particulars. We argued that:

- Defendants are entitled to a specification of the wire(s) serving as the basis for Count Ten.
- The alleged acts occurring in the Southern District of New York must be detailed.
- The "others" referenced as part of the alleged conspiracy must be identified.
- The personal benefits expected from the alleged disclosure of material, non-public information must be clarified.

We concluded by requesting the court order the government to specify:

- Dates, times, senders, recipients, locations, and amounts related to the wire fraud alleged in Count Ten.
- Acts committed in furtherance of each count in the Southern District of New York.

- The identities of individuals whom Rep. Collins and his son anticipated disclosing material, non-public information to, as alleged in the indictment.

On April 2, 2019, the US House of Representatives, with Nancy Pelosi as speaker, filed an Amicus Curiae brief supporting our motion and addressing the Speech or Debate Clause scope and application. Key points included:

- The Justice Department's interpretation that the clause does not provide a privilege of non-disclosure is flawed.
- The clause broadly protects legislative materials, regardless of their location or storage method.
- Legislative independence is central to the separation of powers, and the clause must be interpreted to preserve it.

The House argued that compelled disclosure of documents poses the same constitutional problems as compelled testimony, citing Supreme Court rulings that broadly apply the clause's protections. The Justice Department's attempts to justify their searches and interviews—by claiming precautions were taken—were dismissed as insufficient. The privilege, they argued, belongs to the member of Congress, not third parties.

In conclusion, the House requested the court base its decision on established principles of the Speech or Debate Clause, as outlined in the brief.

The House of Representatives' Amicus Brief was devastating to Geoffrey Berman and the prosecutors at SDNY. They had been extremely careless in how they conducted interviews and seized cell phones and computers from my congressional staff. Their actions clearly violated my Speech or Debate rights.

Legal Proceedings Proceed

On May 1, 2019, Judge Broderick sent a letter to SDNY listing numerous issues he wanted them to address regarding our three motions. He also directed them to produce certain documents related to the motions.

On May 3 and May 10, 2019, Judge Broderick held oral arguments on our three motions. Our attorneys and the government presented their arguments for and against the motions.

On June 10, 2019, Judge Broderick ordered the government to provide answers to specific questions and produce certain documents, including materials governed by the Federal Rules of Criminal Procedure. Among these were the grand jury transcript related to the indictment.

On August 6, 2019, the government filed a superseding indictment with the court. This new indictment eliminated three counts of securities fraud originally filed against me regarding the sale of Innate stock by people not related to me in any way.

In the superseding indictment, I was charged with eight felony counts:

- Conspiracy to Commit Securities Fraud
- Four Counts of Securities Fraud
- Conspiracy to Commit Wire Fraud
- One Count of Wire Fraud
- One Count of Making a False Statement to Law Enforcement

On August 7, 2019, Judge Broderick held a telephone conference to discuss the implications of the superseding indictment on the pending motions. He directed both parties to submit their positions on how the new indictment affected the case.

On August 26, 2019, my attorneys submitted a "Statement of Defendants' Position Regarding the Superseding Indictment" (ECF No. 107). They argued that the superseding indictment did not impact the requested relief, specifically the disclosure of materials related to Brady material or the Speech or Debate Clause of the Constitution. They respectfully requested that the court grant the motions as a necessary step before substantive pre-trial motions.

The statement concluded that the government's opposition to the requested relief was an attempt to avoid disclosure. Without the requested information, the defendants would be unable to mount an adequate defense.

On September 3, 2019, the government submitted a letter responding to our August 26 submission. They expressed concerns that I might use interlocutory appeals to delay the trial, scheduled for February 3, 2020.

They disagreed with our position on appellate rights but emphasized their commitment to the trial date, even if it meant proceeding against only my son and Steve.

On September 6, 2019, my attorneys countered the government's letter. They highlighted that any delays stemmed from the government's actions, including their August 6 reversal on withholding grand jury materials. They also criticized the government's contradictory stance on judicial economy, arguing that their proposal for separate trials was inefficient and inconsistent.

On September 6, 2019, Judge Broderick issued an opinion on the pretrial motions but did not immediately file it publicly. He requested a joint letter from the parties by September 11, 2019, outlining any proposed redactions and their rationale. A hearing on the motions was scheduled for September 18, 2019.

On September 12, 2019, I pleaded not guilty to the charges in the superseding indictment. This indictment was modified to address concerns raised by my attorneys about violations of my Speech or Debate rights. Geoffrey Berman, the US Attorney for SDNY, stated that the changes aimed to prevent pretrial litigation delays.

My attorneys maintained that the Speech or Debate issues remained relevant and part of the case. On September 18, 2019, Judge Broderick ruled against our motions to compel the government to produce evidence supporting our Speech or Debate arguments. He also denied a motion requesting additional evidence that could prove our innocence, citing the precedent set in Brady v. Maryland (1963).

The trial was scheduled for February 3, 2020, as a joint trial involving myself, my son, and Steve. A hearing was held on September 19, 2019, to address the issues surrounding motions filed by my attorneys and Judge Broderick's denial of those motions. My attorneys were prepared to file an interlocutory appeal of Judge Broderick's ruling and informed him of this during the hearing. An interlocutory appeal is a request for an appellate court to review a specific legal matter within a case before the trial concludes.

As a member of Congress, I had unique rights regarding appeals related to the Constitution's Speech or Debate Clause. Judge Broderick and

US Attorney Geoffrey Berman were well aware that I had the right to appeal directly to the Supreme Court, which was obligated to hear such an appeal from a member of Congress. The appeal process concerning Judge Broderick's ruling on my attorney's motion involving Speech or Debate rights would likely delay my trial by at least two years.

The SDNY prosecutors, recognizing that the trial would be postponed for an extended period due to their flawed investigation and violations of my Speech or Debate rights, promptly moved to sever my case from the trial scheduled for February 3, 2020. They proposed proceeding with the trial of my son and Steve independently, deferring my trial to a much later date. Judge Broderick granted their motion.

I was confident that I would not be convicted at trial. I had not sold any stock in Innate Immunotherapeutics. When I called my son to share the negative trial results—a decision I deeply regret—I was unaware that his stock had been transferred from Australia to the United States. At the time of my call, the US stock market was closed, and a trading halt had been issued in Australia at 10:53 PM EST Thursday night. I went to bed that evening expecting NASDAQ to honor the trading halt, not anticipating that trading would proceed in the United States.

The false statement charge against me was, in my view, textbook entrapment. A judge would likely dismiss the charge as entrapment, and even if not, a jury would not have found me guilty of making a false statement to law enforcement. I had truthfully told the FBI that I did not share the negative trial results with my son to enable him to sell stock and avoid losses.

The FBI's conduct on the morning of my interview was unjustifiable. They arrived at my condo at 6:00 AM despite knowing I was represented by attorneys regarding my ownership in Innate Immunotherapeutics. They should not have questioned me without my attorneys present. In my opinion, their sole intent was to entrap me into making a false statement that could be used against me.

The FBI does not record interviews. Instead, one agent questions the individual while another takes notes on what they "think" is being said. This widely criticized practice is prone to abuse. It appeared to me that the agents had rehearsed their approach to entrap me. The FBI is also permitted to lie during interviews, further undermining the fairness of their process.

When the agents steered the conversation toward my son's selling Innate Immunotherapeutics stock on NASDAQ on June 23, 2017, I recognized their trap. NASDAQ's failure to honor the Australian trading halt was unbelievable. I told the agents to leave, asserting that I had nothing further to say and that they should not have been at my condo without my attorneys present.

The FBI's FD-302 report—a written summary of the interview—stated that I said, "I did not share the drug trial results with my son." Since the interview was not recorded, I had no definitive proof of what was said or not said. Moreover, the prosecution never provided the FD-302 report for my defense attorneys to review.

Concern for My Son

I was overwhelmed with frustration, anger, and concern for my son—concerns that proved to be justified. At the same time as my interview, six FBI agents were at my son's and his fiancée's townhouse in Asbury Park, NJ. They ultimately entrapped my son into making a false statement to law enforcement, just as they had done to me.

I was certain that my son and Steve would be convicted in a separate trial. While the evidence against them was circumstantial, it was compelling enough to lead a jury to find them guilty. My son faced numerous charges, including Conspiracy to Commit Securities Fraud, five counts of Securities Fraud, Conspiracy to Commit Wire Fraud, one count of Wire Fraud, and one count of Making a False Statement to Law Enforcement. If convicted on all charges, my son and Steve could have faced decades in prison.

I found myself with no viable options. To protect my son as much as possible, I instructed my attorneys to contact the SDNY prosecutors and offer to drop my interlocutory appeal in exchange for leniency for my son and Steve.

On September 20, 2019, we reached a plea agreement with SDNY. Under the agreement, SDNY would drop all but one charge against my son and Steve. They would plead guilty to one count of Conspiracy to Commit Securities Fraud. In return, I agreed to plead guilty to one count of Conspiracy to Commit Securities Fraud and one count of Making a

False Statement to Law Enforcement, and I would withdraw my interlocutory appeal.

The plea deal was signed by Geoffrey Berman, United States attorney, along with Assistant United States Attorneys Scott Hartman, Max Nicholas, and Damian Williams. It was approved by Jason Cowley, co-chief of the Securities and Commodities Fraud Task Force.

Geoffrey Berman's book confirms his tactics of pressuring me to plead guilty by using my son as leverage. The tactics employed by the SDNY in my case are a stark example of the abuses rampant within the DOJ, as identified in the recently published American Bar Association (ABA) Plea Bargain Task Force report.

To quote Geoffrey Berman's book, *Holding the Line*:

> "It can be a little complicated to try a sitting Member of Congress. The speech or debate clause in the Constitution gives lawmakers certain protections against having things they say or do during their official duties used against them in criminal or civil actions.
>
> "His lawyers invoked it in a filing with the court, claiming we swept up protected materials during our investigation. It could have delayed the matter for some time. He likely had the right to appeal all the way to the Supreme Court before we could try him.
>
> "Damian Williams was the lead prosecutor on the Collins case. He is brilliant, highly analytical, and, by nature, a consensus builder. With the Collins case potentially delayed by his lawyers' tactical invocation of congressional privilege, our team made a pivotal decision suggested by Damian to separate Collins from the case.
>
> "We informed the judge that we would like to proceed to trial with the other defendants. This would force Collins to make a choice: confront the evidence against him in court or bide his time on the sidelines while his son faced the music alone for a crime initiated by his father.
>
> "At the end of the day, the congressman could not stand to see his son face trial for something that was largely his fault and for his son to be convicted while he was still avoiding his day in court. Collins dropped his appeal, pleaded guilty late in 2019, and resigned from Congress.

Judge Broderick sentenced him to twenty-six months in federal prison and levied a fine of $200,000."

I was thrilled beyond words when President Trump fired Geoffrey Berman on June 18, 2020—a day of celebration in the Collins household.

I resigned from Congress on September 30, 2019, and stood in Judge Broderick's courtroom on October 1, 2019, along with my son and Steve, as we all pleaded guilty to the felony charges agreed to in the plea bargain with SDNY on September 20, 2019.

My Sentencing Date is Set

Judge Broderick set my sentencing for January 17, 2020. He set my son's sentencing for January 23, 2020, and Steve's for January 24, 2020.

We couldn't demand anything related to our ultimate sentencing, but at least the charges against all of us had been reduced. There is a reason that 98 percent of all criminal cases in the federal courts end with a plea "bargain." A recent report from the ABA refers to plea bargains as the primary way to resolve criminal cases, a practice that emphasizes efficiency over fairness and innocence.

A task force that included prosecutors, judges, defense attorneys, and academics cited "substantial evidence" that innocent people are coerced into guilty pleas because of the power prosecutors hold over them, including the prospect of decades-long mandatory minimum sentences and manipulation of family members.

"Trials have become rare artifacts in most US jurisdictions, and even nonexistent in others," the ABA Plea Bargain Task Force wrote in a report released on February 22, 2023. The task force worked for three years, collecting and reviewing testimony from experts in the field. The report noted that plea bargains are often the only option for defendants to deal with the excessive harshness of the modern American criminal system.

My Sentencing

I flew to New York City from Marco Island on January 16, 2020, for my sentencing the next day.

The prosecutors at SDNY had aggressively pushed for a fifty-seven-month prison sentence—the maximum term under the DOJ sentencing guidelines. Meanwhile, my attorneys advocated for home confinement and supervised release.

I knew prison time was inevitable. My attorneys informed me that the judge would most likely follow the recommendation of the independent Probation Department and sentence me to a year and a day.

This sentence, while seemingly minor, equates to nine months in prison when accounting for good-time credits. Sentences longer than one year qualify for these credits, enabling the possibility of serving less than the full term. Hence, the peculiar sentence of a year and a day.

With the First Step Act, signed into law during my time in Congress, inmates over the age of sixty would serve only two-thirds of their sentence in prison, with the remaining one-third in home confinement. Based on this provision, we believed my prison time would be just eight months. This was my mindset as I stood before Judge Broderick on January 17, 2020.

We submitted 137 letters from my family, friends, fellow Boy Scout leaders, business associates, constituents, and other Members of Congress, all pleading for leniency. Submitting letters for leniency is common practice, though the typical number ranges from three to ten. The submission of 137 letters was staggering and unprecedented. These letters were heartfelt, reflecting the breadth of my life's work. Reading them was humbling, like witnessing a preview of my eulogy.

Quotes from the 137 Letters

- "In my opinion, Chris' success with Nuttall Gear was nothing short of a miracle."
- "When Constellation Capital purchased Nuttall in 1997, employees split more than $3 million in proportion to their ESOP ownership."
- "Chris is a sincere and caring advocate for helping less fortunate individuals better their circumstances and improve their family's future."

- "Chris employed formerly incarcerated people and extended them personal loans to help them get back on their feet."
- "Chris told me he ran for Erie County Executive to secure a better future for the next generation."
- "Chris formed the Brighter Future Fund and donated his entire salary as County Executive to local non-profits."
- "For the first time in the United States, Chris implemented Lean Six Sigma in a large municipal government with remarkable results: a $250 million surplus."
- "His selfless dedication to Buffalo helped revitalize a dying city."
- "In February 2009, our community was devastated by the crash of Flight 3407. As County Executive, Chris managed the emergency response with compassion and humanity."
- "Chris' efforts to honor Vietnam Veterans are heartwarming. Many of these brave men never received a proper welcome or thanks for their service."
- "Chris drafted and sponsored the Firefighter Cancer Registry Act, enabling the CDC to study and track cancer among firefighters."
- "Chris Collins was the only government official to help my family. He reached out when no one else would."
- "Chris brought the same humility, humanity, and commitment to Congress that he demonstrated throughout his professional life."
- "Chris is an Eagle Scout who has always supported Scouting with his time, talent, and money."
- "Chris' selfless acts and desire to serve have made a lasting impact at every level."
- "My friend was on the verge of losing her home to foreclosure. Chris intervened, purchased her mortgage, and allowed her to remain in her home."
- "Chris didn't know me, but when he learned I was having twin babies and couldn't afford cribs, he bought cribs and bedroom furniture without seeking recognition."

- "The best measure of Chris' character is that his family and friends have remained steadfast in their love and support despite how easy it would have been to walk away."

The Unusual Sentencing

It is highly uncommon for a federal judge to disregard the independent Probation Department's sentencing recommendation. It is also unusual for a judge to weigh factors unrelated to the crime. However, during my sentencing, Judge Broderick emphasized that my status as a member of Congress significantly influenced his decision. He pointed out that my initial not-guilty plea, and subsequent re-election, left my constituents in NY-27 without representation between my guilty plea and the special election to fill my seat.

These considerations shaped a decision that felt both extraordinarily biased and personal.

As Judge Broderick spoke, my attorneys' faces were etched with deep concern. It became increasingly clear that Judge Broderick was likely to ignore the Probation Department's recommendation of a year and a day.

The Department of Justice (DOJ) Guideline Provisions for my sentence were forty-six to fifty-seven months, a maximum of three years of supervised release, and a fine ranging from $20,000 to $200,000. These guidelines were based on the twenty-three points calculated by the Probation Department.

My base level offense was calculated at eight points for one count of conspiracy to commit securities fraud. The guidelines added fourteen points because the total amount of avoided losses, attributed to my son and others selling Innate Immunotherapeutics stock, slightly exceeded $550,000. An additional two points were added for breach of fiduciary duty, and two more for making a false statement. These adjustments brought the total to twenty-six points. However, since I had accepted responsibility, three points were subtracted, resulting in a guideline calculation of twenty-three points.

With no prior criminal history, I fell into Category I on the sentencing table. A base level offense of eight points corresponded to a sentencing range of zero to six months of imprisonment. However, the addition of fifteen points raised the sentencing range to forty-six to fifty-seven months. The thought of spending over four years in prison, based on a single six-minute phone call after living an exemplary life, was overwhelming.

The Probation Department conducts extensive research when making sentencing recommendations to judges. While they are not bound by the sentencing guidelines, these guidelines often influence their recommendations. My exemplary life was considered during their evaluation. I had not personally sold any stock and had spent eleven years in public service as Erie County executive and a member of Congress. Additionally, I had held numerous volunteer roles, including significant contributions to the Boy Scouts of America, and had mentored and advised over one hundred small business owners through the Center for Entrepreneurial Leadership at the State University of New York at Buffalo (UB).

Taking all of this into account, the Probation Department recommended a significant reduction from the guideline range of forty-six to fifty-seven months. Their Pre-Sentence Report (PSR) recommended the following to Judge Broderick:

- Imprisonment of a year and a day
- One year of supervised release following incarceration
- A $200,000 fine

When I stood before Judge Broderick, my primary goal was to plead for leniency in my son's sentencing, scheduled for January 23, 2020. Overcome with emotion, I took full responsibility for the events that followed my fateful call to my son on June 22, 2017. I apologized to Mary for the trauma I had caused our family. Though not present in the courtroom, I also apologized to my son for the situation I had placed him in and for the lasting impact of a felony conviction on his life.

Ex-New York congressman Chris Collins sentenced
to 26 months for insider-trading tip to son

Judge Vernon Broderick, appointed by President Barack Obama, ultimately sentenced me to twenty-six months of imprisonment, one year of supervised release, and a $200,000 fine. He recommended that I serve my sentence at the Federal Prison Camp in Pensacola, Florida, with a report date of March 17, 2020.

My attorneys had prepared me for a sentence of up to four years, though they considered it unlikely. After the sentencing, they speculated that Judge Broderick had initially intended to impose a thirty-six-month sentence but reduced it by ten months after hearing my plea for leniency for my son. A twenty-six-month sentence was unusual and seemed to reflect the judge's emotional response to my statement.

Following the sentencing on January 17, 2020, I returned to Marco Island, Florida, the next day in a state of mental turmoil. The prospect of going to prison was daunting, and I was sick with worry about my son's impending sentencing.

Practically every news outlet covered the story of my sentencing. Public opinion was divided. Many comments suggested that the sentence was fair, likely influenced by reports emphasizing the potential forty-six to fifty-seven-month range. Few acknowledged the independent recommendation of the Probation Department, which had suggested a significantly lighter sentence of a year and a day.

Meanwhile, the "Collins Haters" reacted vehemently. They inundated news outlets with comments expressing outrage that my sentence was too lenient. Some demanded the maximum fifty-seven months, though they knew such a sentence was unlikely. For them, even twenty-six months seemed insufficient.

In the midst of this storm, I faced the difficult reality of preparing for prison while grappling with the consequences of my actions and the impact on those closest to me.

My Son's Sentencing

The prosecutors at the Southern District of New York (SDNY) wanted blood. It wasn't enough that they had pressured a guilty plea out of me; they wanted more. Judge Broderick had already demonstrated a willingness to ignore judicial norms when he sentenced me to twenty-six months in prison, even though the unbiased, independent US Probation Department for SDNY had recommended, after an extensive investigation of the facts, a sentence of only a year and a day.

I knew the prosecutors at SDNY were very upset with the recommendations of the Probation Department. I knew they would aggressively push for my son to be sentenced to significant time in prison. They understood that sending him to prison would have a devastating impact on me, and that would be the "frosting on the cake" of their successful persecution—or prosecution—of me. They didn't care at all about the impact incarceration would have on my son. The thought of his going to prison was too much for me to wrap my mind around.

The US Probation Department had recommended a sentence of six months in prison for my son. The DOJ sentencing guidelines listed thirty-seven to forty-six months as the maximum prison term for him. Judge Broderick had completely ignored the Probation Department's recommendation for my sentence, and I didn't expect him to treat my son any differently.

The DOJ wanted me to serve the maximum time listed in the guidelines, and they wanted the maximum for my son as well—forty-six months in prison.

I was "optimistic," to use the term loosely, that the maximum prison sentence my son would face would be less than my sentence. I hoped for a sentence close to the Probation Department's recommendation of six months. I was all but certain my son would join me at the Pensacola Prison Camp for some period of time. At least we would be together.

Mary stayed in New York City with my daughter as she awaited our son's sentencing hearing on January 23, 2020. My son and his fiancée stayed at his townhouse in Asbury Park, NJ.

We had all decided that I would not attend my son's sentencing hearing. My presence in the courtroom would be a negative influence, and we certainly didn't want that.

My son stood in front of Judge Broderick, expecting the worst but hoping for the best. Mary was an emotional wreck. She knew I would survive my time in a prison camp but couldn't fathom the impact that prison would have on her son. She cried hysterically every night at the thought of his going to prison.

The prosecutors were arrogant, confident, and cocky when they addressed Judge Broderick. They knew he would not sentence my son to the forty-six months in prison they wanted, given that I had been sentenced to "only" twenty-six months. They pushed for twenty-four months as they addressed Judge Broderick. Mary wanted to jump over the railing and punch the arrogant bastards in the face. She didn't, although she does hope that someday they will face some form of comeuppance for their indefensible persecution of me and my son.

Judge Broderick shocked everyone in the courtroom when he sentenced my son to five years of probation, six months of home confinement, 500 hours of community service, and a fine of $150,000. *No jail time.* The prosecutors looked as if they had been run over by a bus. The relief for Mary, my son, and his fiancée was beyond description.

The judge addressed the courtroom and said, "I decline to adhere to the idiom that the sins of the father are visited upon the son," paraphrasing a passage from the Book of Exodus in the Bible. When I was sentenced, I had told the judge that I had made a "stupid, tragic, rash, inexcusable decision" to share the negative results of the Innate Immunotherapeutics clinical trial before they were released to the public. My plea to Judge Broderick on January 17 was to hold me solely responsible for the entire nightmare that followed my phone call to my son on that fateful night in June 2017. I asked him to "save your mercy for my son." He obviously listened to me, threw the book at me, and felt that was enough to justify no prison time for my son.

One of the prosecutors flippantly addressed Judge Broderick about my son, in an almost demanding tone, urging the judge to send him to prison for twenty-four months. Judge Broderick responded to the young, arrogant prosecutor and said, "Show me where any other twenty-four-year-old has ever been charged criminally as opposed to just a civil disposition."

Wow. Judge Broderick had summed up the undeniably unethical strategy used by Geoffrey Berman and the prosecutors at SDNY. They indicted my son for only one reason—to pressure me as my case moved forward.

My son was their "ace in the hole" to coerce me into pleading guilty if that became necessary.

The prosecutor was caught completely off guard by Judge Broderick's question and tone. He didn't answer, likely because the judge's tone indicated he wasn't looking for a response. He was chastising the prosecutor for his indefensible position and attitude.

It's hard for any parent to celebrate the sentencing of their remarkable son, convicted of a felony that will hang over him for the rest of his life, but we celebrated with the biggest smiles on our faces you could imagine.

Judge Broderick had redeemed himself, ever so slightly, by sentencing my son to five years of supervised release and probation.

When Mary called me with the great news, I was so relieved I couldn't think straight and had to ask her to repeat herself. I sat down and cried uncontrollably.

Steve's Sentencing

The day after my son's sentencing, Steve was sentenced by Judge Broderick. That event was somewhat anticlimactic, but after my sentencing and my son's, we felt fairly confident that Steve would be given leniency by Judge Broderick.

Steve was sentenced to four years of probation with four months of home confinement and 250 hours of community service. He was not hit with a fine.

CHAPTER 28

Federal Prison Camp

AFTER BEING SENTENCED, AND WAITING to go to prison on March 17, I spent my days sitting outside on the lanai by our Marco Island pool, smoking cigars, and solving Sudoku and Kakuro puzzles. Kakuro, a math puzzle, is like Sudoku but more complex. I rode my bike around Marco Island, trying to distract myself from thoughts about the prison camp.

With the First Step Act passed by Congress and signed into law by President Trump, I estimated serving about sixteen months at FPC Pensacola. This included a reduction of over eight and a half months under the First Step Act and an additional month for good behavior and work credits. Despite this, I was consumed by stress and anxiety about being away from my family for so long.

Mary, my son, and his fiancée returned to Marco Island on January 28, 2020. Judge Broderick allowed my son some flexibility in starting his six months of home confinement, enabling him to plan around my March 17 reporting date to FPC Pensacola.

My son and his fiancée got married on February 3, 2020 in a civil ceremony at the Naples, Florida courthouse, officiated by the county clerk, with Mary and me as witnesses. To celebrate, we dined at the JW Marriott Hotel.

My son began his home confinement on February 10, 2020. He was fitted with an ankle bracelet, and the Probation Department installed monitoring equipment in our Marco Island home. This marked a stark new chapter for us, a "guess what, now what" moment.

In preparation for prison, I researched federal prison conditions and restrictions. Discovering contact lenses weren't allowed, I sought an alternative since I had worn contacts since age thirteen. LASIK surgery was ruled out due to my age, so I opted for cataract surgery, which gave me 20/20 vision without contacts. It was one of the best decisions I've ever made.

Knowing prisons lacked adequate dental care, I visited a dentist for a thorough check-up. Two problematic teeth were extracted to avoid issues during incarceration. I planned to get implants after my release, but didn't disclose this to the dentist.

COVID-19 Delays

On February 28, 2020, my attorneys filed a motion with Judge Broderick to delay my report date, as I had not yet been designated to a facility. The motion was granted, postponing my report date to April 21, 2020.

My daughter and her boyfriend visited Marco Island on March 4, 2020, just before my scheduled report date. A week later, COVID-19 drastically changed our lives. On March 11, the World Health Organization declared COVID-19 a pandemic. Governors in New York and Florida declared states of emergency, and President Trump declared a national emergency on March 13.

Lamplighter Drive home in Marco Island.

With stay-at-home orders in place, our household grew to include my daughter, her boyfriend, my son, his wife, their two dogs, and our cat. Our five-bedroom, five-bathroom home accommodated everyone comfortably.

On April 1, 2020, my attorneys filed another motion, citing the escalating pandemic and my high-risk status due to age and underlying health conditions. They referenced the CDC's warnings and a revised Pre-Sentence Report highlighting the dangers of incarceration during the pandemic. The prosecution did not object, and the report date was extended to June 23, 2020.

The pandemic worsened throughout 2020. My attorneys filed another motion on May 28, 2020, requesting an extension to August 18, 2020, due to surging COVID-19 cases and deaths worldwide. The motion was granted without objection.

CARES Act

On March 27, 2020, Congress passed, and the president signed into law, the CARES Act (Coronavirus Aid, Relief, and Economic Security Act). This legislation expanded the authority of the attorney general and the Bureau of Prisons (BOP) director to release prisoners to home confinement. It also encouraged the release of eligible individuals under the Elderly Home Confinement Program, which was established through the Second Chance Act.

On the same day, Attorney General William Barr issued a memorandum directing the BOP to prioritize home confinement for inmates who met specific criteria: (a) those at risk due to health problems, (b) individuals convicted of non-violent offenses, and (c) inmates posing a minimal likelihood of recidivism. The conclusion was clear: certain inmates would be safer at home than in BOP facilities.

On March 30, 2020, Congressman Jerold Nadler, chairman of the House Judiciary Committee, sent a letter to Attorney General Barr outlining Congress's concerns regarding COVID-19. He emphasized the importance of the CARES Act and referenced the first death of a federal inmate due to COVID-19, stressing the urgency of preventing further avoidable deaths.

Chairman Nadler reminded Attorney General Barr that the DOJ and BOP had the authority to modify sentences and release medically compromised and elderly prisoners under their custody. Congress expressed its concern that elderly prisoners were at significant risk of dying from COVID-19 and urged proactive measures to mitigate this risk when appropriate.

The CARES Act mandated that the BOP "place elderly prisoners with lower risk levels and lower needs in home confinement for the maximum amount of time."

On April 3, 2020, Attorney General Barr directed the BOP to "immediately maximize appropriate transfers."

Request to Transfer to Home Confinement

On June 16, 2020, my attorneys filed an Administrative Remedy Request with Warden Joseph at FPC Pensacola. They asked him to use his authority under the CARES Act and Attorney General Barr's directive to transfer me to home confinement due to the COVID-19 pandemic. Alternatively, they requested that the BOP file a motion with Judge Broderick to reduce my sentence to time served and impose home confinement.

My attorneys emphasized that my age (seventy) and pre-existing medical conditions, including asthma, hypertension (high blood pressure), and hyperlipidemia (high cholesterol), placed me at a high risk of severe illness or death if incarcerated at FPC Pensacola.

On June 19, 2020, Warden Joseph denied my request, stating that I was not yet in BOP custody. He failed to address the merits of my request, even though I had been under the control of the BOP and DOJ since my sentencing on January 17, 2020.

On July 7, 2020, my attorneys filed a Level II appeal with the regional director of the BOP Southeast Regional Office. After forty-five days passed without a response, the appeal was deemed denied.

On August 1, 2020, another motion was filed to extend my report date to October 13, 2020. With no objection from the SDNY prosecutors, Judge Broderick granted the motion.

On August 21, 2020, my attorneys filed a Level III appeal with the National Inmate Appeals Administrator in Washington, DC. Despite follow-ups on September 21, 2020, no response was received.

Continued Stress and Uncertainty

During this time, my son served six months of home confinement and completed 500 hours of community service from February through August 2020. While on home confinement, individuals are permitted to work or perform community service. My son volunteered at the YMCA in Marco Island, FL, and Shy Wolf Sanctuary in Naples, FL. Despite the YMCA being closed to the public, they welcomed my son for maintenance and computer system assistance.

Ironically, while others were confined to their homes, my son was able to spend eight hours a day performing community service, even while serving a sentence of home confinement. He completed over three years of probation—60 percent of his sentence—and was released early from probation on May 19, 2023. He regained his passport and the freedom to travel without restrictions. My son and his wife welcomed a baby boy on June 8, 2023, a joyous reminder of the importance of family.

In contrast, I spent this time in limbo. Smoking cigars, solving Sudoku and Kakuro puzzles, riding my bicycle, and reading a new book daily could not alleviate my anxiety. Weekly trips to the library to borrow books became my routine, but the uncertainty about my future persisted. Despite repeated delays in my report date to FPC Pensacola, I received no credit toward my sentence for the time spent waiting. I was stuck in purgatory, desperate to begin my sentence so the clock could start ticking toward my release.

As October 13, 2020, approached, the risks and uncertainties related to COVID-19 remained unchanged. With no vaccine and limited treatment options, prisons continued to pose significant dangers for elderly individuals with underlying health conditions like mine.

Resistance to Delays

The SDNY prosecutors opposed my attorneys' request to extend my report date to December 8, 2020, despite the ongoing pandemic. Their stance was perplexing, given the unchanged risks to someone of my age and health. They claimed that FPC Pensacola was safer for me than Marco Island, citing no reported COVID-19 cases among inmates at the facility. This position contradicted the DOJ's official stance that federal prisons were unsafe, especially for elderly inmates with pre-existing conditions.

On October 1, 2020, my attorneys filed an Emergency Motion with Judge Broderick to delay my report date to December 8, 2020, or to modify my sentence to home confinement per Attorney General Barr's directives. Repeated calls to Judge Broderick and his staff went unanswered.

I feared contracting COVID-19 if forced to report to FPC Pensacola. The indifference shown by the SDNY prosecutors and Judge Broderick felt like a game of Russian roulette with my life. Rumors of a potential presidential pardon seemed to fuel their insistence that I serve jail time, regardless of the risks.

Reporting to FPC Pensacola

With no ruling on the Emergency Motion, I had no choice but to prepare for my report date. On October 12, I made the nine-hour drive to Pensacola, hoping for a last-minute reprieve that never came. After a sleepless night, I turned in my rental car, called an Uber, and made my way to FPC Pensacola. My only contact with loved ones would be through phone calls and letters, as visitation was suspended due to COVID-19.

Unbeknownst to me, I would be unable to contact my family for three weeks. Restricted movement within the camp, limited phone access, and a closed library added to the isolation. This was my reality as I began serving my sentence in a federal prison camp amidst a global pandemic.

Quarantine

The Uber driver dropped me off at the guardhouse. FPC Pensacola is located at Saufley Field, a naval base. It's not unusual for a prison camp to be situated at a US military installation. Inmates at minimum-security prisons often provide "cheap labor" for landscaping and other maintenance tasks.

A corrections officer (CO) met me at the guardhouse to escort me into the prison facility. There are no fences or barricades at FPC Pensacola. The COs don't carry guns, and there aren't any prison cells. The camp includes four dormitories, an administration building, commissary, food service building, woodworking shop, laundry, library, chapel, visitor's center, and medical facility.

I was processed in an area designated for new arrivals. Everyone was pleasant and polite. While I didn't feel comfortable, I didn't experience any apprehension or anxiety either. In fact, I felt a small sense of relief to finally begin my sentence. The clock was ticking, and in approximately eighteen months, I'd be heading home.

After changing into prison-issued khaki pants and a green shirt, I was given a pair of uncomfortable work boots. My street clothes and shoes were boxed up to be sent home. I underwent a COVID test and a general health physical as part of the intake process.

I had brought cash to deposit into my commissary account. Waiting for someone at home to wire money could delay access to funds for a week or more. I deposited $2,000 into my account. My inmate number was 86014-054.

I also brought my Maui Jim sunglasses, necessary for my recovery from cataract surgery. Although this raised some eyebrows, I was allowed to keep them. Additionally, I had my prescribed medications for hypertension, hyperlipidemia, and asthma, along with supporting documentation from my doctor. These were placed in my file, and I was informed that the camp would prescribe medications as needed once my supply ran out.

The three books I brought were not allowed and were added to the box containing my clothes to be sent home.

I spent about three hours sitting in the processing room, uncertain of what was happening. Finally, a CO opened the door, escorted me outside, and directed me to a van. Another inmate, Jorge Garcia, was already inside. When I asked where we were going, the CO informed me that Jorge and I were being transported to Federal Correctional Institution (FCI) Marianna for fourteen days of quarantine.

This news left me concerned and confused. I had been told there was a quarantine dormitory at FPC Pensacola for new arrivals, a fact confirmed in writing by the Bureau of Prisons (BOP) to my attorneys. That turned out to be false.

Other promises from the BOP were also untrue. They had stated in writing that inmates at FPC Pensacola had access to email and telephones for social calls. In reality, the computers for email were located in the library, which was closed due to COVID, and access to phones was sporadic at best.

The biggest misrepresentation was that there would be no lockdown and that inmates would have access to the library, recreation, and programming. In fact, FPC Pensacola was in full lockdown. The library was closed, there was no recreation, and programming was unavailable. Inmates were restricted to their dormitories twenty-four/seven, except for those assigned to work details. Recreational opportunities were limited to walking in circles around the baseball field for one hour.

FCI Marianna

I discovered all of this later. For now, Jorge and I were on our way to FCI Marianna for quarantine. After a two-hour drive, we were dropped off at the front guardhouse. Unlike FPC Pensacola, FCI Marianna had tall fences topped with barbed wire. This was a "real" prison. I learned that FCI Marianna is a medium-security prison housing violent felons in two-person cells. It also served as the quarantine facility for new arrivals to FPC Pensacola.

A lieutenant escorted Jorge and me to processing. He acknowledged he knew my background as a former member of Congress but assured me that this information was not being shared with the guards. Only he and the warden were aware of my prior position.

During processing, we exchanged our khaki pants and green shirts for orange jumpsuits, and our black work boots for orange sandals. We were handcuffed and led to the Special Housing Unit (SHU), a section of the prison used to punish inmates for bad behavior, and also used to quarantine new arrivals to the Pensacola prison camp. I was stunned—what was happening?

The SHU consisted of a hallway lined with about twelve cells on either side and two floors of cells, totaling approximately forty-eight. It was immediately clear that this was a grim place.

Jorge and I were kept together and escorted into a small eight by twelve concrete cell. The walls were painted white, and the room contained a bunk bed, a metal toilet and sink, and a small metal table bolted to the wall. The door had a narrow slit for food trays and a three-inch glass window. Another small, frosted window, about five inches wide, was located on the back wall.

Despite his bad hip, Jorge was assigned the top bunk since he was younger than me. The reality of our situation began to sink in: this was going to be an incredibly challenging experience.

Daily Diary in the SHU

The schedule was structured and monotonous. A razor was provided for shaving on Mondays, Wednesdays, and Fridays. Showers were available on Tuesdays, Thursdays, and Sundays. Outdoor recreation, limited to one hour, was scheduled for Mondays, Wednesdays, and Fridays. Inside the cell, activities were scarce: talking, exercising, and reading (if a book was available) were the only options. There was no television. Lights were turned on at 6:00 AM and off at 10:00 PM. Meals followed a strict timetable: breakfast at 6:45 AM, lunch at 10:45 AM, and dinner at 4:30 PM.

Day One: Tuesday, Oct. 13

Jorge and I arrived at Marianna. After processing, we were led to our assigned cell around 4:30 PM. Dinner was served shortly after we settled in. The correctional officer (CO) pushed a cart down the hallway, stopping at each cell to deliver food in a clamshell through a slot in the metal door. Sleep was elusive. I felt trapped in a nightmare, unsure of how I had ended up in this situation.

Day Two: Wednesday, Oct. 14

The cell was cold, and the bunk bed was uncomfortable, lacking even a pillow. Throughout the night, guards shined lights through the glass slot in the door four times to check for escapees. Lights came on at 6:00 AM. Breakfast consisted of bran flakes, powdered milk (no sugar), an apple, a donut stick, and a packet of instant coffee—also without sugar. Hot water was obtained from the sink.

At 9:00 AM, we were taken outside for one hour to a fenced area resembling a narrow basketball court, approximately eight feet wide and sixty feet long. Jorge and I were alone in our pen, while four other fenced areas each housed two inmates. We conversed with other inmates, who revealed they had been in Marianna quarantine for twenty-two days. At 10:00 AM, I was taken to see the nurse, handcuffed for the visit. She checked my blood pressure but wasn't wearing a mask.

Lunch at 10:45 AM included a hamburger, an apple, fries, and water. Dinner at 4:30 PM was pizza and salad. At 5:00 PM, a guard delivered a single-use razor for shaving and collected it two hours later. We learned that a "book lady" pushed around a cart of books on Saturdays. Lights went out at 10:00 PM.

Day Three: Thursday, Oct. 15

Breakfast was the same as the previous day, but without the apple. I felt deeply sad, missing Mary, our cat Mia, bike rides, my son and his wife, my daughter and her boyfriend. I longed for Dunkin' Donuts coffee. Anger welled up inside me at the Department of Justice (DOJ), the Southern District of New York (SDNY), and Judge Broderick for my imprisonment and the false promises about Pensacola.

At 9:30 AM, I had a private shower and received clean boxers, a t-shirt, and socks. At 10:15 AM, I requested a book and was given a Bible. A Sudoku puzzle and a news brief were later delivered to the cell. Lunch at 10:45 AM was surprisingly good: BBQ chicken, mashed potatoes, a cookie, bread, and an apple. At 2:00 PM, a kind guard provided a PIN number needed to make a phone call, but we lacked an approved phone list. Dinner at 4:30 PM was a hard-boiled egg, salad, and bread.

Day Four: Friday, Oct. 16

Breakfast remained unchanged. At 9:00 AM, we were taken outside to the fenced area. I had a long conversation with a friendly guard who had previously delivered the Sudoku puzzle. I recommended he try Kakuro puzzles. Lunch was a fish sandwich and an apple. At 2:00 PM, a nurse checked my temperature. When I inquired about phone access, she explained that we still didn't have a phone list from Pensacola. She suggested submitting a request to the Trust Fund for permission to make at least one call home. The razor was delivered again. Dinner was lasagna, which was quite good.

Days Five to Twenty-Two

Life blurred into a monotonous routine, locked in the cell twenty-four/seven except for occasional showers or one-hour outdoor walks in the fenced area. The food was consistently subpar.

Day Twenty-Three: Wednesday, Nov. 4

Finally, we were headed to Pensacola. We turned in our jumpsuits and changed into our Pensacola clothes. At 10:30 AM, the bus arrived, and by 12:30 PM, we reached our destination.

FPC Pensacola

On November 4, 2020, the bus from FCI Marianna arrived at FPC Pensacola at 12:30 PM. There were six of us on board. Although we had been together in the SHU at Marianna, we had not interacted with each other. Each of us had a cellmate, but we were locked in our individual eight by twelve concrete bunkers twenty-four/seven.

- Jorge Garcia—My cellmate
- Edward Newton
- Gregory Parker
- Shane Conrad
- Randy Thomley

Ed Newton, a towering six-feet eight-inches tall, was nicknamed "520" because he humorously measured five-feet twenty-inches tall. He had been assigned a top bunk shorter than his height, leaving his feet to dangle almost a foot off the bed.

We were all relieved to be going "home." It's amusing that we referred to FPC Pensacola as home, but compared to the medium-security SHU at FCI Marianna, the Pensacola camp felt like a JW Marriott.

Processing at FPC Pensacola

Upon arrival, we were processed through the intake center and issued extra clothing, two bed sheets, a pillow, three towels, two blankets, two laundry bags, and a thin cloth mask for COVID protection. Before leaving, a correctional officer (CO) sternly reminded us that cell phones were prohibited in federal prisons. Using one at FPC Pensacola would result in removal to a higher-security facility. Hearing that, I couldn't imagine anyone risking it.

Life in A-Dorm

We were escorted to A-Dorm, one of four dormitories at FPC Pensacola. A-Dorm is a single-story building with two wings, each housing approximately sixteen cubicles. Each cubicle contained six or seven bunk beds. Due to the COVID-19 pandemic, the camp's occupancy was reduced from about 700 inmates to around 325. A-Dorm housed roughly one hundred inmates at that time.

The bunk beds were sparsely occupied—one inmate per lower bunk, with the upper bunks left empty—as part of the BOP's supposed social distancing measures. The effort seemed laughable, given the communal setting. Inside the dorm, inmates rarely wore masks, even in the TV room, where forty chairs were arranged closely. If anyone wore a mask, it usually didn't cover their nose.

When we entered the dorm, a group of inmates gathered in the lobby area to see who was arriving. Someone recognized me and shouted, "that's Congressman Collins!" Word had evidently spread that I would be serving my time in Pensacola.

Settling In

Jorge Garcia and I were assigned bunk beds in the first cubicle on the left side of the aisle. I was relieved we'd remain together after sharing a cell for three weeks in the SHU. We had bonded for life during that time.

One wing of A-Dorm was predominantly Puerto Rican, while our wing was a mix—approximately one-third Mexican, one-third White, and one-third Black. Each inmate was assigned a small locker for personal items and a numbered plastic chair corresponding to their bunk.

As I settled into my new surroundings, an inmate named Juan Almeida approached and introduced himself. He was assigned to the last cubicle on the left side of the aisle and invited me to join what he called the "power cubicle." Juan was something of a celebrity at the camp, known for being the subject of the 2018 Netflix documentary *Operation Odessa*. The film depicted his attempt, along with a Russian mobster and a Cuban spy, to sell a Russian nuclear submarine to a Colombian drug cartel.

I was initially overwhelmed and hesitant, pointing out that I was already assigned to cubicle number one and couldn't simply move. Juan assured me he'd get approval from the unit manager. I reluctantly agreed.

Daily Routine

At 4:30 PM, inmates gathered near the lobby. Due to COVID restrictions, we were confined to our dorms except for mandatory work assignments. The cafeteria was closed except for meal pickups. Wearing gray sweatpants and gray T-shirts, we lined up to collect our meals in Styrofoam clamshells. Masks were worn only as a performance—a show for passing vehicles to create the illusion of compliance with COVID protocols. Inside the dorm, masks were mostly ignored.

After dinner, Juan reiterated his invitation to join his cubicle, introducing me to his cellmates.

Inmates in Juan's Cubicle:

- Brian Day
- Marc Levene
- Beto Carrejo
- Jeff Grospitch
- Tony Bell
- Ed Gire

Though all the lower bunks were occupied, Ed Gire offered to move to an upper bunk to accommodate me. I declined, saying I'd be fine on an upper bunk if my transfer was approved.

After dinner, inmates congregated in a circle in Juan's cubicle to chat. Snacks like cookies and potato chips were passed around, along with soda purchased from the commissary. Commissary orders were submitted using forms dropped in a lobby basket. The orders were filled and delivered the following day.

Juan's cubicle turned out to be the "power cubicle" of our wing. It became evident that he controlled who could join the group's nightly discussions. Meanwhile, the Puerto Rican inmates in the other wing had their own power structure.

Lights Out

By 8:30 PM, everyone returned to their cubicles for the 9:00 PM headcount. Two guards conducted the count, verifying each cubicle's occupants. Talking was strictly prohibited during the count. Afterward, we were free to move around the dorm until lights out at 10:00 PM. Some inmates used headlamps to read after lights out, while others played dominoes in the lobby.

Life at FPC Pensacola was certainly different, but for now, it was home.

I was surprised to see Puerto Rican inmates stationed near various entrances to our dorm. They appeared to be watching for someone or something. It turned out they were keeping watch for COs (correctional officers) who might sneak into the dorm to catch someone using a cell phone, which happened occasionally. When a guard did sneak in—or, on at least one occasion, when multiple guards burst into the dorm simultaneously—the Puerto Rican inmates would shout a loud warning in Spanish. This allowed inmates using cell phones to quickly ditch them or, in the worst-case scenario, throw the phones onto the floor. If a CO found a phone on the floor, they couldn't determine the owner. By the time the CO had the phone in their hand, it was locked.

On one occasion, the "guard" inmate failed to notice a CO entering the dorm, and no warning was shouted. The CO managed to grab a cell phone out of an inmate's hand before it locked and kept pressing the screen to prevent it from locking. The camp administration was able to compile a log of all the calls made on that phone, including the numbers involved.

Since the phone had been passed among at least twelve different users, multiple inmates' phone records were assessed.

The next day, a procession of inmates was escorted out of FPC Pensacola and taken to County Jail for processing. The entire camp watched in dismay as friends were led away.

Inmates from B-Dorm and C-Dorm, who traveled off the camp for work assignments, were able to smuggle cell phones and other contraband back to camp. Those working at Eglin Air Force Base had cell phones strategically hidden for use during work hours.

You can't blame someone for wanting to stay in touch with family. By the time I arrived at the camp, visitation had been suspended for over nine months. Inmates were restricted to two five-minute calls per week. Often, they didn't know when they'd be taken for phone calls, which meant that many times no one was home to answer. Using forbidden cell phones was the only reliable way for inmates to stay connected with their families.

Life In Camp

On Thursday, November 5, the lights came on at 6:00 AM. Inmates came and went from the bathrooms near the lobby area. The bathrooms had several sinks in a row and six private shower stalls with curtains. Breakfast lineup was at 7:00 AM.

Breakfast was always bran cereal, a carton of milk, and a banana or apple. The milk was often spoiled. After collecting breakfast, we returned to the dorm to eat.

Everyone in A-Dorm worked within the camp. Inmates from B-Dorm and C-Dorm worked at Eglin Air Force Base or UNICOR, the federal prison factory. They gathered for buses to transport them to work assignments Monday through Friday at 5:30 AM, with breakfast at 4:30 AM.

The inmates assigned to Eglin had a ninety-minute bus ride covering seventy-four miles from FPC Pensacola to the base. They handled landscaping and operated heavy equipment and lawnmowers. Those working at UNICOR traveled a shorter distance and worked in a laundry facility.

A-Dorm inmates had various camp jobs, including food service, laundry, woodshop, commissary, business office, naval base ground maintenance, and mechanical services (HVAC, electricians, plumbers, mechanics, welders, painters, carpenters, roofers).

Inmates were paid between fifteen cents and forty-five cents per hour. A forty-hour work week earned roughly six dollars to spend at the commissary.

On Thursday, my second day at camp, I completed admission and orientation (A/O). I met with the unit manager, unit counselor, and case worker for A-Dorm. They explained the camp's rules and regulations. The unit counselor approved me to move into Cubicle number six with Juan Almeida. I moved my belongings and took the upper bunk over Ed Gire. Though I was sad to leave Jorge in Cubicle number one, he was happy to stay there.

Everything at the camp had been upended due to the COVID-19 pandemic. Visitation, recreation, and education were all suspended. The library was closed, and there was no computer access for email. Phones were in a separate building and could only be accessed twice a week with an escort for a five-minute call. When not working, inmates were confined to their dorms twenty-four/seven.

There was effectively no dress code during COVID. Beds didn't have to be made, and cubicles weren't required to be neat. Masks weren't required inside the dorm. A-Dorm lacked heating, as the heat pump had been broken for months. Nighttime temperatures in the dorm dropped into the fifties, and the thin blankets provided were inadequate. Inmates layered thermal clothing and wore ski caps to stay warm.

A sign in the dorm lobby warned about black mold, but no corrective action was taken to remove it.

The commissary truck arrived at our dorm around 2:00 PM on Thursday. Many items were out of stock. I learned that sneakers or work boots had to be special ordered, taking about three weeks to arrive.

Fortunately, I had planned ahead and brought $2,000 to deposit in my commissary account. While food purchases were limited to twenty-five dollars per week, newcomers could buy clothing, dishes, watches, MP3 players, and other items without restrictions. Unfortunately, none of the electronic items I ordered were in stock, and only half of my food items arrived. The inmate delivering my order shrugged and said, "We get what we get." No one in the commissary seemed to care about fulfilling orders accurately.

On the way to dinner, Juan introduced me to Captain Holly, the second in command at FPC Pensacola. COs lined the walkway to the cafeteria as we picked up our food. Juan introduced me as Congressman Collins, but Captain Holly snickered and corrected him, saying I was now "Inmate Collins."

On Friday, my third day, I discovered that camp "currency" consisted of one dollar stamps. The barber shop was closed due to COVID, but an inmate nicknamed "Cheese" cut hair in the bathroom for five one dollar stamps.

I entered a list of phone numbers I might call once I had phone access. This was a requirement for making calls.

Settling In

The camp routine was simple: lights on, lights off, and standing headcounts at 4:00 PM and 9:00 PM. Meals were served at consistent times except on weekends. Juan, Ed, and I often discussed politics and life at camp. Our "circle of friends" gathered nightly in our cubicle to talk and vent.

With the library closed, a rack in the lobby held books. I loaded up on James Patterson novels and passed time reading. Each night after lights out, I grabbed a cup of coffee and went to the lobby to read under the lights. A few regulars gathered there to play dominoes, including Jorge.

On Saturday, November 6, we were allowed outside for an hour to walk around the baseball field. Some inmates sat in the bleachers and chatted. Marc Leven gave me an old pair of sneakers, which, though worn, were better than the uncomfortable work boots I'd been issued. Another inmate, noticing my sneakers, offered me a better pair without asking for anything in return, emphasizing the camp's familial spirit.

Juan, Ed, and I walked around the field, and they answered my many questions. Later, our dorm was escorted to the phone shack, where I made my first call home to Mary and my daughter. It was a short but uplifting conversation. Calls were recorded, and I asked Mary to send me a Kakuro puzzle book.

Due to COVID, my entire family was living in our large house on Marco Island. The house had five bedrooms, five bathrooms, an infinity pool, and a dock with a boat and jet ski. Everyone had their own space, and the setup allowed for some semblance of normalcy during the pandemic.

On Sunday, November 7, we had another hour of outdoor time. Recreation was limited to walking around the baseball field or sitting in bleachers. I filled out a second commissary order form, hoping for better luck with fulfillment.

After five days at camp, I felt comfortable in my surroundings and had established a workable routine. I preferred showering at night instead of mornings.

Mail call occurred at 5:00 PM daily. While many inmates skipped it, having lost touch with family, I regularly received mail. Mary, and my three children often wrote to me. My grandchildren sent drawings and pictures, which brightened my days. Other inmates joked that I was the most popular inmate at FPC Pensacola.

When I left Pensacola, I transferred my *Wall Street Journal* subscription to fellow inmate Dr. Douglas Moss ("Doc Moss"), ensuring he received daily mail. I continued to renew his subscription and send quarterly funds to support other inmates who didn't have any family assistance.

I hadn't yet been given a work assignment. Ed, who worked in the woodshop, and Doc Moss, who managed the tool crib, both encouraged me to apply for their respective areas. Each seemed like a good option.

On Monday, I put out my laundry bag, which was returned cleaned later that afternoon. Commissary frustrations continued, with most of my order missing again. However, I received a headset for listening to TV or radio, and a headlamp for nighttime reading.

On Tuesday, November 9—my seventh day—I had a medical exam at 7:00 AM and a legal call at 2:30 PM. Each night, a call-out sheet was posted in the lobby, listing inmates scheduled for appointments the next day.

Legal Call

The purpose of my legal call with Jon Barr, my attorney, was to discuss my situation and outline the next steps to pursue compassionate release under the CARES Act. At FPC Pensacola, I was the oldest inmate—most were in their forties or fifties, with a few in their sixties. No one else had reached seventy.

Legal calls were held in the Unit Office. They weren't monitored or recorded, and there was no time limit. I had listed Jon Barr as one of my attorneys, along with my daughter. Although she was family, her status as an attorney allowed her to be included on my legal list.

At 2:30, I joined a conference call with Jon Barr, Jon New, and my daughter to discuss our compassionate release strategy. My daughter updated me on the negotiations to sell ZeptoMetrix and explained the closing date had been postponed from November 30 to December 31 due to the need for Hart-Scott-Rodino antitrust approval filings.

Some inmates had waited up to six months for approval for legal calls, so my name appearing on the call-out sheet twice a week didn't go unnoticed. There was grumbling that I received "special treatment" due to my former position as a congressman.

The camp secretary, Mr. Smith, was responsible for approving and scheduling legal calls. His first interaction with my daughter had left a lasting impression. When he hesitated to approve her request for a call, my daughter—fierce and determined—asserted that she would schedule calls as needed, and he would comply or face severe consequences. From then on, her requests were promptly approved, not because of my past role in Congress, but because Mr. Smith feared my daughter.

Learning the Ropes

My counselor, Ms. Bertran, was kind but not particularly industrious. At my attorneys' suggestion, I filed a request with her to transfer to home confinement due to my age and the COVID-19 risk factors.

Wednesday, November 11, was Veterans Day, which brought schedule changes at the camp. Lunch was served at 10:30 AM, and dinner at 1:30 PM—far too early for dinner.

On Thursday, I ventured into the TV room for the first time. It had four TVs on the wall, each tuned to a preset channel. Inmates could listen to the audio by tuning their headsets to the appropriate number. Seniority dictated not only the channels but also the seating arrangements. With the camp at half capacity, each inmate had two plastic chairs instead of one.

Food Service Work Detail

On Friday, November 13, I was assigned to food service as my work detail, though I hadn't requested it. A correctional officer (CO) had specifically requested me for his team. I reported to food service on Monday, November 15, under the supervision of Mr. Griffin, a political enthusiast who was eager to work with "the congressman." Despite his eccentricity, he was pleasant to me, and I didn't mind the assignment.

Food service turned out to be a high-risk environment for COVID-19. Masks were only worn when inmates picked up meals, and external visitors, like truck drivers and repair workers, never wore masks.

Mr. Griffin didn't assign me specific tasks; I helped with various duties like preparing meal trays and handing out food. He provided me with a comfortable office chair, which made me feel out of place since the others sat on hard plastic chairs.

Mr. Griffin's demeanor alternated between friendly and abrasive. He often bragged about his finances and intelligence while belittling others. He also gave me access to the Officer's Mess, an area off-limits to most inmates, to assist Lance Mullins with preparing meals for COs. These meals featured superior ingredients compared to what inmates received. Interestingly, COs were supposed to pay for their meals, but most did not, effectively stealing their lunches daily without consequence.

After two weeks, I requested a transfer out of food service to the woodshop or tool crib, hoping to avoid further dealings with Mr. Griffin. Instead, I was summoned to the unit manager's office, where I was informed that I had to remain in food service. As a former congressman, I was classified as a special security risk, requiring constant supervision. Food service was one of the few assignments where COs were always present.

Transfer to Veggie Prep

On Friday, November 27, Mr. Griffin, annoyed by my transfer request, reassigned me to "veggie prep," starting Monday. He revoked my access to the Officer's Mess and took away my office chair.

On Monday, November 30, when I arrived at the food service area, CO Heatrice locked me in the veggie prep room. The room, containing sharp knives, was considered a security risk. Despite my special security designation, it seemed acceptable to place me in a room with another inmate who might pose a threat.

A kind inmate nicknamed Santa, who worked in veggie prep, was assigned to train me as his assistant. However, he admitted that he didn't actually need an assistant. I felt claustrophobic in the small, locked room and was tasked with peeling onions—a task I had never done before. The moment I began, my eyes started burning intensely. Having undergone cataract surgery before arriving at FPC Pensacola, my eyes were highly sensitive to light and prone to dryness, making them particularly reactive to onions.

Frustrated, I pounded on the door to be let out. CO Heatrice eventually sent me back to the dorm.

The next day, Tuesday, Heatrice attempted to trap me into "refusing a direct order," a serious violation in Federal Prison. He locked me in veggie prep again, expecting me to refuse entry. Instead, I observed Santa perform his duties without intervening. Once he finished, we were both let out after about an hour.

On Wednesday, December 2, I informed Mr. Griffin that I couldn't work in veggie prep due to medical reasons related to my cataract surgery. He was visibly upset and reassigned me as a "cook," scheduling me to work Sunday through Wednesday, four days a week. My hours were grueling: 7:00 AM to 5:00 PM on Sundays, and 4:00 AM to 5:00 PM Monday through Wednesday—a total of forty-nine hours per week at a pay rate of fifteen cents per hour.

I was assigned more hours than any other inmate at FPC Pensacola, despite being the oldest inmate in the camp. Most inmates over sixty didn't have work assignments.

December 6—December 22

For the next three weeks, from December 6 to December 22, I followed this punishing schedule. I woke at 3:30 AM, dressed, and waited for a CO to flash a signal light into the dormitory lobby window, indicating it was time to walk to the cafeteria. Movement within the camp was tightly controlled under COVID restrictions—permission was required for every action, and inmates had to proceed directly to their destinations.

Although my job title was "cook," I was anything but. I merely assisted other inmates who were actual cooks before their incarceration. Many sought food service jobs because the food for workers was better than what other inmates received. Excess fresh produce, left out after COs finished their meals, was fair game for food service workers to take. I brought extra food back to my cubicle to share with my cellmates, while others sold theirs as part of a "side hustle."

Side hustles were common, as many inmates had lost contact with their families and relied on their meager wages to buy commissary items. One inmate cleaned cubicles for a bag of Raisinets, sweeping and mopping floors in exchange.

On December 9, 2020, Juan Almeida, a fellow inmate, was released to home confinement. He had served 50 percent of his sentence and qualified for compassionate release under rules fabricated by the BOP—rules not required under the CARES Act. While I was sad to see him go, I took his lower bunk, which came with a heavy blanket. This was a significant improvement, especially during the bitterly cold nights. With long underwear, sweats, a ski cap, and Juan's blanket, I managed to stay warm.

After Juan's departure, some of us in the cubicle painted our bunk beds with fresh gray paint from the shop, and Ed Gire polished the concrete floor with wax and a buffer. Our cubicle became the cleanest and most attractive in the camp.

On Friday, December 10, I filled out a "cop-out" form and handed it to CO Travers, asking him to deliver it to Warden Joseph. I demanded reassignment from food service due to CO Griffin's failure to wear a mask, which put me at heightened risk of contracting COVID-19. I requested a dormitory orderly position, which involved cleaning shared spaces and aligned with my special risk designation.

Meanwhile, I hadn't abandoned my pursuit of compassionate release due to my age and health issues. On November 30, 2020, with my attorney Jon Barr's assistance, I filed a formal request with Warden Joseph. It included a detailed letter citing the CARES Act and Attorney General Barr's directives.

On December 22, 2020, at 2:00 PM, Camp Secretary Smith delivered Warden Joseph's denial of my request. Ironically, the same evening at 8:00 PM, Smith processed my debit card for remaining commissary funds as I prepared to leave FPC Pensacola for good. News of my full and unconditional pardon by President Trump broke around 7:00 PM.

I never saw Mr. Griffin again, but I doubt he'll forget me—especially after I reported his abuses in a letter to the director of the BOP following my pardon. I've attached a copy of that letter as Appendix B.

Negotiations to Sell ZeptoMetrix

When I arrived at FPC Pensacola, I was informed it was a significant violation of rules to conduct business from a federal prison. At the time, I was in the middle of negotiating the sale of ZeptoMetrix and selling my Washington, DC condominium. Upon my return to Pensacola Camp on November 4, 2020, I informed the unit manager of A-Dorm about these transactions, emphasizing that neither involved running the businesses.

The unit manager appreciated my honesty and assured me that finalizing these deals would not be an issue.

Once my daughter addressed Secretary Smith, she secured the ability to schedule legal calls whenever necessary.

The sale of the DC condo was the simpler issue. Although the condo was beautiful, it was on the first floor—something that deterred many potential buyers, especially women concerned about safety. After a year on the market with no offers, I reduced the price to what I had paid eight years earlier, taking no profit. A male buyer quickly agreed to the reduced price. My daughter prepared the contract, mailed it to me, and the unit counselor notarized my signature. I mailed it back, relieved to close that chapter.

Although I covered the sale of ZeptoMetrix in Chapter 10, I think it makes sense to cover it again as my daughter did conclude the negotiations while I was in prison in Pensacola.

The ZeptoMetrix negotiations were more complex than selling the condo in Washington. On October 5, 2020, the private equity firm made a sizeable offer with a bonus contingent on achieving specific financial results in 2021. It was a staggering amount, but the offer only accounted for operating results through August. By October, I knew our September results were extraordinary and anticipated continued growth through the year.

I assumed I could monitor developments from prison camp, but I was unexpectedly sent to FCI Marianna and placed in isolation for three weeks. When I finally spoke with my daughter on November 10, I was relieved to learn that the closing date had been postponed to December 31 to meet FTC Hart-Scott-Rodino pre-merger reporting requirements. I instructed her to ensure that Shawn Smith, president of ZeptoMetrix, kept her updated on the company's performance.

On November 13, during a legal call, my daughter reported that October sales and profits had surpassed September's impressive figures. I was astonished.

The FTC filing was submitted on November 23, locking in the December 31 closing date. After my return to the dorm on November 30, my daughter updated me that November sales would likely exceed October's.

At 4:00 PM on December 15, my daughter called and told me the deal was done, with the closing scheduled for December 31, 2020. The outcome was monumental —a multi-generational windfall.

Reason My Request to Delay My Report Date Was Denied

I am convinced that the Southern District of New York (SDNY) and Judge Broderick refused to grant an extension of my report date—from October 13, 2020, to December 8, 2020—to counter the possibility of President Trump pardoning me. They wanted to ensure I served jail time.

When the SDNY objected to our motion to delay my report date, and Judge Broderick effectively denied it by not issuing a decision on our emergency motion, COVID-19 was ravaging the country. Severe outbreaks were occurring in several federal prisons, and inmates were dying.

Their justification for sending me to prison during this perilous time, before vaccines or effective treatments were available, was that COVID-19 had not yet hit FPC Pensacola. However, it was only a matter of time before it did.

Trump Backstory

Not many people knew the full extent of my backstory with President Trump. Everyone knew I was the first sitting member of Congress to endorse him on February 24, 2016. Many knew I seconded his nomination at the Republican Convention. Few insiders knew I had formed the Trump Caucus in Congress, and that the original eleven members of the caucus met with President Trump in the Oval Office. Only a handful knew I had flown with him on *Air Force One*.

Fewer than ten people knew that, after the Associated Press called the election at 2:29 AM on election night, President-elect Trump and Ivanka Trump called me at 9:00 AM to thank me for my involvement in the campaign. I was his first call as president-elect—even before he contacted the prime ministers or presidents of Britain, France, or Germany, or any other heads of state.

One of the most compelling aspects of my relationship with Trump involves the Billy Bush tapes. In 2005, Billy Bush and Trump were traveling on a bus to film an episode of *Access Hollywood*. Their conversation, which was videotaped, was extraordinarily lewd. Trump infamously said, "When you are a star, they let you do it. You can do anything."

The tape aired on October 7, 2016, a month before the presidential election. It was widely seen as the death knell of Trump's campaign. After the tape's release, Speaker of the House Paul Ryan publicly disowned Trump and withdrew his support. Many others followed suit. Trump seemed politically toxic.

Chris Cuomo invited me to appear on his CNN show, *New Day*, on October 8, 2016, to discuss the tapes. I had appeared on dozens of CNN *New Day* shows since endorsing Trump in February. At that moment, I was the only Trump supporter willing to address the controversy on air. It was a tense interview, but I finally said the now-famous line: "It was all locker room talk."

Unbeknownst to me, Trump was watching that interview. After the election, during our twenty-minute phone call, President-elect Trump told me he would never forget seeing me defend him. He thanked me for being his only supporter willing to go on national television during such a tumultuous moment.

With Ivanka on the call, we discussed a potential role for me in the Trump administration. I told him I didn't want to join the administration but preferred to support him from Congress. I proposed becoming the congressional liaison to the White House. Two hours later, Paul Ryan called, saying the president-elect wanted me in that role, and would make me the gatekeeper for any congressional recommendations for administration appointments. Ryan also asked me to second his nomination for speaker of the house as a signal of reconciliation with Trump, which I did.

Mark Meadows Connection

My unique connection to Trump extended to Mark Meadows, who later became his chief of staff. Mark and I served in Congress together starting in 2012, and our families became friends. When I reported to FPC Pensacola, my wife Mary reached out to Mark about the possibility of a presidential pardon. Despite the tense election period, Mark expressed a willingness to help. We communicated about the pardon indirectly, using code phrases, as phone calls were monitored and mail was inspected.

By December 20, 2020, I was desperate. My work assignment at the prison was grueling, and COVID-19 continued to be a serious concern. I anxiously awaited updates from Mary during our phone calls, always using our code to ask, "How does it look for Christmas?" She reassured me that things were on track, and I held onto hope for a pardon before the year's end.

Mary researched hotels in Pensacola and car rental requirements. I was in camp without a credit card. My driver's license was in my personal file at camp, but that was all I had. My clothes had been sent home.

My daughter's boyfriend discovered that he could make a hotel reservation and rent a car in my name using his credit card.

My last call with Mary on December 20 ended with her confidently assuring me she would see me for Christmas.

Trump Pardon

On December 22, I had a terrible day in Food Service. At 2:00 PM, Secretary Smith informed me that my request for compassionate release had been denied. It was crushing news.

At 5:00 PM, as I sat on my bed in our cubicle, someone shouted down the aisle that Collins was wanted up front. This was usually a bad sign. By 5:00 PM, most of the administration had gone home, and the Camp largely shut down. When a correctional officer (CO) looks for you at that time, it's rarely good news.

I went to the lobby, where a CO instructed me to follow him outside. The other inmates watched intently, curious about what was happening. As we walked down the sidewalk, I asked the CO where we were headed. He replied, "Medical." I asked why, but he didn't have an answer.

In the medical facility, a nurse took me into an examination room. To my surprise, the doctor was there—something unusual, especially at night. I asked him what was going on. He explained he was there to administer a COVID test.

My mind raced. I connected the dots. They couldn't release anyone from prison without a negative COVID test. Was I being released?

I left the medical unit with cautious hope. Back in the dorm, about fifty inmates crowded the lobby. Someone shouted, asking what had happened. When I mentioned the COVID test, another inmate exclaimed, "You're going home!"

Despite my hope, I felt uncertain. At 7:00 PM, another shout echoed down the aisle: Collins was wanted up front again.

This time, Ms. Kennedy, a case manager from another dorm, was waiting for me. I entered the office, and she looked at me with a smile. "Mr. Collins," she said, "the President of the United States has pardoned you."

I broke down in tears, sobbing uncontrollably. My time at Pensacola was over. I was going home for Christmas. Ms. Kennedy hugged me and said, "I've studied your case. You never should have been here. I'm so happy for you. This is true justice."

Ms. Kennedy explained I had to leave camp immediately. With a presidential pardon, I could no longer be incarcerated. However, they had no immediate place to take me and needed my wife's consent to release me. My safety was their top priority, so they couldn't simply drop me off on a street corner.

I called Mary and told her I had been pardoned by President Trump. "I know," she replied. "Mark Meadows called me. We've arranged for you to rent a car and stay in a hotel. You can drive home tomorrow." Mary cried as she told me I was coming home for Christmas. Our nightmare was over.

Ms. Kennedy said they needed someone to come in to process my commissary money onto a debit card. Most staff lived over an hour away, but Secretary Smith returned to handle my account. Ms. Kennedy handed me the debit card—a bitter irony, as Secretary Smith had denied my compassionate release just hours earlier.

Ms. Kennedy told me to gather my personal belongings. A CO would drive me to the airport to pick up my rental car.

I stopped at cubicle number one to tell Jorge, "I'm going home." He looked confused, so I explained, "President Trump pardoned me. I'm going home."

Back in my cubicle, the dorm erupted with excitement. News of my pardon had already reached the cable networks. I packed a few souvenirs: my watch, alarm clock, and coffee mug. Dressed in my sweats—I couldn't wear prison clothes—I saw a friend carrying off my locker. He wanted its contents, which made me laugh.

As I walked down the aisle, inmates formed a gauntlet, chanting, "Collins, Collins, Collins!" Many slipped notes into my hand, begging me to contact their families. "Tell them about this awful place," they said. "They monitor my calls and read my mail."

Though elated, I felt a pang of sorrow. I was leaving, but my friends were staying. While I would be home for Christmas, they remained in prison.

Waving goodbye, I walked out the lobby door to cheers and shouts of my name. The raw emotion was overwhelming.

Leaving Pensacola

A CO drove me to the airport. I must have been a sight, wearing prison sweats with a commissary bag slung over my shoulder. Renting the car was easy—my daughter's boyfriend had already charged it to his credit card. At the hotel, I checked in without issue, using my driver's license. He had arranged everything.

In my room, I collapsed on the bed. I was free. President Trump had come through for me. Mark Meadows had kept his promise to Mary. I had my life back.

The next morning, I bought a burner phone with my debit card, activated it, and began my journey home. For ten hours, I talked nonstop on the phone as I drove.

I'm A Free Man

My pardon was national news. President Trump had included me in his first wave of pardons, alongside Roger Stone, Paul Manafort, General Michael Flynn, George Papadopoulos, Charles Kushner, and Duncan Hunter.

This was a devastating blow to US Attorney Geoffrey Berman, Assistant US Attorney Damian Williams, and Judge Vernon Broderick. Their efforts to prosecute me had ended in failure. President Trump had pardoned former Congressman Christopher Collins after just ten weeks in prison.

I had been persecuted and pressured into pleading guilty to a felony I would never have been convicted of in court. My son and Steve were collateral damage in their scheme to target Trump's strongest supporter in Congress.

Berman wasted millions of taxpayer dollars, achieving probation for my son and Steve and ten weeks in prison for me—a man who received a full and unconditional presidential pardon.

With my pardon, I regained my rights: firearms ownership, voting, TSA Pre-Check, and Global Entry Pass.

Three weeks later, COVID-19 swept through FPC Pensacola, infecting 100 percent of the inmates in just five days. At seventy, with asthma, high blood pressure, and high cholesterol, I would have been at great risk. President Trump saved my life.

As for Berman, Williams, and Broderick, they gambled with my life. Their day of reckoning will come. When they stand before the Pearly Gates, they will have to try to justify their actions. I doubt St. Peter will show them leniency.

Executive Grant of Clemency

DONALD J. TRUMP

President of the United States of America

TO ALL TO WHOM THESE PRESENTS SHALL COME, GREETING:

BE IT KNOWN, THAT THIS DAY, I, DONALD J. TRUMP, PRESIDENT OF THE UNITED STATES, PURSUANT TO MY POWERS UNDER ARTICLE II, SECTION 2, CLAUSE 1, OF THE CONSTITUTION, HAVE GRANTED UNTO

CHRISTOPHER COLLINS

A FULL AND UNCONDITIONAL PARDON

FOR HIS CONVICTION in the United States District Court for the Southern District of New York on a superseding indictment (Docket No. S1 1:18-cr-00567-VSB-1) charging violations of Sections 371 and 1001, Title 18, United States Code, for which he was sentenced on January 16, 2020, to 26 months' imprisonment, one year's supervised release, a $200,000 fine, and a special assessment of $200.

I HEREBY DESIGNATE, direct, and empower the Office of the Pardon Attorney, as my representative, to sign a grant of clemency to the person named herein. The Office of the Pardon Attorney shall declare that its action is the act of the President, being performed at my direction.

I ALSO DIRECT the Bureau of Prisons, upon receipt of this warrant, to effect immediately the release of the Pardon recipient (Reg. No. 86014-054) with all possible speed.

IN TESTIMONY WHEREOF, I have hereunto caused this Pardon to be recorded with the Department of Justice.

Done at the City of Washington in the District of Columbia this twenty-second day of December in the year of our Lord Two Thousand and Twenty and of the Independence of the United States the Two Hundred and Forty-fifth.

DONALD J. TRUMP
PRESIDENT

Full and Unconditional Pardon from President Trump.

CHAPTER 29

Life After Prison

Purchase of Our Home in Hideaway Beach

As detailed in my chapter on ZeptoMetrix, the sale of the company closed on December 31, 2020, and the proceeds were transferred into our bank account at 10:00 AM.

Mary and I decided to explore real estate opportunities in Hideaway Beach, knowing that we would be full-time residents of Marco Island. We had owned a vacant lot in Hideaway Beach since 2017, which made us members of the Hideaway Beach Club. We thought it might make sense to become full-time residents of Hideaway Beach.

We saw an advertisement from a local realtor, Cathy Rogers, about a home in Hideaway Beach that was for sale. I called Cathy and arranged to view the home at 1:00 PM. When we arrived, Mary and I quickly realized we were not interested. The house was one of the oldest in Hideaway Beach and lacked curb appeal.

I told Cathy we weren't interested and were looking for a more "upscale" home. Cathy mentioned there was a very upscale property on the beach overlooking the Gulf of Mexico for sale, albeit at a much higher price point. I assured Cathy that price wasn't a concern. She made a call to the listing agent, and we headed to see the house. The key was in a lockbox on the front door.

When we walked in and saw the breathtaking view of the beach and Gulf of Mexico, we were captivated. The house, built in 2008, had never been lived in. It turned out that the original owners, who went through three builders and faced significant delays, had been fined by the Hideaway Beach Association. Bitter and frustrated, they returned to Texas and listed the house at a high price with no urgency to sell.

Hideaway Beach home in Marco Island.

The house was fully furnished with exquisite furniture and artwork, including seven signed Dalí prints, a Picasso sketch, a Picasso mixed-media piece, and an original Matisse sketch.

A humorous aside: about thirty minutes after arriving at the house, I received a call from President Trump. Excusing myself, I said, “I have to take this call; it’s President Trump on the line.” Cathy’s expression was priceless.

The house was listed as fully furnished. Interestingly, the listing agent was set to lose the listing that very day, December 31, 2020, making her motivated to close a deal. I made a cash offer, anticipating a counteroffer. However, the agent convinced the owner to accept my offer without a counter. We closed the purchase on January 29, 2021.

Sale of 9660 Cobblestone Drive, Clarence, NY

Due to the COVID-19 pandemic and travel restrictions in 2020, we were unable to sell our home in Clarence, NY. Thankfully, our fully furnished five-bedroom house in Marco Island was spacious enough to accommodate

Mary and me, along with our kids, their significant others, our cat, and my son's two dogs.

In February 2021, after receiving my COVID-19 vaccination, I returned to Buffalo to begin the process of selling our house in Clarence, where we had lived for twenty-eight years. We purchased the house in 1993, shortly after my son was born. My daughter was two years old at the time. Before moving to Clarence, we lived in a house I bought in 1976, when I relocated to Buffalo from Alabama to work for Westinghouse Electric.

Since our Marco Island house was already fully furnished, we decided to list the Clarence property as a furnished home. We moved only personal items and some odds and ends to Florida, leaving most of the furnishings behind.

Home in Clarence, New York.

At the time, the Buffalo real estate market was struggling. Years of job losses and population decline had put significant pressure on property values. Ultimately, I sold the house for the same amount we had paid for it in 1993, including the cost of improvements. There was no financial gain. To close the sale, I also had to agree to hold a ten-year mortgage for the full purchase price—an unfortunate outcome.

Life After Prison: Dealing with Uncertainty as a Pardoned Felon

Reflecting on life after being pardoned and leaving the Pensacola Prison Camp, I realize I was struggling with depression and uncertainty about the future. I had resigned from Congress in disgrace and was unemployed. Although I retained substantial ownership interests in Volland Electric and Audubon Machinery, both based in Buffalo, I was no longer involved in their day-to-day operations.

Having worked since I was sixteen, I wasn't ready to retire. I had enjoyed both my private-sector career, and my time in public service as Erie County executive for four years and a member of Congress for seven years.

In many ways, 2021 felt like a lost year. The COVID-19 pandemic was still a major concern, with mask mandates and limited social interactions. Florida had fewer restrictions than most states, but caution remained widespread. Despite being financially secure, I was still grappling with depression and an uncertain future. My kids were also financially set for life, having owned 33 percent of ZeptoMetrix.

From February to September 2021, we focused on settling into our new home in Hideaway Beach. The time passed quickly, and although I remained somewhat depressed, my outlook began to improve. I didn't know what the next thirty years would hold but remained optimistic, hoping to live to one hundred.

Having avoided golf since my legal troubles began in 2018, I decided to start playing again. Hideaway Beach has a convenient nine-hole executive course just three minutes from our house. The club hosts two weekly events, offering an easy way to meet other golfers in the community.

Mary and I also joined the popular bocce league at Hideaway Beach. Bocce is a game well-suited to older players, requiring only the skill to toss a ball down a ten-by-sixty-foot court. The objective is to get your bocce ball as close as possible to the smaller target ball, the pallino. It's a mix of skill and luck, and we found it both enjoyable and social.

Over the past four years, I've kept active by playing golf, bocce, biking with Mary around our gated community, and participating in events with the local chapter of the Young Presidents Organization (YPO) based in Naples, FL.

The Challenging Reality of Being a Convicted Felon

Beyond the personal humiliation of being a convicted felon, the reactions from organizations I was affiliated with felt like a series of devastating blows.

- In August 2018, after my indictment, Speaker Paul Ryan removed me from my membership on the powerful Energy and Commerce Congressional Committee.
- Following my re-election in 2018, Republican Leader Kevin McCarthy denied me membership on any congressional committee.
- I was removed as chairman of the Scout Caucus in Congress and was asked not to attend its meetings. Additionally, I was asked to remove the Scout flag displayed outside my Washington, DC, Congressional office.
- The local Boy Scouts of America chapter in Buffalo, NY, required my resignation from their board, where I had served for over thirty years.
- My thirty-five-year membership in YPO International was terminated, though my chapter in Naples, FL, allowed me to retain local membership.
- At the Brookfield Country Club in Clarence, NY, where I had been a member since 1977, I was required to transfer my membership to my wife, Mary Sue.
- My plaque as a member of the Hendersonville High School Hall of Fame was removed.
- Several of my credit cards were canceled, including those from Neiman Marcus, Bloomingdale's, TJ Maxx, Capital One, and A/X, despite my being a loyal customer for over forty years.
- After the sale of ZeptoMetrix, the financial manager I hired had to find a new institution to manage my investments, because all their existing fiduciaries refused to handle them.

The Comfort of My Cat

When your world is turned upside down, you look to family for comfort and support. If you're fortunate to have a pet, their loyalty remains steadfast, no matter how others treat you.

In my case, our beloved cat, Mia, provided unwavering companionship during the turbulent years from 2018 to 2022.

Mia, a Ragdoll cat, joined our family in 2000 and lived an extraordinary life, passing away on June 11, 2022, at the remarkable age of 22. She was my loyal sidekick during some of my darkest days.

It took me over a year to recover from her loss. Eventually, in 2023, my wife and I decided to welcome a new cat into our lives. After searching online, I found Sabina, a Lynx Ragdoll, whose picture was posted by a breeder the very day I started my search. We arranged for Sabina to join our family on October 13, 2023.

A Return to Politics

I never anticipated returning to politics after my guilty plea to insider trading on October 1, 2019, and my subsequent sentencing to twenty-six months in federal prison on January 17, 2020.

My plea ensured that my son received probation rather than imprisonment, a critical outcome for his future. He began his probation in February 2020 and was released from probation in May 2023.

During my son's probation, I avoided any media attention. I knew that Judge Vernon Broderick and US Attorney Damian Williams were very upset when President Trump pardoned me, and I couldn't take the chance that anything I did or say would impact my son not being released early from probation for good behavior.

In July 2023, I was invited to financially support and speak at the "United We Stand" Trump Flotilla near Marco Island. This event reignited my political ambitions, coinciding with local Congressman Byron Donalds and his potential career shift, including a possible gubernatorial run or a Trump administration role.

July 2, 2023 United We Stand Trump Flotilla announcement.

On July 2, 2023, I gave a passionate speech at the Trump Flotilla, announcing my intention to run for Congress in FL-19 if Byron Donalds vacated the seat. This announcement, alongside the prospect of being the first member of Congress to represent two different states in over 50 years, sparked significant media attention.

I subsequently joined the Collier County Republican Executive Committee as an elected representative for Marco Island and began participating in local conservative organizations. I also established regular meetings with Roger Stone and Michael Caputo, who were prominent figures in the Trump campaign.

July 2, 2023 Trump Flotilla speech announcing my candidacy for Congress in FL-19.

The Washington Post Profile

On January 18, 2024, *The Washington Post* published a three-page feature, "The Art of the Rebound," profiling my potential return to Congress. The article, written by Manuel Roig-Franzia, was based on a two-day interview conducted in September 2023, followed by a photo shoot later that month.

The article's publication was delayed for four months as *The Washington Post* needed to pick a publication date when they could devote three pages to the feature story.

The article received a lot of national and local coverage, and reinforced the narrative of my political resurgence.

2026 FL-19 Congressional Election

Palm Card for 2026 congressional campaign in FL-19.

I have officially announced that I am running for Congress in 2026 as a candidate to replace Congressman Byron Donalds in FL-19. The primary will be held on August 18, 2026. My website is www.CollinsFL19.com.

APPENDIX A

Young Presidents Organization

IN 1985, I RECEIVED A call from Norm Ernst, a member of the Empire State Chapter of the Young Presidents Organization (YPO). I had never heard of YPO, but Norm informed me that I qualified for membership if I was interested in joining.

A new YPO member needed to be the president of a company before age forty, with a minimum of fifty employees and sales exceeding $5 million. At the time, I was thirty-five years old, and Nuttall Gear met both the sales and employee qualifications.

I went to lunch with Norm, who shared how much he enjoyed YPO and how it positively impacted his management skills.

YPO was formed in 1950 by Ray Hickok. At just twenty-seven years old, Ray became the head of his family's Rochester-based company, Hickok Belt, which employed 300 people. Feeling the need for advice and counsel from other young presidents, he gathered a group of fifty young executives at the Waldorf-Astoria Hotel in New York City for the first meeting. Among the attendees were actor Douglas Fairbanks Jr., who was leading his own production company, and Willard Rockwell, later the founder of Rockwell International, a major aerospace firm. The keynote speaker was General Robert Wood Johnson of Johnson & Johnson, the renowned healthcare company. These young presidents continued to meet regularly to share experiences and learn from one another.

What began as a single YPO chapter in New York has grown into 460 chapters worldwide, with over 34,000 members in 142 countries.

I joined the Empire State Chapter in 1985, when YPO International had eighty chapters and 6,000 members. Our chapter consisted of fifty-five members and another forty in our sister organization, the World Presidents' Organization (WPO).

WPO members were YPO members who had reached age fifty and retired from YPO. We referred to them as "49ers." I am, and always will be, a 49er. Incidentally, WPO was reorganized a few years ago and is now known as YPO Gold. I like to think of it as "gold means old."

In 1988, I was elected education chairman for the 1988–89 membership year. After three years in the chapter, I then served as chapter chairman in 1989–90 and became membership chairman for 1990–91. Holding leadership positions within YPO was both enjoyable and rewarding.

We held monthly meetings nine months a year, from September through May. One of the most impactful meetings I attended was a seminar titled "Guess What—Now What."

At the event, we were given stickers reading "GW-NW" to wear on our shirts. The meaning became clear during the seminar. A "guess what" moment refers to any unexpected or unpleasant event, such as spilling a drink, hitting a deer on the way to the airport (yes, I've done that), splitting your pants, or losing your cell phone.

The seminar emphasized not dwelling on the negative. Instead, it taught us to immediately switch to "now what" mode. Spill a drink? "Now what." Hit a deer? "Now what." This mindset fosters problem-solving and reduces stress, anger, and anxiety. "Guess What—Now What" has become a guiding principle for my family and me. When our son came home with a disappointing report card and handed it to me saying, "Guess What—Now What," all I could do was laugh.

Beyond monthly meetings, most YPO members participate in smaller forum groups of about eight people. These forums allow for deeper, confidential discussions on personal and professional issues.

My forum included Cole Bergan, Jim Buzzard, Louis Ciminelli, Ken Drake, Burt Notarius, Bob Skerker, and Mark Sidebottom. YPO members are often categorized as entrepreneurs, hired guns, or silver spoons. Entrepreneurs founded their companies; hired guns were brought in to lead; silver spoons inherited leadership roles in family businesses. Our forum had five entrepreneurs, one hired gun, and two silver spoons. Hearing about the challenges faced by others, especially those with complex family dynamics, was incredibly enlightening.

One of the most memorable sessions we had was a three-day seminar based on the book *Please Understand* Me by David Keirsey and Marilyn Bates. We explored the Myers-Briggs personality test, identifying our personality types among the sixteen possibilities. I'm an ISTJ: Introvert, Sensing, Thinking, Judging. Understanding the personality traits of my peers was an eye-opening experience, shifting perspectives from "I'm right, you're wrong" to "we're just different."

The corporate world is dominated by ESTJ and ISTJ types, who are naturally drawn to business. Learning about other types, such as ENTPs (often inventors) or ISFPs (typically artists), broadened my understanding of different temperaments and how they interact.

This newfound knowledge was transformative. Back at Nuttall Gear, I had all salaried employees take the Myers-Briggs test and wear their four-letter designations on name tags for a week. This exercise improved team understanding and collaboration.

Forum retreats were another highlight. We traveled to destinations like Park City, the Caribbean, and New Mexico, focusing on topics such as mission statements, strategic planning, and core values. These retreats, always guided by skilled moderators, were invaluable for both personal and professional growth.

Everything YPO does is first-class—from travel and accommodations to speakers and unique experiences. Mary and I were married on January 9, 1988, and just days later, we attended a two-week YPO University in Australia for our honeymoon, celebrating Australia's bicentennial. We enjoyed extraordinary experiences, from touring Taronga Zoo to attending the Governor's Formal Ball.

YPO also hosted events in collaboration with other chapters. We traveled to Toronto for a joint event with the Ontario chapter, and to New York City for extravagant holiday weekends. These experiences were always unforgettable.

Today, as members of the Naples, FL chapter of YPO Gold, we remain active. Whether it's learning about tequila in Mexico, attending Formula 1 races in Miami, or touring Italian wineries, YPO continues to enrich our lives. We look forward to being part of this incredible organization for the rest of our lives.

APPENDIX B

Director Carvajal Letter

Congressman Chris Collins
317 Lamplighter Drive
Marco Island, FL. 34145

January 6, 2021

Director Michael Carvajal
Federal Bureau of Prisons
320 First Street NW
Washington, DC. 20534

Re: FPC Pensacola

Dear Director Carvajal:

I am writing to you as a former Member of Congress and a former inmate at FPC-Pensacola to express my concern surrounding the unconscionable, unprofessional, unethical, and inhumane conditions at FPC-Pensacola, which is directed by Warden M.V. Joseph.

The Mission Statement of the Bureau of Prisons is as follows:

> It is the mission of the Federal Bureau of Prisons to protect society by confining offenders in the controlled environments of prisons and community-based facilities that are safe, humane, cost-efficient, and appropriately secure, and that provide work and other self-improvement opportunities to assist offenders in becoming law-abiding citizens.

The conditions at FPC-Pensacola do not reflect the standards of this mission statement. Based on my own personal experience, I can assure you that the facility is not safe, humane, or cost-efficient. In this letter, I will enumerate the many ways in which FPC-Pensacola fails to meet these basic standards.

First, the most urgent concern is the unsafe conditions related to contracting COVID-19. The inmates have an exponentially increased risk of contracting the virus because of Warden Joseph's negligence. Guards routinely do NOT wear masks, or if they do, they do not wear them properly. There is no such thing as social distancing at the facility. Warden Joseph and the Correction Officers (COs) make a mockery of common sense COVID safety precautions. Hand sanitizer, wipes, etc. are not generally available to inmates. The cloth masks issued to inmates are totally inadequate. Immediate action must be taken to remove Warden Joseph and have a competent warden implement COVID safety procedures to protect the lives of the inmates.

Common sense dictates that the main risk of introducing COVID-19 into FPC-Pensacola comes from the COs, who live in the community and are exposed to COVID on a daily basis. In fact, many COs at Pensacola have already contracted COVID. The inmate population is generally at risk of contracting COVID every single day, but this is needlessly compounded by the unsafe actions of the COs.

To illustrate the magnitude of the problem I will relate my experience working in food service. The COs working in food service (Food Service COs) are Mr. Paul, Mr. Griffin, Mr. Heatrice, Mr. Thomas, Mr. Brazile, and Mr. Jiles. (As an aside, the inefficiency and waste of having six COs work in food service, when two or three would be more than sufficient, is in direct contrast to the BOP's stated Mission of being cost-efficient.) The six Food Service COs rarely wear masks. They "put on a show" when inmates walk through to collect their food containers to bring back to the dorm. As soon as the inmates walk out the door, the masks come off. The Food Service COs interact with the thirteen inmates that work in food service on a typical day with no masks and no respect for social distancing.

Warden Joseph and his staff are all well aware that the Food Service COs do not follow proper COVID safety protocols. Many other COs come and go from food service, each and every day, and obviously notice that the Food Service COs do not wear masks, or if they do, do not wear them to cover their noses.

Older inmates with underlying medical conditions, such as myself, are deliberately forced into an unsafe work environment in food service. I am seventy years old with health conditions (asthma, high blood pressure, and hyperlipidemia) that put me at significant risk to experience severe illness or death if I were to contract COVID-19. I sent a written request to Warden Joseph, personally delivered to him by CO Travers, to be removed from my food service work assignment and to be returned to my dorm as an orderly. Warden Joseph ignored my request.

Additionally, I made two separate requests to the two COs in charge of food service—Mr. Paul and Mr. Griffin. I was turned down both times.

Beyond CO behavior, inmate co-mingling policies also contribute to the increased risk of contracting COVID at FPC-Pensacola. There are three open dorms at this time (A, B, and C). The facility claims to keep inmates in dorms A, B and C separated in order to prevent the older inmates in dorm A from contracting the virus. Dorm A (my former dorm) never leaves campus. All work assignments for inmates in this dorm are on campus, including work in commissary, laundry, food service, etc. Inmates in dorms B and C leave campus to do their work assignments. That means they are interacting with the public every weekday and are at a very high risk of bringing COVID back into the prison. That is why the dorms are never *supposed* to mingle. However, they do mingle—church service includes inmates from all three dorms. Work crews in food service include inmates from dorms A and B. No one wears masks. It's a ticking time bomb, with contradictory rules in place within the prison, where one rule by definition contradicts another rule.

Beyond contradictory rules, there are additional policies in place that blatantly break COVID-related guidelines. FPC-Pensacola has signs posted about social distancing and masks that are not followed at all. In order to pretend to promote social distancing, there is a sign that says only ten inmates are allowed in the TV room and that they must wear masks. This is totally ignored. The COs are well aware that there are thirty or more inmates together in the TV room every day. The offices for the unit manager, case manager and secretary are right outside the TV room. Furthermore, since inmates don't wear masks in the dorm, the sign that limits the TV room to ten inmates doesn't even make sense in the first place.

Although inmates do not wear masks in the dorm, they are required to wear them when walking to food service to pick up their food, because the inmates are visible to cars driving by. This is all a show—Warden Joseph wants the public to think that FPC-Pensacola follows COVID-19 safety precautions. Additionally, truck drivers that deliver products to FPC-Pensacola do NOT wear masks. Contract repairmen do NOT wear masks.

I provide these examples to point out the hypocrisy of the situation at FPC-Pensacola.

Beyond the dangers of contracting COVID, the inmates face other unconscionable conditions at FPC-Pensacola because of the COVID-related lockdown in place at the facility. For example, as the oldest inmate at Pensacola, I was forced to work forty-nine hours a week with a ten-hour shift on Sunday (7:00 AM–5:00 PM) followed by three straight thirteen-hour shifts on Monday, Tuesday and Wednesday (4:00 AM–5:00 PM). There is a fair amount of down time during the workday, but because of the COVID lockdown, inmates cannot leave the food service facility. The only place to sit is on a hard stool connected to the tables. Inmates are not allowed to bring a more adequate chair from the dorm to sit on during the day. I am beyond the standard retirement age, and all other inmates over the age of sixty were taken off their work assignments due to COVID-restrictions. Not only was I working thirteen-hour shifts, but just to add insult to injury, they wouldn't even let me have a comfortable chair to sit on during breaks. That is a simple example of unnecessary inhumane treatment of inmates.

Additionally, I complained to Mr. Griffin that my work schedule was not fair to me, or the other three inmates who were forced to work the same four-day schedule. There are two work crews that split the week, and typically, these crews alternate between three-day work weeks and four-day work weeks. However, this trade-off did not happen—my crew was unofficially, permanently assigned a four-day work week. When I asked Mr. Griffin who I should contact to correct this unfair situation, he threatened me with adverse consequences if I were to complain. Simply put, he said he could make my life miserable, and since inmates "have no rights" he could do whatever he wanted. Is this the professionalism and excellence that the BOP claims to adhere to?

Besides a lack of professionalism and excellence, the policies at FPC-Pensacola also contradict the stated core value of integrity and ethical conduct. There is an Officer Mess (OM) where COs eat lunch and are "required" to pay for their lunch. However, only one or two COs bother to pay, and the other COs steal their lunch on a daily basis.

Other unconscionable conditions at FPC-Pensacola during the COVID-19 lockdown include:

1. Pensacola is one of only a few prisons without phones in the dorms. Rather, the phones are in a separate building. As a result of COVID lockdown, inmates are limited to three phone calls per week. Prior to COVID, prisoners could make unlimited phone calls any time they wanted. The phones should have been moved into the dorms months ago.

2. The phone building is limited to ten inmates at a time during the week, to promote social distancing, which makes no sense since the inmates don't social distance in the dorms. However, the COs allow twenty inmates at a time during the weekends when the Warden isn't present.

3. There is no sanitation of phones, which are used by inmates from all the dorms.

4. Inmates at Pensacola were denied access to emails for the first nine months of lockdown. Only recently were inmates allowed access to emails three times per week. Other BOP facilities have the computers located in the dorms, along with the phones, for unlimited inmate access. Much like the phones, the computers should be moved into the dorms ASAP.

5. Inmates at FPC-Pensacola have NO recreation, NO education, NO access to the library, and NO visitation. Inmates are supposedly allowed outside to walk for one hour, three times per week. However, depending on an inmate's work schedule, that is not the case. Dorm A inmates are allowed outside on Saturday, Sunday and Tuesday, but since I worked every Sunday and Tuesday, I only got outside once a week for one hour.

6. There is NO heat in dorm A and no plans to repair the HVAC equipment to fix the heat pump. Temperatures routinely drop into the fifties during the night with inmates sleeping in long underwear, pants, shirts, socks, jackets and hats. The blankets are thin and inadequate. There is no excuse to not repair the HVAC equipment.

7. There is a sign on the door into dorm A that warns that there is black mold in the dorm and to be cautious. Inmates are locked in the dorm twenty-four/seven other than work details. There is no excuse for not taking corrective action to eliminate the mold and risk to the inmates' health.

8. The mail situation at FPC-Pensacola, managed by CO Durphy, is inadequate with unbelievable delays in getting outbound mail to the post office. Delays of ten days are not uncommon. Incoming mail is not delivered to inmates in a timely fashion. I subscribed to *The Wall Street Journal*, which is delivered to FPC-Pensacola every day, but I did not receive my copy on a daily basis, and in many cases received three or four issues at a time.

9. Legal mail is only supposed to be opened in front of the inmate, who signs for the mail. In my case, my legal mail was opened in the mail room, illegally examined, and then delivered to me along with the regular mail drop. This is just another example of the unprofessional, unethical behavior of the COs at FPC-Pensacola.

10. FPC-Pensacola is a minimum-security facility that should be preparing inmates to return to society. Because of COVID restrictions, the facility operates as a low-security facility with controlled movement of inmates. Some COs, such as CO Church, take pleasure in treating inmates with no respect. For example, I was in a group waiting to go to food service when one inmate walked out the right-side door of a two-door entrance, while other inmates walked out the left-side door. CO Church

barked at all the inmates, forced everyone back into the dorm, and then threatened to issue a "shot" to any inmate who walked out the right-side door. Treating inmates in such a manner does not prepare inmates to return to society.

11. FPC-Pensacola has totally inadequate dental care for inmates. An incarcerated individual is entitled to medical and dental treatment. Having to wait eighteen to twenty-four months to get your teeth cleaned is not adequate dental treatment.

12. While it is understandable that the BOP would seek to save money with generic medications, there are instances where an inmate has an adverse medical reaction to the standard generic medication and therefore needs a different generic prescription. While I was at FPC-Pensacola, an inmate with a thyroid problem could not take the standard generic medication without an adverse reaction, and his pleas for a different generic prescription were ignored. After several weeks of not being able to take his medication, he collapsed in the dorm and had to be rushed to the hospital. This is another example of the inhuman treatment of inmates at FPC-Pensacola.

In summary, the situation at FPC-Pensacola MUST be addressed immediately or the dire consequences of COVID-19 spreading through the inmate population will occur. It's not a matter of "if," it's a matter of "when."

Warden Joseph should be immediately relieved of his position. He is totally indifferent to the egregious violations of the BOP mission, vision and core values that occur on a daily basis at FPC-Pensacola.

I have attached a separate summary of the numerous, flagrant violations of inmate rights that occur every day at FPC-Pensacola.

I have copied other BOP staff as well as members of Congress to alert them to the deplorable situation at FPC-Pensacola. I suspect that FPC-Pensacola is not the only BOP facility exhibiting a total disregard for the core values published by the BOP. Actions, not words, matter when the lives of human beings are at stake.

I trust that this summary of the situation at FPC-Pensacola will be taken seriously with appropriate action to rectify the issues I have highlighted.

Respectfully submitted,

Christopher Collins
Former Member of Congress—NY 27 (2013–2019)
Former Erie County Executive—(2008–2011)
Former BOP inmate #86014-054 (10/13/2020–12/22/2020)
Issued a Full and Unconditional Pardon from President Trump on 12/22/2020

cc:
Mr. Gene Beasley—Deputy Director Federal Bureau of Prisons
Mr. J.A. Keller—Regional Director, BOP Southeast Regional Office
Mr. M.V. Joseph—Warden FPC-Pensacola
Congressman Matt Gaetz—FL-01 (Pensacola)
Congressman Jerry Nadler—NY-10 (Chairman House Judiciary Committee)
Congressman Jim Jordan—OH-04 (Ranking Member House Judiciary Committee)
Senator Lindsey Graham—Chairman Senate Judiciary Committee
Senator Dianne Feinstein—Ranking Member Senate Judiciary Committee

APPENDIX C

Volunteer Service

OVER THE YEARS, I HAVE devoted my time and energy to supporting various organizations, holding multiple roles and responsibilities:

- **1978–1996**: Active volunteer with the United Way of Buffalo.
- **1988–1996**: Member of the House of Delegates for the United Way of Buffalo.
- **1985–1987**: Volunteer with Junior Achievement, teaching at a local high school.
- **1985–1996**: Active member of the Young Presidents' Organization (YPO), serving as:
    - Education Chairman
    - Membership Chairman
    - Chapter Chairman
    - Chairman of the Executive Committee for the Empire State Chapter.
- **1985–1991**: Member of the Board of Directors for Kenmore Mercy Hospital.
- **1986–1989**: Member of the Board of Directors for the American Gear Manufacturers Association (AGMA).
- **1992–1995**: Member of the Small Business Advisory Board (nine-member committee) to the Federal Reserve Bank of New York.
- **1994**: Volunteer with the Buffalo Financial Planning Commission, collaborating with the City of Buffalo public schools to reduce expenses.
- **1999–2011**: Volunteer with the Center for Entrepreneurial Leadership (CEL) program at the State University of New York

at Buffalo (UB). Served as a Mentor and Reactor for various small businesses participating in the program.

- **1998–2018**: Member of the Executive Board for the Greater Niagara Frontier Council (GNFC), Boy Scouts of America.
- **1999–2002**: Cub Master for Pack 568, Boy Scouts of America.
- **2003–2011**: Assistant Scout Master for Troop 93, Boy Scouts of America.
- **2001–2017**: Chairman of the National Scout Jamboree Committee for GNFC.

This extensive volunteer history reflects my dedication to community service and leadership across various organizations and initiatives.

Bibliography

Berman, Geoffrey. *Holding the Line.* "Chapter - The Pardoned, pages 116–118." Penguin Press, 2022.

Bianculli, David. "Jew Bashing: Collins calls Shelly Silver the Anti-Christ." *New York Daily News,* October 25, 2009.

Carberry, John. "Candidate says he has right stuff to beat ultraliberal LaFalce in the 29th District." *The Daily News,* September 30, 1998.

Craig, Gary. "A novice is giving LaFalce a tough fight." *Democrat and Chronicle,* October 17, 1998.

Davis, Henry. "Doctors healed ECMC – Kaleida rift." *The Buffalo News,* June 29, 2008.

Eustachewich, Lisa. "Chris Collins begs friends to write letters in bid for leniency." *New York Post,* October 8, 2018.

Fisher, Bruce. "Tell Us What You Really Think, CHRIS. Why Collins Calling Sheldon Silver the Anti-Christ Is No Joke." *Artvoice,* October 29, 2009.

Gaudiano, Nicole. "Once-obscure Rep. Chris Collins sees his star rise with Trump." *USA Today,* February 21, 2017.

Hudson, Mike. "LaFalce fights battle of career versus Collins." *Record-Advertiser,* October 21, 1998.

Hudson, Mike. "LaFalce, Collins face off on issues." *Tonawanda News,* October 24, 1998.

Hudson, Mike. "LaFalce, Collins square off." *Niagara Gazette,* October 24, 1998.

Jagord, Steven. "Collins bounces back, ready to take on Washington." *Clarence Bee,* November 9, 2012.

McBride, Ann. "Businessman announces candidacy." *Niagara Gazette,* May 7, 1998.

McCarthy, Robert. "Broad-based team to get Collins rolling." *The Buffalo News,* November 9, 2007.

McCarthy, Robert. "Buffalo News endorses James Keane for Erie County executive." *The Buffalo News*, October 28, 2007.

McCarthy, Robert. "Chris Collins builds his campaign." *The Buffalo News*, July 8, 2007.

McCarthy, Robert. "Collins all set to tee off in new post." *The Buffalo News*, January 3, 2008.

McCarthy, Robert. "Collins challenges LaFalce with personally financed TV ads." *The Buffalo News*, August 31, 1998.

McCarthy, Robert. "Collins claims victory over Hochul." *The Buffalo News*, November 7, 2012.

McCarthy, Robert. "Collins enters race with all the trimmings." *The Buffalo News*, March 28, 2007.

McCarthy, Robert. "Collins eyes GOP county executive bid." *The Buffalo News*, March 3, 2007.

McCarthy, Robert. "Collins launches campaign for Congress in 27th district." *The Buffalo News*, March 25, 2012.

McCarthy, Robert. "Collins opens bid against LaFalce with big cash supply." *The Buffalo News*, May 6, 1998.

McCarthy, Robert. "Collins sprints through first 100 days on the job. County executive ruffles feathers but sticks to pledge to streamline government." *The Buffalo News*, April 11, 2008.

McCarthy, Robert. "Collins surges ahead in new poll. Leads Keane by 9 points in county executive race." *The Buffalo News*, October 12, 2007.

McCarthy, Robert. "Collins trips over his tongue again." *The Buffalo News*, January 14, 2010.

McCarthy, Robert. "Collins update." *The Buffalo News*, April 11, 2008.

McCarthy, Robert. "Collins widens lead over Keane to 46%-33%. 18 percent are undecided as Election Day nears." *The Buffalo News*, November 4, 2007.

McCarthy, Robert. "Collins wins in a landslide." *The Buffalo News*, November 7, 2007.

McCarthy, Robert. "County executive race called a dead heat. Zogby poll finds Keane and Collins running even with five weeks to go." *The Buffalo News*, October 2, 2007.

McCarthy, Robert. "Dems will be bruised, battered, and penniless when the Democratic primary is over." *The Buffalo News*, April 29, 2007.

McCarthy, Robert. "Erie County fiscal stability authority shifts to advisory status." *The Buffalo News*, June 15, 2008.

McCarthy, Robert. "Ex-Paxon aid signs on with campaign." *The Buffalo News*, March 29, 1998.

McCarthy, Robert. "Hepatitis scare raises concerns, offers glimpse into nightmare of a flu pandemic." *The Buffalo News*, February 18, 2008.

McCarthy, Robert. "Hochul, Collins await what may be a long night." *The Buffalo News*, November 6, 2012.

McCarthy, Robert. "LaFalce could face tough GOP challenge." *The Buffalo News*, March 29, 1998.

McCarthy, Robert. "Opinion Column." *The Buffalo News*, October 15, 2007.

McCarthy, Robert. "Private sector savvy – can Chris Collins' business expertise save Erie County?" *The Buffalo News*, September 23, 2007.

McCarthy, Robert. "Rising again, Collins heads for Capitol Hill." *The Buffalo News*, November 8, 2012.

Morris, David. "Donald Trump Taps Little-Known Lawmaker to be 'Eyes and Ears' in Congress." *Fortune*, November 15, 2016.

Peterson, Kristina. "Lawmaker Is Talent Scout for Trump." *The Wall Street Journal*, December 16, 2016.

Peterson, Kristina. "Want a Job in Trump's Administration? Get on Chris Collins's Spreadsheet." *The Wall Street Journal*, December 15, 2016.

Politics. "Congressional candidate blasts president's conduct." *Niagara Gazette*, September 15, 1998.

Reporter, Staff. "Westinghouse to Sell Its Gear-Making Assets." *The Wall Street Journal*, January 7, 1983.

Robinson, David. "Collins wants tighter rules on tax breaks." *The Buffalo News*, February 17, 2008.

Schroeder, Richard. "Westinghouse will lose another division, but the Buffalo area will gain an independent manufacturer." *The Buffalo News*, January 7, 1983.

Spina, Matthew. "Adept at using political chokehold – cutting off money to the other side of the table is how Collins the negotiator flexes his muscle." *The Buffalo News*, June 15, 2008.

Spina, Matthew. "Collins orders more part-timers hired – Their paid time off is half that of full-time, rank-and-file employees." *The Buffalo News*, January 31, 2008.

Spina, Matthew. "Collins' aides put on county payroll." *The Buffalo News*, November 30, 2007.

Spina, Matthew. "Need cell phone, car? Collins wants proof." *The Buffalo News*, February 3, 2008.

Tatum, Sophie. "Rep. Chris Collins: I could be 'go-between' between Trump and Ryan." *CNN*, November 9, 2016.

Thomas, Vanessa. "Collins reaches out at black service." *The Buffalo News*, December 3, 2007.

Zremski, Jerry. "Collins emerging as a power broker. Vocal supporter of Trump is helping fill 4,000 positions." *The Buffalo News*, December 4, 2016.

Zremski, Jerry. "Collins to speak at GOP convention." *The Buffalo News*, July 15, 2016.

Zremski, Jerry. "Collins wins seat on major House panel. Energy post a forum to promote fracking." *The Buffalo News*, December 4, 2014.

Zremski, Jerry. "Collins' early loyalty to Trump prompts talk of 'Mr. Secretary.'" *The Buffalo News*, July 20, 2016.

Zremski, Jerry. "LaFalce challenger first in area to call for president's resignation." *The Buffalo News*, September 18, 1998.

Zremski, Jerry. "LaFalce duels with Collins over trips." *The Buffalo News*, October 22, 1998.

Zremski, Jerry. "LaFalce, Collins differ sharply at forum over ways to improve the local economy." *The Buffalo News*, October 24, 1998.

Zremski, Jerry. "Trump appoints Collins to his transition team." *The Buffalo News*, December 12, 2016.